Contemporary Women Teachers

Balancing School and Home

Dee Ann Spencer
Central Missouri State University

Longman
New York & London

To my son, Todd,
and my parents, Henry and Jeanne Fries

Contemporary Women Teachers: *Balancing School and Home*

Copyright © 1986 by Longman Inc.

Executive Editor: Raymond O'Connell
Cover Design: Eileen Beirne
Compositor: Graphicraft Typesetters Limited

Library of Congress Cataloging in Publication Data

Spencer, Dee Ann.
    Contemporary women teachers.

    Bibliography: p.
    Includes index.
    1. Women teachers—United States—Case studies.
I. Title.
LB2837.S66   1985   371.1'0088042   85–4251
ISBN 0–582–28427–9

85 86 87 88 9 8 7 6 5 4 3 2 1

Contents

Research on Teaching Monograph Series

PUBLISHED TITLES

JERE E. BROPHY AND CAROLYN M. EVERTSON, *Student Characteristics and Teaching*

SUSAN URMSTON PHILIPS, *The Invisible Culture: Communication in Classroom and Community on the Warm Springs Indian Reservation*

HARRIS M. COOPER AND THOMAS L. GOOD, *Pygmalion Grows Up: Studies in the Expectation Communication Process*

THOMAS L. GOOD, DOUGLAS GROUWS, AND HOWARD EBMEIER, *Active Mathematics Teaching*

ROBERT E. SLAVIN, *Cooperative Learning*

LEONARD S. CAHEN, NIKOLA FILBY, GAIL McCUTCHEON, AND DIANE W. KYLE, *Class Size and Instruction*

PHILIP A. CUSICK, *The Egalitarian Ideal and the American High School*

LARRY CUBAN, *How Teachers Taught: Constancy and Change in American Classrooms: 1890–1980*

GARY NATRIELLO AND SANFORD M. DORNBUSCH, *Teacher Evaluative Standards and Student Efforts*

DAVID BERLINER AND CHARLES FISHER, *Perspectives on Instructional Time*

BARBARA LARRIVEE, *Effective Teaching For Successful Mainstreaming*

GRETA MORINE-DERSHIMER, *Speaking, Listening, and Learning in Elementary Classrooms*

DEE ANN SPENCER, *Contemporary Women Teachers: Balancing School and Home*

Preface

American schools have serious problems and teachers have often been blamed for them. Media reports have criticized that teachers are burned out, do not care about students—are, indeed, even afraid of them—and lack control over classrooms. Perhaps the most serious indictment, however, is that teachers are barely more literate than the students they teach. What support can be found for these charges? Unfortunately, the lack of confidence in teachers' literacy is not without foundation. A recent Carnegie Foundation report describes the people who are now going into teaching (Feistritzer, 1983, p. 76). According to this report, the quality of education majors is lower than the quality of those in almost every other academic area, if the SAT scores of high school students are used as the basis of comparison.

In addition, fewer students choose teaching as a future career. As Feistritzer points out, the reasons are not difficult to understand. Teachers' salaries are lower than those of every other professional, and they work under poor conditions, have little opportunity for advancement, and have low status in our society. Women have traditionally comprised the largest pool of potential teachers, but today the best and brightest female college students are choosing fields that pay more and are more prestigious and more challenging.

Who *is* the typical American teacher? Literature on education gives us few clues. An exception is found in the following description.

> A "typical" American teacher today would be a woman still in her thirties who had taught for 12 years, mostly in her present district. Over those dozen years, she would have returned to her local college or university often enough to acquire enough credits for a master's degree. She would be married and the mother of two children. She would be white and not politically active. Her formal political affiliation, if she had one, would be with the Democratic Party. She would teach in a suburban elementary school staffed largely by women, although, in all likelihood, the school principal would be male. She would have about twenty-three pupils in her class. Counting her after-hours responsibilities, she would put in a work week slightly longer than that of the average blue-collar worker in industry, but bring home a pay check that would be slightly lower. (Feistritzer Associates, 1983, in Feistritzer, 1983, pp. 24, 26)

We can see from this description that the typical teacher, a woman who has taught 12 years, chose teaching as a career at least 16 years ago, during the 1960s, when women had basically three choices of careers—nursing, secretarial work, or teaching. She also has characteristics that extend beyond the classroom. Women teachers have families and, perhaps, political affiliations. Today's teacher is not an "old maid" who dedicates her life to schoolchildren, nor a married woman with children who teaches because working hours and vacations fit in with family life, nor someone who builds a teaching career around the birth of children or the fact that extra "pin" money is needed for the household budget. Yet Feistritzer's description tells us little about the everyday reality of teachers. How does the fact that they are married and have two children affect their teaching? What is the effect of a male administrator on female faculties? How do long hours and low pay affect teachers' home lives? And what effect does comparing them with blue-collar workers have on teachers' perceptions of themselves as professionals? These questions and others are addressed in *Contemporary Women Teachers*. The book is an examination and description of the relationships between women teachers' home and school lives.

My interest in women teachers developed from several sources. Undoubtedly, my own years as a public school teacher and working mother and years of research in schools talking with teachers in classrooms, lounges, and cafeterias were important influences. After 18 years, I knew that studies of teachers, no matter how detailed, are depersonalized and out of touch with reality. They make teachers the object of study rather than the subject (Hoffman, 1981). Also, they do not attend to the other important aspects of teachers' lives—their families and personal lives— that are inextricably entwined with their teaching. Teachers, like all people who work, do not neatly compartmentalize various aspects of their lives. In fact, quite the opposite is true. For example, when developing the research design for this study, I thought of Emily, a 37-year-old, seventh-grade English teacher, who came to school one morning after having deposited her four children at four different schools. Her daughter had forgotten her Brownie uniform and had to be taken home to get it, and one of her sons needed a clean gym suit at the last minute. Walking into school, Emily slipped on the ice in the parking lot; after she got into the school, she was so dizzy that she had to sit down briefly. Then, she taught her full schedule of classes. My observation was that she taught as well as usual. At the end of the day she picked her four children up, fixed dinner, did the dishes, helped the children with their homework, and got them to bed. Then she graded papers. Her husband left before she did in the mornings and got home in time for dinner at night, and so child care was part of Emily's responsibilities. Emily had no time to herself except an occasional hour after all the children were in bed. I wondered how her home life could be separated from her school life, and how anyone could understand teachers without information about their total lives. I did not think it was possible. The result of that belief provides the focus for this book. I hope it will provide insight and understanding into teachers' lives and serve as a balance to the weight of criticisms about teachers. It makes teachers the subject of study, not the object.

Women were chosen for the study because they are the typical teachers. They represent 83 percent of elementary teachers, 46 percent of secondary teachers, and 66 percent of the total number of teachers (Grant & Eiden, 1981). Another reason is related to the fact that teachers work because they need to earn a paycheck, not for extra money. Even so, women teachers have been criticized for their inconsistent or lack of commitment to teaching. For example, some have asserted that teachers' lack of power, autonomy, and status is due to women's lack of consistent career patterns, their submissiveness to administrators, and their decision to put their families before their jobs. Teaching has been assumed to be congruent with female socialization, prestigious and monetarily rewarding (compared to other alternatives for women), compatible with family life, and work that allows women to be away for periods of time without loss of skills when they return (Lortie, 1975). These assumptions about women's presumed lack of commitment and its effects on teaching as an occupation needed critical examination.

Women were also selected because studies of working women show that they continue to take major responsibility for housework and child care (e.g., Pleck, 1977). Although working women spend less time on family tasks than those who do not, men contribute the same amount of time to household work whether or not their wives work outside the home. Presumably, teachers are like other working women in that their home responsibilities are different from those of male teachers in ways that would have important effects on their lives at home and at school. A final reason for selecting women was that the intimate rapport needed to gain in-depth life history data necessitates long-term close contact. I believed women would feel more comfortable sharing their lives with me.

To provide the detailed descriptions of teachers' lives to illustrate these points, I used research methods that focused on women's day-to-day intimate experiences (see Appendix A for a description of research methods). Eight women—of differing marital status who taught different grade levels in different-sized school districts from rural to urban—were observed at school and in their homes, interviewed continually, and asked to write diaries. The study lasted two years, although contact with the teachers has continued for over four years.

To the extent possible in a research relationship, the women shared their lives with me. We discussed and interacted with students, graded papers together, made bulletin boards, went to meetings, left school together, shopped for groceries, shared meals, and baby-sat. We went to family reunions, fished, traveled, attended the theater, and played piano duets—depending on the leisure activities each woman enjoyed. Although the eight teachers' lives provided the foundation for my intensive examination of women who teach, I collected additional data through interviews with 42 other women teachers who had the same marital, school-level, and district-size characteristics in different areas of the country (see discussion in Chapter 10). This book is the result of the integration of my observations and analyses, illustrated by the teachers' words and perspectives.

Chapter 1 presents a history of women's roles in teaching and women's influence on the emergence of teaching as a quasi profession, the contradictory factors in teaching that contribute to the problems of working in a quasi profession, and the interrelationship of teacher's home lives with these contradictions and problems. Each of the next eight chapters describes a case study of a teacher's life. The chapters are ordered by marital status, beginning with single women, then married women without children, married women with children, and last, divorced women with children. There are two women in each marital category so their lives can be compared, as can differences between the lives of those who were or were not married and did or did not have children. In each chapter a typical day is described to show the pattern of the woman's life and how she shifted between her home and school roles. Next, her life history is presented, and each situation, at school and at home, is examined in detail. Obviously, after observing and interviewing these women and their keeping diaries for nearly two years, I had hundreds of pages of data. From these pages, I selected representative examples of experiences and behaviors to illustrate their lives.

In Chapter 10, comparisons are made to the larger sample of interviews with the 50 teachers; and in Chapter 11, I return to the themes of Chapter 1 and discuss the implications of this study for education and, especially, for teachers and classrooms.

The research reported in this book was made possible by a grant from the National Institute of Education.[1] At NIE, I had the pleasure of working with Ursula Piñero, project officer, who was (and continues to be) consistently warm, supportive, and enthusiastic. She was a motivating force in a morass of data and bureaucratic paperwork, and she is a valued colleague.

I was fortunate to have the consultation of several people. Arlene Daniels, Northwestern University; Peter M. Hall, University of Missouri-Columbia; Barbara Heyl, Northern Illinois University; Sara Lightfoot, Harvard University; Caroline Persell, New York University; and Thomas L. Good, University of Missouri-Columbia, all provided insightful comments, criticisms, and suggestions throughout various stages of the research and writing. Hugh Mehan, University of California, San Diego, followed the study from its inception to its completion and continued through the preparation of this manuscript to provide energizing, thought-provoking, supportive comments. His help was invaluable to the successful completion of this work.

I am deeply appreciative of the office space and facilities provided by Bruce J. Biddle, director of the Center for Research in Social Behavior, University of Missouri-Columbia; of the sensitive and thorough interviews of Josephine Ingram, Mary Statz, and Harriet Yelon; and of Carolyn Backer's meticulous and thorough coding of data. And finally, I gratefully acknowledge the patience and excellent work of Mary Harbourt, who typed several thousand manuscript pages, transcribed dozens of tapes, and complete several reports.

Most important were the teachers who shared their lives with me for two years, as well as those who allowed me and my assistants to come into their homes for several hours of interviews. To them I express my deep gratitude.[2]

NOTES

1. The National Institute of Education (Contract No. NIE-R-79-0008). The research reported here does not necessarily reflect the views of that agency.

2. Portions of the book appeared in articles titled The home and school lives of women teachers and The home and school lives of women teachers: Implications for staff development. *The Elementary School Journal*, January 1984, *84*, 283-314.

1

Women Who Teach

TEACHING AS A QUASI PROFESSION

An understanding of women's role in teaching is crucial to understanding
this book. The question is, how did teaching become a female-dominated
profession—"women's work"—and, in the process, become a quasi profession rather than a profession?

The quasi-professional status of teachers has often been attributed to
the notion that women lack commitment to building careers; they go in and
out of the labor market to bear and raise children and work only for "pin"
money rather than for necessities (Simpson & Simpson, 1969; Geer,
1968; Lortie, 1975). To support her perception of the weak commitment of
teachers, Geer cites the high dropout rate of graduates in education and
those in their first years of teaching and the entrance and exit of women
from the teaching field to tend to family commitments. She offers five
characteristics of teaching to explain this movement.

1. Unlike other occupations that create knowledge or build on past
   skills and knowledge, teaching requires the transmission of others'
   knowledge and skills. It does not create new knowledge.
2. The teachers' clientele, students, are involuntarily present. There
   is little pleasure derived from daily work, because any rewards for
   success are divided among colleagues and the school. A student's
   success is not seen as one teacher's success.
3. There is a lack of collegial relationships among teachers, which in
   other occupations helps to increase work excellence; there is no
   shared community to bind them to the profession. Instead, each

teacher generally operates within the privacy of her own room to a small audience of children.
4. There is no real system for advancement or mobility; a teacher is not rewarded for achievement.
5. The length and frequency of vacations increases the possibility of "moonlighting," which can eventually conflict with commitment to teaching.

Although I agree with Geer's five points, I see them as evidence of the problems in schools and the quasi-professional status of the occupation rather than as evidence of teachers' lack of commitment. There is no doubt that the reason for high dropout rates among education graduates and first-year teachers is that they realize that better pay and more prestige are found in other fields—not because women lack commitment to teaching. The job market for teachers has changed drastically in the 15 years since Geer's work was published. Experienced women teachers no longer have the option of going in and out of the market even if they are so inclined. Often no jobs are available because of severe financial cutbacks and declining enrollments in most school systems. Moreover, it is not economically feasible to quit. Families could not survive financially without the mother's paycheck. The economic realities make commitment or the lack of it a moot issue.

Historical evidence shows that the issue of commitment was never relevant in understanding why women stay in teaching. Based on the diaries and journals of women who taught, Hoffman (1981) shows that teachers began working because they needed to work and that the image of teachers as angels of mercy is inaccurate. She adds that women were not preoccupied with fears of being old maids but chose to work and enjoy independence from married life. They worked to earn a paycheck and to gain satisfaction.

Even though women work because they need a paycheck, they are often unwilling to admit they are teaching for that reason. Many consider it unprofessional to do so. In fact, there are many references to teachers who are critical of others who are in teaching "just for the paycheck" (Lortie, 1975; Carew & Lightfoot, 1978). An example is found in the case study of Phyllis, in Chapter 6. If she had quit teaching, her family of four would have qualified for welfare, based on her husband's salary. Her family needed her paycheck, but she refused to use that reason for working.

Reconsidering part of Feistritzer's (1983) description, cited in this book's preface, of the typical American teacher as one who "would put in a work week slightly longer than that of the average blue-collar worker in industry, but bring home a pay check that would be slightly lower" (p. 26), it is not inappropriate to consider teachers as part of the working class rather than as professionals. For example, in 1981–1982, the starting salary for a teacher was $12,769 (National Education Association, 1983, in

Feistritzer, 1983). This was $3500 less than a starting salary for a college graduate in business administration ($16,200), the next lower-paying profession. Teaching salaries also showed the smallest gains since 1973–1974 of any professionals except accountants. When compared to all workers, teachers are closest to city employees, although some of those, such as police and fire fighters, make more. Teachers do make more than civil service workers, although we cannot compare the monetary differences in fringe benefits that are typically available to civil service workers. The longer teachers are in the profession, the wider the gap between their salaries and those of other white-collar workers. It is not surprising that low salaries have led to widespread dissatisfaction among teachers. As Feistritzer (1983) points out, "In addition to concerns of status and prestige, sheer economic necessity is driving women into high paying professions. More than one in seven families (9.1 million) are headed by women, a 65 percent increase since 1970. A teaching salary of $17,000 cannot support a household, many find" (p. 83). That teachers make low salaries contributes to their nonprofessional status.

AN EXPLANATION OF TEACHING AS A QUASI PROFESSION

Whether or not an occupation is considered a profession depends on the extent of control and autonomy of an individual in that occupation. According to Grimm (1978), professionalization is "the process by which an occupation claims and receives the legal autonomy to exercise a monopoly over the delivery of an important service" (p. 294). By this definition, teaching, and other female-dominated occupations such as library work, nursing, and social work, have not achieved professional status.

An analogy can be made between the historical development of clerical work and that of teaching. The basis for this analogy is found in the work of Glenn and Feldberg (1977), who trace clerical work from the nineteenth century, when the individual was visible and key to the successful operation of a business, to the present with its highly bureaucratized organizational structure in which the individual has become depersonalized. Over the years, clerical work has shifted from white-collar to blue-collar and tasks have become externally structured and controlled as activities became manual rather than mental and jobs were simplified. Workers lost control over their tasks and had less contact with managers as the size of organizations grew and technology and organizational goals changed.

I would argue that teachers, like clerical workers, shifted in occupational status as the bureaucratic structure of schools grew. In the nineteenth century, schools expanded throughout the country, a large pool of teachers was needed, and women were there to fill that need. Hiring women was considered "cost effective" because they were paid less than men, and by 1840, most teachers were women (Lightfoot, 1978). By 1919, 86 percent of teachers were women—the largest percentage of women in teaching before or since that time (Shakeshaft, 1981). Although women are still predominant (66 percent), since 1919 there has been a major change at the secondary school level. Males have increasingly dominated that level.

According to Glenn and Feldberg, managerial control in organizations was possible, in part, because managers were men and clerical workers were women. Males also occupy a disproportionate share of the elite positions in schools. Nearly all administrators are male, and, as pointed out by Grimm and Stern (1974), "when the administrative component of a 'female' profession is itself expanding, the increasing demand for administrators will enhance the tendency of males to dominate the field" (p. 703). Male domination in administrative positions means a hierarchical arrangement in which decisions in schools are made by males and carried out by females—a situation comparable to clerical workers and managers. In both situations, relationships between those in control and the workers become strained and impersonal and contacts between them decrease.

With the expansion of schools has come increased specialization of teaching tasks. This too constricts teachers' options; choices are narrowed and control is limited. Teachers have become subject to local, state, and federal requirements that specify expectations more so than ever before. Although accountability is not undesirable, the increased demands on teachers' time and energy has made teaching more mechanical and less creative or spontaneous.

Glenn and Feldberg explain that standardization of tasks makes it easier for managers to monitor work. The problem is that teachers, like clerical workers, become more vulnerable because they are open to constant inspection. This undermines their internal motivation and separates them from one another, because it creates a competitive atmosphere rather than one of cooperation and interdependence.

As pointed out, Glenn and Feldberg said that the fact that workers are women and managers are men has contributed to women's lack of control in female-dominated professions. Managers capitalize on the stereotype that women work to please others and are more sensitive and honest and less mercenary than men. Because "niceness" is stressed, orders given to women are disguised as personal requests that they find difficult to refuse. These same characteristics have been attributed to women teachers with the additional "ideology of 'true womanhood' that emphasized woman's nurturant qualities and hence her suitability for teaching" (Shakeshaft, 1981). Teachers, like other women in female-dominated professions, have been linked to qualities of nurturance, caring, and socialization (Grimm, 1978). Teaching became an extension of mothering.

The result of viewing work as blue-collar rather than white-collar, continuing with Glenn and Feldberg's argument, is a downgrading of the work itself and a change in the workers' relationship to it. These changes remove the very features that attracted people to the work situation. Workers become less knowledgeable, less involved, less committed, and less able and willing to respond to variation. In clerical work and in teaching, this process is counterproductive because workers become alienated or "burned out." As loss of control over the work place becomes a significant feature of teachers' work, teaching becomes more similar to blue-collar work. Teachers' perceptions of their loss of control over working conditions were expressed by a 30-year-old elementary school teacher when she compared teachers and waitresses.

> I think it [stress] is something that most people who are working, as either public employees or . . . with the public, feel when they are with people over whom they have no choice—like a waitress. People come in and she has to serve those people and has no control over who she wants in there. Teachers and public employees are in the same situation. The view from the classroom is that you have no control over the situation.

In summary, teaching is considered a quasi profession because of low pay and teachers' lack of control over their work place. The conditions under which teachers work are more similar to those of blue-collar workers than to those of professionals. The way in which the organizational structure of schools has developed over time and the predominance of women in teaching have created and perpetuated these conditions.

CONTRADICTIONS IN THE TEACHER ROLE

Why do teachers continue to work under adverse working conditions? Why do they insist that teaching is indeed a profession when their experiences tell them something quite different? I was often puzzled by the reactions of teachers with 15 years' experience to problematic situations. They were genuinely disappointed with the reality of a situation. At the same time, they believed that if they tried hard enough, the ideal could be achieved —that they would be professionals—although their loss of control over the work place did not allow change. They were perpetually caught in double binds—situations that posed contradictory sets of expectations for their behavior yet that they were powerless to change. When the situations did not change, the teachers blamed themselves and tried harder to achieve the ideal. The result was a cycle of disappointment, a "catch-22" from which there was no escape.

In the following sections I have identified contradictory situations I found typical of the experiences of teachers. They are organized around the concepts of roles and role conflict. Role conflict of public school teachers has been the subject of many studies (e.g., Drabick, 1971; Katz & Kahn, 1966; Wright & Tuska, 1969). In these studies, examination and

discussion have adhered to definitions of role conflict found in the literature—as that which develops "between two or more roles an individual is
expected to enact simultaneously, but between the person's own expectations for a role enactment and the expectations other people have for that
enactment" (Zurcher, 1983, p. 78). The teacher role is described as a
complex set of expectations for behaviors. These expectations are often
ambiguous, inconsistent, and discrepant and make problems difficult for
teachers to identify, explain, or resolve. Role conflict is seen as a
consequence of the dilemma in which teachers encounter simultaneous yet
contradictory sets of expectations.

Contradictions in Normative Expectations for Role Enactment

Normative expectations for teachers' behavior derive from long histories
and traditions in education. Always in the public eye, teachers have been
expected to be "paragons of virtue"; as a result, school systems have
imposed rules, regulations, and procedures that reflect societal definitions
about what teachers should do in relationships with students and administrators. Many of these norms are concerned with control (over students in
the classroom) and acceptance of control (of administrators), which creates
a contradiction in expectations for teachers.

These contradictions in expectations also reflect historical "swings of
the pendulum" found in education—at some times, teachers were
expected to be models of control, and at other times, they were expected to
relinquish that control to students; for example, in open classrooms
(Ravitch, 1983).

Power over Classes versus Powerlessness in School Organizations. Classrooms are social settings in which teachers hold the most powerful
positions. Teachers are expected to gain and maintain control over
students, and students are expected to comply with rules and obey their
teachers. Teachers can manipulate their power through positive or negative sanctions over which students have no control. However, within the
context of the school or school system as an organization, teachers take a
subordinate role to administrators. Whether or not teachers have control
over their students is a major basis of their evaluation by administrators.
Although administrators expect teachers to keep their classes under
control, teachers are often treated in infantile ways. Principals can assign
teachers to such duties as monitoring restrooms or detention rooms, can
enter and observe classrooms without notifying the teachers, and can
schedule meetings without consulting teachers. In a few cases, principals
go through teachers' desk drawers and grade their lesson-plan books.
Teachers therefore feel a contradiction between the expectation that they
play a superordinate role with students and a subordinate role with
administrators. Their role shifts continually throughout the school day.

Spontaneity versus Self-control. Teachers are expected to be enthusiastic in their classes, exhibit warmth toward students, and motivate students by exhibiting a positive and dynamic example. At the same time, teachers are expected to be in control. Too much noise or laughter is viewed by administrators or other teachers as a lack of control over classes. The contradiction between maintaining control while generating enthusiasm is difficult and often exhausting, because there are few times throughout the day when teachers can relax.

Being Well Liked versus Constraining Affection. Teachers who are well liked by students are given positive evaluations by administrators, because the teachers' popularity is seen as evidence of good rapport and is considered conducive to learning. Yet secondary teachers have to refrain from being overly friendly toward students and must limit displays of affection, particularly toward students of the opposite sex. Close friendships are not acceptable and overt displays of affection are judged by others as morally and ethically unacceptable behavior. This places teachers in a contradictory set of expectations.

Contradictions in Personal Expectations and Normative Expectations

While schools are social settings with long histories and traditions of rules reflecting expectations for teachers' behavior, teachers' personal expectations or self-concepts do not always align with these expectations and are frequently contradictory. Many studies of these contradictions have focused on teachers in their first year(s) of teaching when they come to the stark realization that their ideal of teaching is drastically different from the reality (Wright & Tuska, 1968; Edgar & Warren, 1969; Ryan et al., 1980). In 1981, 15 percent of those graduates qualified to teach did not apply for teaching jobs. Of the 85 percent who did apply for jobs, 20 percent were not teaching one year later (Feistritzer, 1983). This indicates over a one-third attrition rate. The ideal of teaching often does not meet the real.

Teaching as a Profession versus Working-Class Job Characteristics. The development of teaching as a quasi profession with working-class characteristics was explained earlier. That the process can be explained, however, does not change teachers' desire to perceive themselves as professionals, even though they have little choice about what, when, or where they teach; their classes are interrupted by announcements over intercom systems; and they have to engage in such demeaning tasks as monitoring bathrooms and performing janitorial duties in their classrooms.

Teachers who are against unionization usually feel that way because they think it is unprofessional. However, because they are not in an organized group oriented toward change, poor working conditions are perpetuated.

Desire for Autonomy versus Desire for Administrative Competence. The development of teaching as a quasi profession has also meant a loss of control over work and working conditions. Teachers want freedom to teach and control their classrooms without constraint or censorship but have to comply with stringent curriculum plans and guidelines. These determine what they teach, how they teach, and when they teach. In open schools or schools that were once open and have constructed thin folding walls, their autonomy is further constrained because they can see and hear what other teachers are saying and doing throughout the school day. However, while teachers want autonomy over their classes and working conditions and input into decisions that affect their classrooms, they also want to be relieved of certain kinds of decisions they define as administrative. Principals who do not carry out certain responsibilities, such as enforcing student discipline, are seen as ineffective and as burdening teachers with unnecessary work that takes time away from their teaching. Teachers' expectations are contradictory in that they want autonomy but only within carefully defined limits.

Teaching as Hard Work versus "Rate Busting." Teachers are committed to the work ethic. Not being prepared is unthinkable to most teachers and they are critical of colleagues who are unorganized, poorly prepared, or remiss in making classroom assignments. There is a fine and fuzzy line between doing the best job possible and "rate busting," which creates contradictory expectations for what is defined as "normal" work and what is considered "overdoing it." Rate busting refers to teachers who always take work home, stay after school, or come to school on weekends. Teachers who work hard during the regular work day are critical of those who do too much work; and those considered rate busters are puzzled by the others' reactions because they think their extra hours are necessary.

Contradictions in Schools As Social Settings

Contradictions in role enactment were often complicated by contextual problems in school social settings, problems and situations that in themselves were also contradictory.

Teaching as Respected Work versus Public Criticism of Teachers. Teachers choose teaching as a career because they believe it is respected work. But, as pointed out earlier, they are often blamed for problems in the schools. In mass media reports, which reach even the smallest communities, teachers have been accused of being illiterate and the cause of students' low scores on standardized tests. Teachers are disturbed by these reports and the knowledge that people in their communities are reading them but are uncertain about how to respond. Thus, teachers experience contradictions between their conception of teaching as respected work and the public's criticism, as well as the low status accorded teaching in our society.

Teaching as a Helping Profession versus a Low Salary.   Among the reasons teachers choose teaching as a career is that they want to "help" people, particularly children. They anticipate that rewards will be intrinsic and that pleasure will be derived simply from watching children learn. They find, however, that all children do not want to learn and that all children are not desirable people with whom to work. For most teachers, intrinsic rewards are minimal. In addition, the reality of a low salary forces some teachers to live under extreme hardship. Thus, the lack of intrinsic rewards is not balanced or offset by extrinsic rewards. In fact, teachers have difficulty determining whether there are any rewards at all in teaching.

Teaching as Easy Work versus Exhaustion.   Teachers contend with the common assumption that teaching is an easy job because the work days are short, vacations are long, and groups of children are easy to control. The reality is that teachers' work days often extend into the evenings, that summers are spent in school or working at other jobs, and that control over children is demanding and exhausting. Paper grading and extracurricular duties take inordinate amounts of teachers' time outside the school day—as do meetings, workshops, and parent conferences. The strain of standing all day, monitoring students' work and behavior, and dealing with problems and disruptive behaviors is draining and difficult. Unlike other workers, teachers often have no coffee breaks, lunch hours away from their work setting, or places to prop up their feet and complain. Despite these conditions, they know that the common perception is that they have an easy job.

Female Teachers versus Male Administrators.   The disproportionate number of males in administrative positions has been noted, as has the negative effect of this arrangement on relationships between teachers and administrators. Despite the fact the research has shown that women are more effective than men in the principal role, males continue to fill administrative positions. Some reviewers have even concluded that hiring males has been detrimental to schools (Gross & Trask, 1976, in Adkison, 1981).

The inequitable power relationships between teachers and principals affect the nature and frequency of interaction in schools. For example, women teachers feel constrained when interacting and negotiating with male principals, so the teachers tend to be passive and subservient when interacting. Contacts are often limited to formal settings, such as faculty meetings, infrequent classroom visitation by principals for the purpose of teacher evaluation, or teachers' requests for materials. Male teachers, however, have interactions on both a formal and informal basis; they play golf with their principals, go hunting or fishing with them, or join them for an after-work drink.

At times, teachers encounter overt sexist remarks or sexual harrass-ment (are kissed or pinched). Even where principals have more collegial relations with women teachers, there is often a subtle undercurrent in which they refer to faculty as "the girls" or expect them to cook dishes for school gatherings.

Isolation versus No Privacy. Teachers feel a sense of isolation from other adults. Although surrounded by students all day, teachers (particularly elementary school teachers) see other teachers only briefly; and when they do, they rarely talk about instructional practices. Feiman-Nemser and Floden (1984) point out that this problem makes it difficult for teachers to evaluate their own practices. Even in open schools, where teachers in adjoining classroom areas see each other all day, they cannot talk because their total attention has to be on their classes. But despite this isolation, teachers have no moments of privacy when they can let down and relax because they are always before an audience of children. Teachers have to eat lunch under crowded conditions, sometimes with several hundred noisy children; and breaks in the day are filled with hall duty, playground duty, or bus duty. There is no place, including the restroom, to sit quietly by oneself. Some schools do not have separate restrooms facilities for teachers, and in extreme cases, the restrooms do not have doors. Thus, teachers have no privacy yet feel isolated.

Loving Children versus Unlovable Children. One of the reasons teachers cite for choosing teaching as a career is that they like (or love) children. The implication is that "children" means *all* children. However, teachers find that *real* children in *real* classrooms are not always lovable—or even likable. This results in a serious contradiction because teachers cannot admit not liking a student. To do so is an admission of failure or disloyalty to teaching. For women, particularly elementary school teachers, the admission also reflects their failure as females—to admit not liking a *small* child is "unwomanly."

Teaching as Specialized Work versus Teaching As Something Anyone Can Do. Teachers believe that their degree(s) and experience qualify them for specialized work. When they are dissatisfied or consider quitting teaching, they have difficulty assessing the uniqueness of their skills. Their identities have become so enmeshed in their teacher role that they cannot envision themselves in another work role. Many even see their skills as limited to a particular age of childhood or a particular subject. They have difficulty seeing what they might do in another setting. The fact that schools often hire substitute teachers who do not necessarily have certification to teach the grades or subjects they are asked to teach contributes to the notion that teaching is something anyone can do. Principals also contribute to this perception when they schedule teachers for classes for which they are not prepared—sometimes shortly before the beginning of a school year. The result of this contradiction is that teachers who are extremely dissatisfied with teaching often stay in the classroom because they see no other choices.

HOME LIVES OF WOMEN TEACHERS

The major theme of this book is that the school and home lives of women teachers are inextricably related. Since their work is only a part of teachers' lives, the contradictions in teaching are compounded by the contradictions in their other roles—those of wife, mother, friend, or daughter. Surprisingly, there has been little research about working persons' personal lives, with the notable exception of Lillian Rubin's (1976) interviews with working-class couples.

Historically, the personal lives of teachers were the concern of boards of education, who for decades placed rigid constrictions on teachers' moral behavior—including prohibiting them to marry (unless their husbands were physically or mentally incapacitated) (Woody, 1929, in Shakeshaft, 1981). At the same time, people held peculiar notions about single teachers, as seen in this excerpt from Waller (1932).

> The life history of the unmarried teacher seems to follow a pretty definite pattern. There are a number of years in which the hope of finding a mate is not relinquished. There is a critical period when that hope dies. An informant has suggested that hope has died when a woman buys a diamond for herself. The critical period is an incubation period during which spinsterhood ripens. During this critical period many desperate and pathetic things occur. The woman going through this period falls in love very easily, and may come to make the most open advances upon light or no provocation. The attentions of a lover being absent, the most perfunctory civility may be magnified to that size, and distorted to fit that configuration. Hence arise deep plots to trick the doctor or the dentist into a declaration. Hence, too, pitiful misinterpretations of the most commonplace remarks. It is a period of the most intense conflicts, and no way of solving the problem is left unthought of; these dignified women sometimes attempt, pathetic to record, to learn the technique of sex lure from the twenty-year-olds of their acquaintance. Perhaps this hope of finding a mate always dies hard and slowly, and requires little stimulant to keep it alive after its time....
>
> It is a peculiarity of some of these maiden teachers, a peculiarity which has been observed in several widely separated groups, in order to relieve the loneliness of their lives, to give names to inanimate objects. They populate the universe by naming the things about them, especially those articles which are in daily use and may be thought to have something of a character of their own. Thus a car is John, an ashtray Mr. Johnson, a fountain-pen Mr. Wright, and so

on. It is significant that most of these names are male. The sex starvation, and its attendant isolation from the procession of the generations, are here, and they materially affect the adjustment of maiden teachers to the teaching profession (pp. 408–409).

The balancing act performed by women teachers between home and school is a recent phenomenon if we consider that married women could not teach in many school systems until after World War II. This factor distinguishes teaching from other female-dominated professions and occupations. The personal lives of other working women were not sanctioned as rigidly. However, while Waller's description of single women seems humorous today and even absurd—I met no sex-starved single teachers who bought themselves engagement rings or named their ashtrays Mr. Johnson—we have moved from a time when teachers' marital status and home life were carefully monitored to a time when they are virtually ignored.

The work of Nelson (1982) may demonstrate that moving from one extreme to the other resulted in a loss of benefits from overlap between home and school. In interviews with Vermont schoolteachers who taught between 1915 and 1950, Nelson found that teachers did not attempt to separate their home and school lives. For example, they brought their children to school because they had no satisfactory babysitting arrangements, and when they became pregnant, their own mothers or daughters substituted for them. At the same time, teachers brought their students home with them. The close interaction of school and home life of these teachers resulted in their families cooperating more with housework. Thus, when they left teaching for a pregnancy or illness it was only for a brief period of time because they had a support network within their families and their schools. As the chapters in this book will illustrate, problems that were easily resolved for Vermont teachers several decades ago are a source of constant concern for teachers today.

Some support for the importance of interrole relationships on the teacher role is found in a recent study by Sutton (1984), who examined the effects of coping with multiple role demands among 200 elementary school teachers in 25 public schools. Sutton found that teacher stress was related to three factors: role demands (including role ambiguity, role overload, and role conflict); instructional problems, related to teaching students; and interpersonal relations, related to conflicts among staff members or lack of support from superiors. The strongest effects were found for role demands; they were found to be significantly related to job dissatisfaction and life dissatisfaction.

> The substantial relationships between interrole conflict and job and life dissatisfaction may reflect, in part, the competing demands that many teachers must face between work and family roles. Since 78% of the teachers were married and 63% were female, perhaps these findings reflect the stress of

balancing the demands of two competing roles: wife and teacher. While men also face these competing demands, women in America still tend to do the greater share of domestic chores (p. 22).

Women who work have been described as having a "double day" of work because they do all the housework when they get home from their work place (Eisenstein, 1981). Pleck's (1977) research has shown this to be the case. Men either take work home at night or use that time to recuperate from their day. Women, however, go home to more work. In fact, I found that teachers had a "triple day" of work. They taught all day, did most of the housework (including child care), and then did more school work, such as grading papers. When one considers the contradictory situations in which they teach, understanding their "balancing act" becomes even more difficult.

In summary, the historical development of the structure of schools and the predominance of women in teaching has led to the quasi-professional status of teaching. As a quasi profession, working conditions in schools are similar to those in working-class, or blue-collar, jobs. Those conditions take the form of contradictory sets of expectations for teachers' behavior, which create and perpetuate dilemmas and problems and, at the same time, hold teachers in their jobs. The effect of low salaries on teachers' lives is particularly crucial because it forces a working-class life-style on them. How women survive and even thrive under such conditions is described in the next eight chapters.

2

Lee: A Single Elementary School Teacher

Lee was a 26-year-old single woman who taught elementary physical education and coached secondary level girls' sports in a small school in the Midwest. Lee's story is one of stamina, perseverance, and vigor. Reared in a poor family where violence and struggle for survival were everyday occurrences, Lee believed that teaching was a means of gaining upward mobility. No matter how difficult the working conditions in schools, Lee was motivated toward achieving the respectability she never had while growing up. She never quite escaped her family background, however, and one of the reasons was that she taught in rural schools similar to the ones she had attended. Conditions in these schools, especially in the state where Lee taught, were often quite bleak because of a lack of money. Financial problems in the schools translated into personal problems for Lee because her low salary forced her life-style to be severely limited.

Lee's story also illustrates the problems of single women. Living alone, single women have a difficult time managing expenses. After necessities are paid for each month, little is left for savings. Therefore, it is improbable that Lee would ever accumulate enough money to purchase a house, make investments, or even take a vacation.

Being single also signals to school administrators that a teacher's time is more flexible and, therefore, she is available for school activities. As a coach, Lee was expected to spend every afternoon and evening throughout the school year involved in sports activities. However, in the three schools in which she taught, she was either paid nothing for her extra time or an insignificant amount compared to the money the male coaches received.

TYPICAL DAY

Lee's day began at 6:30 A.M., when she hurriedly showered, dressed in a sweatsuit and tennis shoes, and ate a doughnut before leaving the house she shared with a roommate. Her morning ritual was simplified because her short, curly hair required only a towel drying and she wore little makeup. She arrived at school by 8:00 A.M. after a 20-mile drive on a winding road. Her new Mustang took the curves easily at 60 MPH and she arrived in time to drink a Dr. Pepper in the teachers' lounge, a former shower room the teachers referred to as "the pit."

Leaving "the pit," Lee walked across an icy driveway to her office, located above a stage at one end of the gym building. In her office, which also served as a storage room for athletic equipment, she greeted a male coach who was pumping up a volleyball. The two of them shared the responsibility for 30 sixth-graders who came into the gym at 8:30 A.M. A third male coach was also scheduled for the class but usually did not arrive until 9:00 A.M.

The male coach sat on the stage while the students did calisthenics; then he divided them into teams for a basketball tournament. Lee refereed a game at one end of the gym while he refereed a game at the other end. After an hour, Lee put a large electric time clock into a suitcase and carried it back to her office. Perspiring after the exertion of running for an hour, she put on a sweat jacket and coat and walked through the ice and snow to the high school building. The shock of leaving the warm gym several times a day and going into the 15-degree outside air gave Lee a chill she hoped would not make her sore throat worse.

Lee walked through the dimly lit halls to the second floor, where she taught drivers' education in the home economics room. From the classroom she took her class to a small theater to see the film *Seatbelts for Suzie*. Although the film was over 20 years old, it was one of the few available. The class found places to sit among the seats, most of which had been broken or had their stuffing strewn around the room.

Lee returned to the gym for a coeducational physical education class, which she shared with the other two coaches. The 30 students played three-way volleyball. The losing teams were required to run around the outside of the gym. Running was treacherous because of the snow but the students ran anyway, some without shirts. Lee had little conversation with the coaches and thought to herself, "I hate this class!"

At noon, Lee paid 50 cents for a soyburger, french fries, and peach halves and sat with the other teachers at a table they shared with students. The teachers talked about school problems and criticized the administrators, despite the proximity of the students.

After lunch, Lee relaxed in "the pit," drank a Dr. Pepper, and talked to other teachers about "Lard Butt," their name for the principal, who had recently required a social studies teacher to teach a math class even though the teacher wasn't certified in math. They also admired their recent redecoration of "the pit." They had painted the walls, hung posters, and added a bookcase, all of which helped distract attention from the shower nozzles and drains, holdovers from "the pit's" years as a shower room.

During the afternoon Lee taught physical education to every elementary student in the school. The first group—kindergartners and first-graders—was team taught with the music teacher in a 100-year-old building, the original school in the community. The children had difficulty walking to the building on the ice so Lee had to help them. When they got into the building, they had to keep their coats on because of inadequate heating. After 30 minutes, they went to the gym building, where they played "killer ball." Lee chased the 50 children around the gym, tapping them with the ball until only one child was left. The screaming children were delighted, but complained of sore throats in the hot, dry room. Lee thought to herself, "I love these kids!"

The last two classes, one of third-garders and one of fourth-garders, were held in the cafeteria. After an hour of "Duck, Duck, Goose," the children hugged Lee and went back to their classes and she returned to the gym to prepare for basketball practice.

Because the boys' team used the gym before the girls' team that week, Lee used the time after school to prepare her softball schedule. At 5:30 P.M., practice began and Lee attempted to raise the spirits of her team, which was having a losing season. At 8:00 P.M. she ended practice and drove the winding road home. Because the night before she had gotten home from the game at 11:00 P.M., she was exhausted; she fixed herself a frozen pizza before lying down on the couch to watch TV. After resting a while, she talked with her roommate about the day's events, prepared a test for her drivers' education class, and went to bed, hoping her throat and chest would be less congested by morning.

PERSONAL HISTORY

Growing Up

Lee was raised in a poor, small mining town in the Midwest. Her memories of childhood were infused with the difficulties of poverty and having parents who were different from other parents because of their age, poor health, and physical disabilities. Her father was 63 years old at Lee's birth, and her mother was crippled and had a severe hearing impairment. They took little interest in Lee's activities throughout her school years.

Interview, May 9, 1980.
           LEE: They [her parents] just really didn't want to let us out. We were in prison.
    INTERVIEWER: Why do you think you were in prison?

LEE: Well, we were really poor for one thing. My dad was 63 when I was born and when I was 2 years old, he was on social security. My mother didn't work and we had no source of income then. I'm not sure what social security was back then but it wasn't very much for sure, with a husband, wife, and three children, and one who died at birth. So there was the concept of being poor. Economically it was bad and when I was 10 years old, my mother went to a mental institution. Later I found out it was because my father beat up on her. Hell, you know, I didn't know that. At 10 years old, your mother and father don't really openly fight in front of you. They kind of hid around and did it. Ten years old when my mother left and, except for an occasional Saturday afternoon visit, I didn't see her again until the night I graduated from the eighth grade when she came home. It was hell growing up in that kind of situation.

During her mother's absence, Lee was responsible for her two younger sisters and all the housework. When the work was not done, regardless of whether her sisters were to blame, Lee was beaten.

Interview, June 18, 1981.

LEE: He [her father] used to beat the hell out of me. I went to school when I was a sophomore with welts from him beating the hell out of me with a razor strap. I'm sure at the time I probably needed it but I don't think I needed it quite so severely. I think he secretly wanted another son and the last child my mother had was a boy and it was born prematurely and died. My dad thought, "Oh, well I'm just going to make Lee into my little boy."

Lee's father died when she was a senior in high school. She lived with her mother through her college years, although her mother was in and out of mental institutions throughout those years. Lee paid all their bills and remodeled the house while working and going to school, but the house burned down during one of her mother's stays in the hospital. When her mother left the hospital, she moved into a small house Lee referred to as a "dump." Lee traveled to this house to clean it and do the yard work. She tried to get power of attorney for her mother because she knew her mother was not capable of caring for herself.

Diary entry, May 12, 1981: My mother sometimes gets me upset. She's in her early 60s, crippled, and her mind is going. She doesn't pay her bills or take care of anything. She never cleans up that house. She represents everything I ran away from. I try to go down once a month to pay bills—take her shopping, but if there's a major problem, I'm upset for a week. I guess I wish she would accept her responsibility of paying her bills and taking care of herself. My sisters don't help the situation. One lives about two miles from Mom but won't go up there and the other lives 30 minutes away and has been home once since Christmas. Sometimes that whole mess really bothers me.

Not only did Lee's sisters ignore responsibility for their mother, but they would not even share the cost of their father's gravestone, which was still not purchased. Lee saved her money and finally bought one.

Education

During high school Lee was part of a group that called itself the "dirty dozen." She said, "We did ornery things; we smoked and we drank." The group was the first to wear jeans to school in the 1960s and staged a sit-in to protest the school's lack of a girls' athletic program. Lee's involvement in sports was a major influence on her decision to go to college and become a coach and teacher.

During Lee's senior year, a coach who supported girls' sports came to her high school and encouraged and inspired Lee to become a physical education teacher. Lee thought she could give students opportunities that she had never had.

Interview, May 9, 1980.
LEE: I like to be a winner and the only way you get to be a winner is through hard work and dedication.
INTERVIEWER: And you've gone on that philosophy?
LEE: Sure, what else is there?
INTERVIEWER: You went to college for that reason?
LEE: Yeah. That man really helped me. He told me that you've got to do what you want to do and the only way you're going to get it is by doing it yourself.

Lee was able to finance her college education with money she earned in a writing contest and with loans. She also borrowed $3000 — which took her 10 years to pay back. To Lee, to graduate from college was to make it in the world.

Interview, May 9, 1980.
LEE: To get a degree and be socially acceptable because I was not socially acceptable in high school. I felt kind of like I wanted to go back and say, "Hey, look, I got out of this hole and made it." I pulled myself up and I got my stuff together and here I am. You know. I'm a coach. And even though it's a small town where the school system has less than 200 kids in it, I am still highly respected in the town, only because of the social role.

Work

After Lee's graduation, she could not find a teaching job, so she worked in a grocery as a cashier for a year. Her first teaching job was in a small town near her home town. She taught reading and science (for which she had no certification) in the fifth and sixth grades and coached all the girls' sports (for which she received no extra compensation). In her second year in the school district, she taught reading, physical education, and health and coached all sports. The first year, Lee's teams had good records but the second year they had losing records. Lee attributed their losing records to a change in the players' attitudes but could not explain why their attitudes changed.

Interview, May 9, 1980.

LEE: I had made the decision that I was going to resign. We had a very bad season and it was that same set of girls that I had the year before that! They just didn't care anymore. And when a student does not care there's just nothing you can get out of them, regardless of what you say. If they don't want to practice you're not going to win. And we just didn't win. We were 3 and 11, and I was so discouraged I wanted to quit. I thought, "Wow, I got myself into this. I had a good year last year, I had a lousy year this year. I hate it. I hate it." I really hate being around them because they just infuriate me.

Lee's eventual resignation was also the result of a dispute between the teachers and the superintendent. The superintendent received state aid for students in special programs and wanted to claim that 85 percent of the student body qualified for those programs. When he asked the teachers to lie to state officials to corroborate his claim, the teachers refused. The outcome was considerable publicity, a state investigation, and the resignation of 15 teachers. Lee was convinced that she and the other teachers would have been fired if they had not resigned. Lee then took a job at the school described in the next section.

Although Lee often questioned why she stayed in teaching, she always answered the same way.

Interviews, May 9, 1980; January 18, 1981.

LEE: Why else? Because everywhere you go there is going to be a new set of kids, and as a coach I'm not hired and fired by my teaching ability, I'm hired and fired by my record. I enjoy being a teacher, but when it comes right down to it, my total enjoyment comes from the coaching.

I don't know what else I'd do. I could check out groceries in a grocery store, probably making more money than I make now teaching. But you can't beat the hours and you can't beat the vacations, but that's not the only reason. I just like kids. I like being around them. If I can help one kid, that's going to make my whole year worthwhile.

Personal Relationships

Because of the responsibility of caring for her mother and her long work hours, Lee had little time for developing personal relationships. She dated during high school and college but never had a serious commitment until she began teaching. This relationship had already lasted for four years and had a stabilizing effect on Lee's life—it was the first time she had felt loved and cared for. She and her friend had much in common; they were both teachers, from rural areas, liked sports, and were satisfied with their friendship without wanting more lasting commitment. The stability of this relationship helped Lee focus her time and energy on teaching and coaching.

SCHOOL LIFE

Cultural Setting

Lee's school was in a farming community in an isolated region of the Midwest. The town, located in rolling hills, was reached by winding roads on which travelers were periodically warned of one-way bridges (whoever reached the bridge first crossed while the other car had to yield). Most of the school's 200 students lived on dairy farms outside the community and were bused to the school. Farm families had difficulties surviving economically, and Lee estimated that two-thirds of the student body qualified for free lunches. Education was not highly valued because children were needed to work on the farms. Lee thought the low value placed on education was reflected in the community members' criticism of the schools and defensiveness of their children.

> Interview, May 9, 1980.
> LEE: I don't know whether they just don't care or they figure, "Well, the school has been there for 60 years, it's going to be there another 60. I went there. I turned out all right. I milk cows. My kid doesn't need to go to school. He can milk cows too." The townspeople are very biased. They all think their kids are right, regardless of what the situation is, and the teacher is the bad guy. Everything is the teacher's fault.

Lee's belief that community members blamed problems on the school rather than on their children was borne out by the conservative ideologies and religious beliefs of the people. Evidence of their belief in "an eye for an eye and a tooth for a tooth" was seen in the rise of a paramilitary unit, which was closely linked to a religious group. Taking the law into their own hands was a common practice—one that extended to the schools. For example, during Lee's first year, the principal attempted to enforce disciplinary measures in the high school and was met with strong resistance from students and parents. One night at a beer party, some students decided to kill the principal. They shot an arrow with a hunting bow through the man's trailer, missing his wife's head by 6 inches. Although footprints were taken and other evidence obtained, the prosecuting attorney dismissed the case on grounds of insufficient evidence.

School Administration

The school system was governed by a six-member school board (all males), a superintendent, and a principal. The superintendent had been in the school system for 20 years, but had been stripped of his authority by the school board, which made all the decisions. The president of the school board came to the school frequently and changed the orders of the superintendent and the principal if parents had complained. In turn, the superintendent changed the orders of the principal if the school board pressured him. The school board's meetings were either closed to the public (including faculty) or were not given advance notice—both violations of state law.

Teachers thought they had no administrative support and that they were helpless victims of the superintendent and the school board. As we saw, Lee's first principal attempted to support teachers, but he was stripped of his authority and nearly killed. Her second principal gave no support to teachers and took no disciplinary measures against students. Lee was evaluated once by the first principal but never again during her four years in that school district. She was therefore never sure of her areas of strength and weakness.

The lack of administrative support and formal evaluation resulted in the school board's having the power to fire teachers at will. At the end of Lee's first year, two-thirds of the teachers were fired or quit. Early in her second year, Lee was relieved of some of her coaching duties, because some parents complained to school board members that their daughters did not like Lee and were quitting the team. Over a cup of coffee with school board members, the superintendent decided a new coach would help recruit more girls for the team. So he hired a student teacher (male) who had been in the school three weeks. Lee, in the hospital at the time, did not find this out until she returned to school. She confronted the superintendent.

> Interview, January 18, 1981.
> LEE: He said I wasn't popular with the kids so that's why they wouldn't play. And I asked him, "You mean to tell me we're running popularity contests up here?" He said, "No, I didn't say that. I didn't say that." I said, "Well, you mean to tell me

that if there is a student in one of my classes that doesn't like me, all his mama and daddy will have to do is to go to the school board and he'll take him out of my classroom and place him somewhere else?" He said, "Yep, we'll do that. Gotta keep peace up here."

Lee was fired at the end of the year.

School Facility

The complex of school buildings in Lee's district was built between 50 and 100 years ago. Some had been renovated but others remained in their original state. On one floor of the high school, the ceilings were 15 feet high and lighting was provided by only a few bare bulbs.

Wires were hanging from ceilings, paint was peeling, toilets were broken and stopped up, plaster was falling from the ceilings, and holes had been punched in the walls. There were no curtains and no air conditioning or fans in warm weather. During the winter, the furnace was turned on only from 7:00 A.M. to noon, in an attempt to save fuel. The temperature was unbearably hot in the middle of the morning, while in the early morning and late afternoon, it was unbearably cold.

Before teachers were allowed to use "the pit" for a lounge they had to use the boiler room for that purpose. The boiler room was in the center of the high school, reached only by a steep, narrow stairway, and contained the furnace, janitors' supplies (including dirty mops hanging from lines), broken furniture, dirt, and mice. The teachers could not smoke there, so those who smoked had to drive around in their cars during lunch in order to do so. "The pit" was reached either through a janitor's storage room or a plywood door from outside; despite its smallness, shower nozzles, and drainholes it was a welcome change from the boiler room.

During the summer between Lee's two years at the school, a janitor used water to clean up a soft drink that was spilled on the gym floor. In the 100-degree weather, it raised the boards up one-half an inch. The school repaired the floor at a cost of $7000. During the winter, snow blew in air vents and made puddles on the gym floor, and one of Lee's basketball games had to be canceled. The floor was salvaged that time but warped once again when a fountain decorating the prom leaked.

The dangerous, unsanitary, unattractive facilities were likely to continue in their current state, because the schools were under serious financial strain and citizens would not pass a bond issue.

Teacher Morale

Teacher morale was extremely low because of poor working conditions, low pay, the lack of discipline, and the lack of administrative support.

Teachers felt dissatisfied, depressed, and helpless because of the administrators' and school boards' misuse of power and threats to their jobs. Teachers tried to discuss the problems with the administrators but were usually successful only in exacerbating conflicts. The only respite the teachers had was meeting informally, either at school or in someone's home, to complain or laugh about their problems. This informal support network was sometimes beneficial to school organization. For example, when teachers discovered two days before school began that the principal had allowed students to enroll in classes but had not made a master schedule, they took matters into their own hands and completed the scheduling process. This prevented considerable chaos on the first day of school.

The informal support network was also cathartic. A group of teachers, including Lee, often met for drinks or dinner in someone's home and shared problems. The evenings helped build a feeling of camaraderie and made the poor working conditions more bearable.

The teachers were similar because most of them were young and single. The school system hired them because they were cheaper than experienced teachers and were easier to fire since they lacked tenure and had no family or power network in the community. Thus, these young, single teachers tended to move from one small school district to another with little gain in salary or improvement in working conditions.

Students

Because students were from poor families, they dressed in jeans and T-shirts. There were no designer clothes, name-brand tennis shoes, or styled hairdos. Some students had no coats or hats, and Lee and other teachers helped provide them. The dropout and truancy rates were high, as were drug and alcohol use. Vandalism and theft were common. Lee frequently caught students stealing money from the locker room but received no administrative support for sanctions. Students had low aspirations—few would go to college or a trade school, and most would work on farms, in factories, or as maids or waitresses in a nearby lake area.

The interaction among the students and between students and teachers was quite informal. This informality resulted in some students looking to teachers as friends and confidants and others ignoring rules.

Interview, January 18, 1981.

LEE: There's no discipline in that building at all so the kids get away with murder. You take a student into the office and the principal laughs at you for it. We have a policy that the boys are not to wear hats in the building. We take their hats off and I give them to him and he gives them right back to them and he tells them it's okay to wear it.

Classes

Lee taught every elementary child in the school and most of the secondary students. Her physical education classes met on altenate days while her drivers' education class met daily for a semester. As described earlier, the lack of space and equipment limited Lee's classroom activities. The three coaches shared classes or shared the gym floor, depending on the season or on classroom activity. During basketball season, the boys' coach let his players practice during their physical education class. This interfered with Lee's class, because their space was limited and basketball players ran through it. Her girls' team was not allowed to do the same.

Asked to talk about her teaching philosophy, Lee wrote the following.

> Diary entry, May 12, 1981: In physical education I try to introduce them to a wide variety of leisure-time activities and make them aware of the benefits of physical fitness for health. My goals are for each individual student to perform the skill and learn the rules of the game. I must keep in mind that not all students have the same skill level but if they try—isn't that all you can ask? Some kids need to have the material presented in a variety of ways. Such as a "fun thing" or maybe as a challenge. After a period of four weeks each student should be performing at a level above what they originally started and do so with the knowledge of rules and strategy. I have always felt that if the majority of my students achieve the goals set in my objectives, then I've helped them to grow.

In the classroom Lee was a strong disciplinarian and maintained good control of her students. But her attitude, demeanor, and behavior changed, depending on the level of the class she was teaching and the sex of the students. She strongly preferred elementary over secondary students and females over males. This was evident in her comments and behavior.

Interview, May 9, 1980.

LEE: I have kindergarten through fourth grade physical education and they're just great. I love those kids. Maybe it's just an ego trip, like, "Oh, Miss _____, you're our best teacher." I'm the one who lets them get out and play every day. They are really great. My 9 through 12 is terrible. Either they didn't want to mind or they just felt like, "Hey, I'm a man and you're a woman so I don't have to pay any attention to what you say." And they were really rowdy and at one point during the school year, they were into breaking up the equipment. The girls I really didn't have that much problem with, because they usually mind about what to do.

While teaching high school classes with male students, Lee's demeanor was serious, and she was unenthusiastic and controlling. But with elementary children, male and female, she was smiling, enthusiastic, spontaneous, warm, and flexible.

Interview, May 9, 1980.

LEE: I enjoyed being with the little kids. Even now I still feel like I can handle the small ones better than the juniors and seniors. Not so much the girls but the boys. They have a tendency to sound off and I get mad. I don't like to be around them. I really don't.

INTERVIEWER: Why?

LEE: They intimidate me, I guess. One thing because of my size. They peer down at me and they start lipping off and cussing at me and I'm at a loss. What do I do now?

Lee preferred coaching to teaching. Although she was puzzled by her teams' change from a positive to a negative attitude and was angry toward those who quit or did not want to work hard, she said she taught in order to be able to coach. She particularly enjoyed being able to help girls who had problems and hoped she was providing them with opportunities she never had.

Leaving School

After Lee was fired, she went through a three-week period of depression and bitterness before she found another job. She found it difficult to teach when her students knew she had not received a contract.

Diary entry, May 12, 1981: No matter how bad it got, I kept going to save my reputation. I wasn't going to have them saying I was irresponsible or anything on that level. Pride—and I was too stubborn to let it show how disgusted I was with the whole situation. Some mornings were more difficult than others. There were a lot of times I didn't want to go. Several mornings I went in late and then I always felt guilty. I guess it was a matter of principle. If I'd been a shit ass about it, it would have only hurt me in the long run. I have a responsibility to my kids. They count on me to be there for class.

To a lot of those kids, P.E. is their favorite class. I'd hate to let them down. Whenever I have P.E. the elementary teachers have their free hours. When I'm not there, they don't get a free hour and somehow I feel they blame me for it. I didn't want any hassles, just finish out the year and get the hell out.

As soon as Lee signed a new contract, her spirits became very buoyant and she was able thoroughly to enjoy chaperoning the senior class on a trip to Florida. Her new contract was in a large district with a better salary schedule, and her salary increased $3000 a year. Although the observation part of this study had ended by the time Lee began her new school year, her diary entries and interviews continued and showed a consistently positive attitude about her new job.

Diary entry, July 23, 1981: You wouldn't believe the feelings inside me. I'm so full of anticipation and enthusiasm for our season to start, I'm about to burst. This is part of a poem that I thought also applies to life itself.

Life's battles don't always go to the stronger or faster but sooner or later, the team that wins is the team that thinks they can.
I love it!

Diary entry, July 24, 1981: Isn't it nice to see my spirits up and my excitement over coaching and teaching again? I think it's great.

Diary entry, September 9, 1981: "If you believe—you can." Nice philosophy, huh?

Diary entry, September 19, 1981: School has been in session now about a month. I really like it down here. My volleyball team shows promise and that helps lift my spirits. I have enjoyed working with those kids more than anything. They are great kids with a lot of talent.

My classes are whipped into pretty good shape. They are well disciplined and organized. It is a relief to know that my principal will support me. He is a nice guy and a strict disciplinarian. If a kid screws up he'll expel him for three days or give him an in-house suspension. He doesn't take flak from anyone. That's the way it should be.

The combination of teaching in a larger district, a better salary, administrative support, a more disciplined student body, teaching girls only, and having fewer coaching responsibilities was more satisfying to Lee and she maintained a positive attitude throughout the school year. Her contract was renewed.

HOME LIFE

Lee rented a two-bedroom brick house with several large trees in a well-kept yard. Because the house was located in a small town 20 miles from her school, she was not bothered by phone calls or visits from students; and so she thought it was worth the commuting time and costs. The large living room was free of clutter and contained only a few pieces of furniture Lee had purchased on a monthly payment plan. The furniture was mostly beige and the room had no splashes of color. A TV and stereo were the focal points in the room. Photographs of Lee's athletic teams and her roommate's family were on the stereo.

Household Duties

Lee and her roommate shared household duties. Her roommate did most of the cooking because of Lee's hectic schedule when coaching, and Lee did the dishes. Lee also did their laundry at a laundromat because her roommate once ruined some sweatsuits by leaving them in a dryer too long. During the week neither of them did much housework because there was no time, so Lee kept the house straightened by picking up any clutter. On the weekends they shared or alternated heavier housework such as vacuuming, mopping, and waxing floors. Because they were at home so infrequently and there were no children to clutter the house, the house stayed reasonably clean and orderly most of the time. Lee worried, however, about not getting enough work done in the house.

> Diary entry, December 16, 1980: I really need to clean the house, but there's something about leaving the house at 7:30 A.M. and getting home at 6:00 P.M. that really turns me off of housework.

Financial Conditions

Lee found it very difficult to live on her salary of $10,000 but her life became easier when her salary increased to $13,000 in her new job. After she paid her half of the rent, utilities, and phone bill, plus her car and furniture payments and insurance premiums, she had only $165 left over for food and gas. Her gas expenses usually amounted to $60 so she had about $100 for food, entertainment, and clothes. Because she was compulsive about paying her bills, she managed financially by buying few clothes and spending very little on entertainment. She had no savings and probably would never have enough money to buy a house.

> Interview, January 18, 1981.
> LEE: I mean I'm not living wildly or have big bills. You know if I was blowing money it would be one thing, but I'm not. I don't go anywhere or do anything. I go home to my mom's about once a month because that's all I can afford.

Leisure Activities

Lee's leisure activities were severely limited by her financial condition. During the week she usually watched TV with her roommate or the person she dated and on the weekends they fished or talked and sipped beer. On rare occasions they went to a large city to visit friends or to go to a bar for drinking and dancing.

> Diary entry, February 22, 1981: Ah! Sunday. Read the paper and napped all day.

> Diary entry, February 25, 1981: How nice it is to come right home after school. No practice or anything. Only problem is I eat constantly. The hips are showing the end results.

> Diary entry, March 1, 1981: A very cheap, relaxing weekend. Sitting around with three good friends playing spades and drinking beer.

Lee had the only vacation of her life when she chaperoned the senior trip to Florida. The school paid her expenses and Lee and the students all rode and slept in a school bus down and back. Most summers, Lee either worked or went to school. The summer after she was fired, however, she rested, went to a coaching camp, and worked occasionally in a friend's liquor store.

Interview, June 18, 1981.

LEE: This is the first summer that I have not worked or gone to school since I was 15 years old. I really like it. I could lie around and eat cherry chocolates and watch soap operas all summer.

Health

Lee was frequently sick with colds, sore throats, or the flu, particularly in the winter. Also, she had a persistent stomach problem, which once caused her to be in the hospital for a week. Doctors could find no specific problem but attributed her pain to stress. Excerpts from her diary show that her sicknesses persisted throughout the school year, although she usually went to school anyway because she could not miss ball games.

Diary entry, September 28, 1980: I'm not feeling well. I have a cold. I'm seriously considering calling in but with all the trouble of getting a substitute, I almost feel guilty about it.

Diary entry, October 31, 1980: What a week! On the 23d I was relieved of my junior high coaching duties and caught some damn virus. I spent the 24th–29th in the hospital. The doctor never decided what it was.

Diary entry, November 29, 1980: Ever since I got out of the hospital, anytime I get the least bit upset, so does my stomach.

Diary entry, December 3, 1980: I can't believe how sick I've been since I got out of the hospital. I've had a sore throat and ear trouble for a week. My stomach hurts whenever I get upset.

Diary entry, January 30, 1981: I've been in bed since 1:30 P.M. I guess I have the flu. I've been throwing up and running a fever. The only thing I've had to eat all day is popsicles.

Diary entry, September 4, 1981: I went to the chiropractor. My back was out in six different places. I've been in more pain than ever. He also told me I suffer from stress. No shit.

There were several contributing factors to Lee's sickness pattern. The stress of coaching and dealing with the impending termination caused her to lose sleep, so she felt tired much of the time.

Diary entry, April 8, 1981: It seems like I'm so tired all the time. A typical teacher—overworked and underpaid.

Being tired lowered Lee's resistance, as did her poor nutritional habits. Breakfast was usually a hurried frozen waffle, lunch was whatever was served in the cafeteria, and dinner was often a hamburger at a local cafe. To boslter her blood-sugar level, she often drank soft drinks and ate doughnuts.

Diary entry, May 25,, 1981: Starting today I'm on a 1500 calorie diet, trying to work down to 1000 calories. I'm about 10 to 15 pounds overweight (check the hip area). On this calorie intake diet I'll lose about a pound a week. It'll be a slow process but I'll look better. I really need to cut down on the Cokes and junk food.

Well shit, I've already blown my diet. I had three oatmeal cookies. Old habits are hard to break.

At the same time that Lee's resistance to sickness was reduced, she worked under conditions conducive to the spread of germs. She was in close proximity to children and, because she enjoyed the small ones, allowed them to hug and kiss her. She worked in buildings where the temperature fluctuated from freezing to unbearably hot, and she ran between the buildings all day, regardless of weather conditions or temperature. The result was an endless cycle of sickness.

CONCLUSIONS: OVERLAP OF HOME AND SCHOOL

Lee's school life frequently overlapped, if not subsumed, her home life, while her home life rarely affected her school life. As a coach, Lee stayed after school nearly every night of the school year, and when there were games, she did not get home until nearly midnight. Because she lived 20 miles from her school, she could not go home between the time school was over and games began, so she ate in fast-food restaurants, which in the rural area where she taught consisted of a small cafe that served greasy hamburgers. Therefore, Lee's eating habits were poor—she ate no breakfast, relied on soft drinks to get her through the day, and sometimes ate school lunches or greasy hamburgers at the local cafe.

Lee's long work hours exhausted her. After games she was usually excited and could not sleep. The cumulative effects of sleepless nights and poor eating habits contributed to a repetitive pattern of sickness. She was exposed to germs all day because she taught nearly every child in the school system, ran between several buildings regardless of the weather, and came to school even when she was sick because she would not miss a practice or a game. In addition, the context in which she worked—poor facilities, an ineffective principal, low pay, and low teacher morale —depressed her and contributed further to the sickness and exhaustion she frequently felt.

Exhaustion, nervousness, and sickness were not conducive to relaxing at home or to building personal relationships. Lee had only weekends to relax, catch up on housework, date, and spend time with friends—if she had the energy or was not sick. Fortunately, the person she dated also taught and had extracurricular duties, so they were tolerant of each other's schedules, problems, and physical ailments.

Lee's home life influenced her school life to the extent that depression or economic conditions were predominant in her thoughts. When this was true, she had difficulty gaining enthusiasm for her work, had low affect, and was less tolerant of students' behavior—particularly that of high school students.

Lee's commitment to the work ethic and continued belief that teaching would afford her a respectable social status contributed to the continuation of her ideal about teaching and schools. There was a refusal to accept the reality of her working conditions. To have accepted that reality as either universal to teaching or as a reflection of her own entrapment in circumstances would have been an admission of the failure of a lifetime of goals, attitudes, and beliefs. By challenging the reality of working conditions and fighting to survive and even change those conditions, Lee was able to maintain strength and the resolution to succeed.

Epilogue

Lee continued in her new job as described above. As of correspondence through the 1984 school year, she had successful sports seasons, was pleased about her continuing personal relationships, and started work on her master's degree. Her five-year goal was to find a job coaching girls' teams in a junior college or a small college.

3

Chris: A Single Secondary School Teacher

Chris was a 29-year-old secondary school social studies teacher who taught in two school districts during the study—a suburban public junior high school and a suburban–urban private school that housed grades K–12. Because the two schools were diametrically different, it was possible to compare the effects of school setting on a teacher's classroom performance and on her attitudes toward teaching. Chris was committed to a teaching philosophy similar to those on which open and free schools were based in the 1960s. Therefore she had difficulty in a traditional setting such as the suburban public junior high school in which she taught during the first year of the study. Chris was bright and assertive and voiced opinions and opposition to her administrators—also traits that caused her difficulties in traditional settings. However, she thrived in the nontraditional setting of the private school, where she taught the second year, and her teaching was much more effective. Chris's optimism and idealism about teaching kept her motivated through all types of situations. She had deep beliefs about what schools *should* be and worked hard to create situations where those beliefs could be fulfilled. Fortunately, she found such a situation in the nontraditional school.

In Chris's case, the effects of personal problems on teaching performance were clear. When problems were particularly stressful, she had difficulty making it through a school day; when satisfied in her personal life, she could tolerate even the most stressful school situations. This is not surprising for an individual in any type of work but is particularly well illustrated in Chris's life story.

TYPICAL DAY

Chris woke up at 6:30 A.M., made coffee, showered, dressed, fluffed her curly hair, drank several cups of coffee, smoked a few cigarettes, and left her trailer home in her immaculate white sports car. She drove through the city traffic and thought to herself how much more comfortable she felt now driving in traffic than she had when she moved to the city a year before. The drive took nearly an hour but she was not worried about being late because her first class did not begin until 10:15 A.M.

She drove up the long wooded driveway to the school, felt a wave of homesickness for her parents' farm, and was thankful for the school's isolated wooded location in the city. She spoke to several students as she walked in the esthetically pleasing glass, wood, and rock structure; they returned her greetings, calling her by her first name.

Chris walked through the carpeted hallways to her office and looked over her plans for that day before getting a cup of coffee. Teachers were in the central office and in the lounge discussing administrative problems they had to solve because their principal had resigned. One teacher took over scheduling responsibilities and asked the other teachers to look over her plan for possible problems and to offer suggestions.

Since there were no bells to signal the beginnings and endings of classes, students moved from one area to another and slowly filled Chris's anthropology class. One student turned his radio on to a rock station and left it on until class began. Chris enjoyed the informal atmosphere in her classes after having spent the previous year teaching in a school where discipline was strict and the principal expected tight control. She allowed students to volunteer answers, make comments, or interrupt her whenever they wished. Although she enjoyed her anthropology classes more than her history classes, she felt relieved that the school encouraged creativity and flexibility in course content, rather than forcing adherence to a rigid curriculum plan. Chris was therefore able to build lessons around some of her areas of expertise. This worked particularly well for her social problems class because she could draw on her background in sociology to give substance to the course.

At lunchtime Chris went to the cafeteria, where a few students were eating at restaurant-style tables—most of the students had left campus, taking advantage of the school's open-lunch policy. She decided to have soup and a sandwich, and took her tray to the teachers' lounge, where the discussion about scheduling, discipline for tardiness, and other administrative problems was continuing. While Chris smoked another cigarette, she noted the jug of wine in the refrigerator and thought how relaxed the atmosphere of the school was compared to that in public schools.

During the afternoon she took her students to the large library–media area in the center of the school. Students used the two-story facility to find sources for research papers. Chris moved around the room helping students locate books and periodicals. Students moved in and out of the area to the restrooms, water fountains, or areas where smoking was permitted.

During her last class late in the afternoon, Chris felt tired because she had been up late the night before talking to friends. She felt less spontaneous, energetic, and able to smile and joke; therefore, she let the students carry the discussion among themselves as they sat in a circle.

After school Chris checked with other teachers to see if there were any meetings and was relieved that there were none. There had been numerous meetings all fall at all times of the day and night concerning the school's financial problems and the subsequent resignation of the principal. Chris was relieved to be able to go home, where she had a drink and relaxed with her cat. She then made plans to meet a friend for dinner, because she had brought no work home, wanted to get out, and needed someone to talk to.

After an evening of food, drink, and talk, Chris returned to her trailer and once again played with her cat to relieve her loneliness. She did a few household chores and went to bed and thought about her uncertain future. She was depressed because she had had to take a salary cut to go to the private school, and she thought about ways to leave teaching. Each alternative was expensive, however, and she would have no way to support herself. But she also thought about how much she was enjoying the school year, the students, and the atmosphere of the private school. Her attitude toward teaching had become more positive, but she almost wished she were having another bad year so she would have been more motivated to leave teaching.

PERSONAL HISTORY

Growing Up

Chris was raised on a farm near a small town in the Midwest by her father, who was a farmer, and her mother, who was a teacher. Chris and her two sisters were expected to do many chores around the farm and invoked the wrath of their father if they did not. Born 10 years after her next oldest sister, Chris, when she was 13, was told by her mother that she was an "accident," that her parents had not wanted another child. Chris thought this might explain her father's deep anger and abusive treatment. She said her father often called her a "dumb shit" and tried in as many ways as possible to show her she was incompetent.

Chris's father beat her mother and many of Chris's childhood memories involved this brutal treatment. When she was 5, she stopped one of his beatings by getting a gun out of a cabinet and threatening to shoot him. The fact that her mother continued to tolerate his abuse puzzled Chris, because she saw her mother as something of a "superwoman"—who taught, helped run the farm, sewed, made quilts, canned food, and provided Chris's only source of support and love. It was even more puzzling to her because her mother once told her that she did not love Chris's father but that her daughters were her life. Chris's mother had always had a separate bank account from her father into which she put her teaching salary, and when her father refused to pay for her and her sisters' college educations, her mother paid all their expenses. Chris's parents lived separate lives after their daughters left home—often living in different houses on properties they owned.

Chris's deep love and attachment for her mother were shaken when her mother developed cancer (during the period of this study). She drove from the city to her mother's home nearly every weekend for several months, and with her sisters helped her mother get on a diet and vitamin regimen they were convinced would halt the spread of the cancer. Chris was devastated by the thought of losing her mother, and her fear, anxiety, and depression were reflected in her teaching and personal life.

Although Chris and her sisters, who were also teachers, became close during their mother's illness, they had not always had such a relationship. Her oldest sister was away from home during most of Chris's childhood, and her sister's attitude toward Chris was similar to that of her father. Chris thought that her sister was a lot like her father and that she was his favorite daughter. Chris's birth when her sister was 10 usurped her sister's central position in the family. Her sister often exceeded some of the normal sibling cruelties—she locked Chris in closets, shot arrows and told Chris to run under them, hung her from a tree by the leg, and laughed hysterically when Chris broke her arm. Even though her sister was now 40 years old, at times during the study she still revealed some of her old anger and animosity. Chris's oldest sister was married and had two children, taught at a university, had a Ph.D., ran a farm, and owned and maintained rental property. She often took a critical mother role toward Chris and reprimanded her for not knowing what she wanted to do with her life. Thus, of all the people in her family, her mother was the one to whom Chris stayed closest. She visited her as often as possible, despite her anxiety at having to see her father and listen to his continued criticism.

Education

Chris's mother was a strong influence on Chris's performance as a student, her decision to go to college, and her decision to go into teaching. During high school, her mother always excused her from farm chores if there was homework to do. Chris was placed in an accelerated classroom in which her mother was the teacher; she thought her mother expected more from her than from the other students and did not like to see her mother in that role. Graduating in the top 10 of her high school class, Chris want to a small liberal arts college near the farm. Later she transferred to a larger university that was somewhat farther from the farm.

Chris said she went into teaching because "my mother told me to and I was an obedient child. I was programmed." She had considered going into a field of science or becoming an X-ray technician but said that when she was in junior high school there was a switch to new math and that "screwed her up." She developed an anxiety toward math and sciences and later decided she "just wanted to do anything that had to do with people." Therefore, she majored in sociology and the social sciences. She also said she tended to set goals that were easily attainable so she would not fail.

Work

During college, Chris had several summer jobs that paid minimum wages. She sold magazines door-to-door throughout the West but made no money because employees were expected to pay their own expenses. She also worked in a pizza parlor and in a packing plant where chickens were processed. She described the latter as the most unpleasant job she had ever had.

Interview, June 9, 1981.

CHRIS: On every chicken butt there is a little oil bag. When they preen, they spread that oil on their feathers, and that's what keeps all the chickens in the world from drowning when it rains. So you take a knife and scale that out, that was my job. So, during the evening there would be about 50,000 chicken butts come flying by and if you were quick enough to grab one of them between the greasy hand, the glove, and the knife, you might accidently slice off a chicken oil bag.

Every two hours they would shut down and hose all the shit out and you'd go into the snack area, where they had the audacity, I might add, to serve fried chicken. I don't know who the hell would eat fried chicken after watching 50,000 chicken butts pass by your eyes.

Chris quit the chicken plant after two weeks, finished school, and took her first teaching job shortly before the school year began. She stayed in the job for six years and found teaching ideal. Teaching three flexible courses —anthropology, sociology, and cultural studies—she was able to experiment, take lots of field trips, play simulation games, design individualized projects, encourage class participation, and, in general, do must of the things she wanted to with the students. She thought the students were cooperative and respectful, that, in fact, they were quite similar to students in the rural area where she grew up. She felt she had a close rapport with them, that they confided in her and joked with her but still did the work she expected.

Chris took a leave of absence for a year to finish her master's degree, so her yearly salary dropped from $11,000 (1978–1979) to $2500 (1979–1980), for an assistantship. At the end of the year, her former school district told her that they had to cut back positions in social studies so they could not let her return. Despite the fact that Chris had tenure and had been promised that she could return, the principal and superintendent refused to change their decision. Chris was angry at the administrators and distraught at not being able to return to a job she found ideal. Although she had sufficient legal grounds to file a suit against the district, she did not because she had no money for legal fees. Also she did not want a negative reputation that would prevent her from being hired in other school districts.

Chris spent the summer working on her degree and looking for a job. Through an assistant superintendent she knew, she was able to gain an interview and, later, a one-year appointment in a suburban junior high school. Chris was anxious about moving to a city because she had always lived in rural areas. However, one of her sisters and several of her friends lived in the area, and she needed the job, so she moved. The junior high school was the first of two schools in which Chris taught during the study and is described in the following section; her other school will be discussed in the section "School Life."

Teaching: Year One of the Study

Chris's school was located in an affluent suburb of a large city (over 500,000 population). Its 600 students were predominantly from white upper-middle-class families, wore designer clothes, and had professionally arranged hair styles. The school facility was new and had been built in an "open-pod" plan—all sections of the building opened into the central cafeteria area. Movable walls had been put up in some areas to partition classrooms from one another. The school was carpeted, well maintained, clean, and attractive. There was a spacious teachers' lounge replete with equipment and supplies, a Coke machine and coffee machine, a microwave oven, and plenty of tables and chairs for large gatherings at lunch. Lunches were usually tasteless because the food was cooked in a central kitchen and then delivered to the school. A typical lunch was a cold soyburger; greasy, limp french fries; a small amount of lettuce with a flavorless dressing; and a dessert that looked like adhesive used to hang things on a bulletin board. Teachers met in the lounge and discussed students, administrators, their union (95 percent were members), the possibility of striking, or parties. As a new faculty member, Chris felt left out of discussions; and because she rarely socialized with the other teachers outside school, she felt even more isolated.

Chris taught ninth-grade civics to six classes a day. Although she only had to prepare one lesson plan each day, the monotony of teaching the same thing six times, particularly in a subject in which she had little preparation, quickly became boring. This was particularly true on days when Chris planned to do something uncreative, such as grading a test. She also found that she was unable to lecture very often because students of 13 or 14 years of age would not listen for long and she was simply not able to talk for six hours straight.

Observations showed that by early afternoon Chris visibly faded. She sat down to teach instead of standing, she had less spontaneity, developed dark circles under her eyes, smiled very little, and was less tolerant of students' behavior or misbehavior. At the end of one day, she laid her head on her desk and moaned, "Why does anyone ever go into teaching?"

Chris's teaching style was mechanical and lifeless, particularly in the afternoons or when she was having personal problems. She frequently reprimanded the class to "quiet down" or "cut it out" but never totally had their attention. Students whispered, punched one another, or combed their hair. At the beginning of classes, Chris never waited for total attention before beginning the lesson; she might start a period by saying, for example, "Okay, you guys, you're supposed to work on your review questions today." Some students worked, some did not, and Chris had to remind them several times to "get busy." Students seemed uninterested in the class, called out without raising their hands, and seemed more intent on finding the specific answers to questions than understanding the context from which the answers were taken.

Chris got satisfactory evaluations from her principal, based on two one-hour observations during the year. Among the principal's positive comments were that she was well groomed, had a good attendance record, related well to students, was cooperative with school administrators, related well to other staff members, had a clear and pleasant voice, and was academically prepared. Overall, she was rated as "acceptable" and recommended for another contract. Among the areas of needed improvement, the principal commented that Chris might develop more of a sense of humor, make her classroom atmosphere more informal, and develop discussion techniques appropriate for junior high students. These latter comments came as no surprise to Chris but were a continual source of conflict. She had a difficult time adjusting to ninth-grade students and thought they were disrespectful and lacking in self-control, compared to her high school students.

> Diary entry, November 18, 1980: Terrible Tuesdays, as my sister calls them, because for some reason both our students seem to be hyper on Tuesdays. Today was no exception. Often, I find discussion very difficult with my ninth-graders. Thursdays I spend a lot of time with them doing written assignments, which keeps the class highly structured. That's the only way they seem to be able to handle it. They must have direction and structure, and I find that hard to accept sometimes. I want them to be able to do something on their own and *think* for themselves.

Thus, Chris found that she could cope with her students by being controlling and that when she relaxed and became less formal, as the principal suggested, the students were what she considered to be out of control. She often saw her teaching as a policing activity.

> Diary entry, September 23, 1980: They're [her students] back to giving me shit. It seems to be a constant battle. If I have to say "Be quiet" one more time, I think I'll scream. I am so sick of being a police person. I want to instruct, to discuss, to interact, but all I seem to be able to do is say "Be quiet" and fill out numerous forms. What a joke!

Chris talked about some of the reasons she was so dissatisfied with her students and with teaching, compared to the satisfaction she felt in her first seen in the following two diary entries.

> Diary, entry, November 17, 1980: My students' lack of consideration and apathy adds to my anxiety and stress. Last week I had an unusal experience. One of my lovely students had made me a surprise in the form of a Chinese star (which is a form of weapon) that is made of metal and filed off into very sharp points and edges. The star was placed above my head so that when it was hit by a paper wad it would tumble down onto my head and hopefully inflict some damage. I was quite shocked at this malicious attempt to let me know that someone did not like having me around. I promptly gave the device to the principal and he assured me he would do some detective work. So far he has not proven to be any Dick Tracy. I have a few ideas but have not been able to come up with any hard-core evidence. Instead of working on my master's degree, I should have gone to the police academy.

> Diary entry, January 5, 1981: Return to school—Blah! This card was on my desk first hour, first day back.
> "If you think you know what's going on, you're probably full of shit."
> They're already giving me shit. It is humorous. I probably am full of shit.

Later in the school year, Chris admitted that part of the problem with her students' attitude may have been the result of her negative attitude toward them.

Interview, March 26, 1981.
CHRIS: I've been a bitch and I know it, but they've been rude too. I've been bad and I know it, but you just put it under your belt and go with it.

Chris talked about some of the reasons she was so dissatisfied with her students and with teaching, compared to the satisfaction she felt in her first job. She realized that the courses she had taught in her first job enabled her to use a variety of activities and her individual creativity, which made it easy for her to build a rapport with her students. In short, the courses were fun, were often held outdoors, and were those students chose to take rather than being required. In contrast, the subject matter of civics was monotonous and the course was required. Another factor was that Chris had difficulty dealing with the maturity level of ninth-graders, although she did recognize that in her first years of teaching her close rapport with her seniors may have been related to the fact that she was close to them in age. She said she knew her sense of humor had changed over the years and that what she found humorous her first years of teaching she no longer found humorous—which made her seem, at age 30, considerably distant from the 14-year-olds she taught.

Interview, March 26, 1981.

CHRIS: It's been awful. It's just hard for me. I just have a hell of a time lately relating to them. I don't know, but things that went on in high school I think I can relate to. I related to those kids and they would do things and I thought they were funny. These kids do things and I just think they're obnoxious.

I think that's the most hellacious years of your life [junior high school]. I think that's the most absolute worst age to work with. Junior high would just never be my choice. I think I would prefer elementary before junior high. They're just as obnoxious as shit.

And they're beating on each other and they can't keep their hands off each other.

A final point of comparison between Chris's teaching jobs was the differences between rural and urban students and the relative poverty that was characteristic of the former and relative affluence of the latter. Chris identified with rural students because of her own background; she understood and had sympathy for their poverty. She valued their attitudes about hard work and respect for teachers. In comparison, she regarded her suburban students as spoiled, indulged, and pampered by their parents. She thought that they wanted things "handed to them on a silver platter" rather than working for them and that they were disrespectful and rude.

Interview, March 26, 1981.

CHRIS: It's a hard thing to explain and it's almost like a sixth sense, but being from a rural area I think people have more of a—I wouldn't want to generalize too much—realistic sense of values. You do know there are limitations to life and that you can't buy everything. Not everything is a new dress or who's got the cutest hair style or whatever. They're very superficial —just a very plastic kind of atmosphere. Any child who comes in that's the least bit different, like some of them are more mature or have a little more depth, they are ridiculed. They all have to look alive. I guess it's the value system. It really irks me and I'm really turned off by it. I know that I'm prejudiced.

At the end of the school year, Chris's school district had a "reduction in force" of 24 teachers. Teachers like Chris—who were on one-year temporary contracts—were the first to be RIFed. The morale in the school lowered considerably and Chris noted a sign in the teachers' lounge that read, "Doing a good job around here is like wetting your pants in a dark suit—it gives you that warm feeling, but nobody notices." Chris was told that she would be rehired if there were openings but that they would not know if this were possible until August. In the meantime, they asked Chris to write a letter of resignation, which Chris found absurd because she had no job from which to resign. She finally deduced that the purpose of the letter was to relieve the district of the responsibility of paying unemployment. She did not send the letter because she found another job soon after school ended. The district did offer her a job in August, but she had already signed a contract with a private school—at which she took a $2000 reduction in salary.

During Chris's year in the junior high school she became increasingly dissatisfied with teaching. She felt she had been "screwed over" by the district she had left in order to work on her master's degree and that she was similarly treated when she was RIFed by the second district.

> Diary entry, September 28, 1980: I am beginning to hate my position as a teacher.

Chris began to think of alternatives to teaching and when she was RIFed, she applied for jobs in other occupations. She did not qualify for the jobs she applied for in insurance companies and found the male interviewers to have sexist attitudes. For example, one man told her she was "cute, nice, and probably bright" but that "we" need teachers and she ought to stick to teaching. So Chris thought about going to law school or running her parents' farm. To go back to school, however, she needed money, so decided to teach to earn enough money for school. Running the farm would isolate her from the professional world and she was not ready for that.

On the other hand, Chris said she could not imagine doing anything else but teaching and that despite all her problems, she still liked students. Her attitude toward teaching and students became significantly more positive during the following school year, which is described in the next section.

SCHOOL LIFE

Chris's new school was a private school that had once been administered by an order of nuns who had lived in a convent in one wing of the school complex. When the nuns gave up their administration, the school became a private day school supported by students' tuition payments ($2400 per year). The convent wing became unoccupied. There were 380 students in the twelve grades, 160 of which were in the high school.

Cultural Setting

The school was in a suburban area adjacent to the same city as Chris's previous school. Parents who sent children to the school tended to be upper middle class but some students were sponsored by wealthy citizens who wanted to provide a "needy" child with an education outside public schools. The school's philosophy was based on experiential learning, self-discipline, and self-motivation—similar to the open-school philosophy of the 1960s and early 1970s. The declining enrollment showed that parents who wanted a "back-to-basics" education for their children were not choosing the school. The school had become known as one that could handle problem children. Its relaxed atmosphere combined with its emphasis on self-control and self-motivation was considered by school officials to be a successful combination for dealing with problem students.

School Administration

Chris's initial impression of the principal was positive. Although the school had a board of directors, the principal was responsible for administrating the everyday activities. Shortly before the beginning of the school year, financial problems led to a tumultuous period. Chris was in shock at the possibility of losing her job before beginning it, particularly after she had turned down a job in her former school, but she was still expected to attend meetings and support decisions made by the majority of the teachers. Various alternatives were suggested for obtaining operating funds. Among them were to cut back several teachers to part-time positions or to cut back all teachers' salaries. After many days of meetings during which classes were dismissed, students became alarmed and they and their parents demanded to be involved. More meetings took place, during which two teachers and the principal quit, but enough money was raised from parents to begin the year.

Chris said she needed a sense of order and organization after the period of chaos but hated to admit it because of her belief in the school's philosophy of individuality and children's rights. During the following months, order was restored but not because a principal was hired. In fact, Chris was able to observe how a school would operate with no principal where teachers made the administrative decisions cooperatively. Interestingly, she found the teachers did quite well at making decisions about curriculum scheduling, discipline, and other administrative functions. Teachers tended to take responsibility for particular duties but with the advice of the other teachers. However, teaching and administrating simultaneously became quite time consuming, and the teachers were relieved when a faculty member they all respected was selected as the principal. Chris described the woman as "brilliant" and said she had been able to "turn the place around."

School Facility

The school building was quite unusual architecturally but its high ceilings and huge expanses of glass were cost ineffective and were partly the cause for the financial problems. The school was designed at a time when there were no energy crises and the nuns were able to raise a large sum of money for an elaborate structure. Although right in the city, the school was on a wooded hill and so not easily seen from the road. Esthetically it was a direct opposite to traditional rectangular brick schools.

Inside, there were three large pods—areas that housed the lower, middle, and upper schools. Each operated separately during the school day although the pods converged in a central media-library, theater, and lobby area. The lower level, equivalent to elementary school, had an open plan; there were some areas where children could climb, crawl, or otherwise move about freely and other areas for reading, where pillows were strewn about for lounging. The middle level, equivalent to a junior high school, was closed, and the teachers had decorated their rooms colorfully. The upper level, or high school, had walls but no doors on classrooms and no decorations in the rooms.

There was a separate hallway for students' lockers where students could study or talk. The noise was contained in this area because of good planning and architectural design. Each pod had its own teachers' lounge, so interaction among teachers in different levels was reduced. Each teacher had an office of reasonable size, where he or she could work and lock up materials.

Teacher Morale

Teacher morale was quite low when Chris first came to the school because of the uproar surrounding the financial problems and the principal's resignation. Chris described the period as extremely stressful, which made it impossible to teach. Teachers who were cut back or who eventually quit were alienated from those who were full time, and teachers who agreed to take a salary cut were alienated from those who refused. Although Chris agreed to a salary cut, she felt caught in an undesirable, uncomfortable situation not of her making. She felt isolated and left out of the teachers' social circles and disenchanted with the school.

Interview, November 3, 1981.

CHRIS: I had had it [referring to the first weeks of school]. I didn't want any more. I considered going to my former school as a permanent substitute. I really wanted to run away. Now, I'm ready to abandon ship. I'm more rigid now than ever. I have a sense of panic. Sometimes I feel as though I live apart from my body. I'm just getting through the days with no enthusiasm.

Chris was able to see the connection between the effect of the events at the beginning of the year and her feelings of disillusionment and hopelessness revealed in this interview excerpt. She said she had merely lived from day to day without taking time to pause and reflect on how she had survived those first weeks.

Chris did survive and found that as order was restored and the new principal organized the school, she herself came to be more integrated socially with the teachers and increasingly more satisfied with teaching. During the second semester she said she was as happy with teaching as she had ever been, even in her ideal first job, but thought that was a "dangerous kind of thing" because she still wanted to try another kind of work. In Chris's words, "It would be easier if things were crappy, then I'd have the incentive to do something else."

Students

Chris consistently made positive comments about her students throughout the school year, which supports her belief that she could motivate and control upper-level high school students better than ninth-graders. Even though most of the students were as affluent as her former ninth-graders, they dressed more casually and individualistically. There were also students who were poor (those sponsored by patrons) or from the working class, and thus there was a wide range of student interests and values. And students were encouraged toward individuality and creativity rather than toward the conformity that Chris found predominant in her previous school. Even during her depression at the beginning of school, Chris said the students were respectful, intelligent, open, and honest.

Students were allowed to participate in meetings with faculty, to interview candidates for faculty positions, and to participate in day-to-day decisions that would affect them. Chris was impressed with the students' ability to handle these situations and found that only a small minority could not handle the responsibility. Discipline was also a problem with this minority. Some could not deal with the freedom from excessive or rigid rules and lacked self-control. Some did not attend classes or were chronically tardy. And some caused disruptions related to drug use. Although the school was quite tolerant, within limits, of most behavior, the chronic problem students were subjected to sanctions. The new principal implemented more rules and worked to gain control of some of the drug problems but found it difficult to establish new standards during the first school year.

Classes

Chris taught five classes a day and had two conference hours. She taught four semester courses—anthropology, social problems, sociology, and psychology—and one year-long U.S. history course. Chris felt confident teaching the classes because she had experience and knowledge in most of the subjects and because the school supported creative approaches. The variety of courses was particularly stimulating to Chris after her year of teaching the same subject six times a day.

The change in Chris's demeanor and teaching style, as compared to the previous year, was striking. She appeared more relaxed, smiled and laughed with students, was more spontaneous in class discussion, and rarely told students to "Be quiet" or "Get busy." This is not to say that all students paid attention or were actively engaged in class work all the time. Chris still tended to begin class without waiting for full attention and interacted only with the most verbal students. Students called out answers and one student finished the ends of Chris's sentences when she paused. The quieter, less assertive students did not participate. Nevertheless, Chris's enjoyment of her students was obvious, and her interaction with them was quite different from her interaction with the junior high students of the previous year. The conflicts resulting from the necessity to keep tight control, her belief in the students' lack of self-control and their rudeness, and her former principal's insistence that she be more informal were absent. Chris said she was relieved not to have to tell students to be quiet all the time and was not bothered by their talking out and having long discussions. In fact, the school offered exactly the kind of situation in which Chris wanted to teach.

Leaving School

Chris's year at the private school was quite different from the previous year in important ways. The context in which she taught, including the school's organizational structure, policies, procedures and rules for teachers' and students' behavior, and the relationship between teachers and administrators, differed considerably, as did the behavior of students and the relationship between teachers and students. The fact that Chris's attitude toward teaching became more positive supports an assumption that teachers do not merely become dissatisfied (or burned out) with teaching per se but do so because of situations in which they find themselves. One would anticipate that for those who are not so fortunate as Chris to be able to move or change schools, dissatisfaction with teaching would increase as the work became irrevocably linked to a particular school.

Chris planned to continue at the private school for another year—if their financial situation allowed them to reopen.

HOME LIFE

Chris's home life had a strong influence on her school life. She had dated numerous people since her teen years, some for long periods of time, but had never married. Chris tended to commit herself to relationships in which she supported people who needed help or boosts in self-esteem. By subsuming herself she lost her own sense of identity. Invariably, the relationships were ended by the other person and Chris was devastated. But she had strong recuperative qualities, which helped her survive these periods.

> Diary entry, August 1981: I trust like a child and when I love someone I trust them to be honest with me. It is interesting to me that I do sort of work backwards. I like people until they give me a reason not to.
>
> Philosophically, however, I believe that to lose one's sense of love and trust leaves only an empty shell to exist. The innocence of youth is truly a beautiful thing. Perhaps this is why I love teaching. I enjoy the spontaneity of youth and the unpredictable behavior that sometimes accompanies it. I find it a very sad fact that pain and reality leads us to be cynical, cold, and hard. It reminds me of the cliche, "Some (wo)men see things as they should be and ask why? Other (wo)men see things as they should be and ask why not?" I guess it is that driving force of "why not" that makes me survive and want to survive.

One of the reasons Chris moved to the city and took the job in the junior high school was to be with a person she had dated for several months. They planned to live together and share expenses. Shortly after the beginning of the school year, however, the other person moved out, began dating someone else, and left Chris with all the expenses of her new home. Chris went through a long period of shock, sorrow, anger, and depression. She began counseling, cried a lot, drank a lot, and had difficulty getting up each morning to go to school. Her deep emotional turmoil was a strong influence on her work at school and contributed to her dissatisfaction with teaching (this will be discussed in more detail in the last section).

Chris gradually came to understand some of the negative patterns she tended to repeat in relationships and, with the help of her counselor, discovered that to change those patterns she needed to develop a more positive self-image. Chris began to like herself and was able to decrease her depression and protect herself from getting into another negative relationship.

> Diary entry, August 1981: Finally in the last months of school, I began to crawl out of my shell a bit. I learned a lot about myself on all those lonely nights. I learned that I could survive and that actually I liked myself. I began to be more comforting to myself and to care for my needs. Unless you have been there, it is hard to understand. But if you do not like yourself, then you look to everyone else to fill your voids, and when that is the case, then you rely on

others too greatly. It is an easy thing to begin to see this and rationalize it, but it is one hell of a hard thing to do. For the first time in my life, I truly am beginning to be able to do this. I guess necessity is the mother of invention or that you have to reach the pits before you can start to crawl up again. I feel as though if I don't find a job by this fall that I should go back to school and try to reach to find my potential. I have always set goals that were easily attainable because I feared failure in the one area of my life that had been secure. Now, I feel I am ready to challenge myself to find what it is I am made of.

Chris did develop another relationship, but very cautiously. The relationship thrived and they were married. They were mutually supportive and loving. Chris did not feel exploited or inadequate and thought that the relationship would remain mutually gratifying, supportive, and tolerant of each other's growth. It was the first time Chris had felt truly loved by anyone except her mother.

Household Duties

Chris lived in a trailer that was permanently anchored to a lot in a well-kept, quiet trailer park in an isolated part of the city. She made biannual payments on the trailer from her savings account. She thought the payments were relatively inexpensive for the city and hoped to be able to sell the trailer at an insignificant loss if she ever decided to move.

Because Chris lived alone and was only in the trailer a few hours a day, there was little housework. One large area contained the living room and kitchen-dining area, and there were two bedrooms and a bathroom. The washer and dryer were in a hall closet. In the living room was an array of traditional furniture, a television set, a stereo, and a small bookcase. One bedroom had only an extra couch in it and Chris's cat slept there. Because the house was uncluttered with furniture and objects and because Chris rarely cooked, the trailer was easy to keep clean. Chris had an aversion to dust and dirt; when she discovered a mouse in a closet, she bought several traps and boxes of poison to kill the one mouse.

Financial Conditions

Chris was constantly worried about her financial condition for several reasons. First, the year she spent in graduate school she had to use up her savings to meet monthly expenses. By selling some cattle she owned on her parents' farm, she was able to survive. Second, when she moved to the city she thought her teaching salary would be adequate to meet expenses because she expected to share expenses with the person who was supposed to have lived with her. (Actually, because she ate little and rarely left the house during her depressed period, she saved money that year.) Third, she took a $2000-a-year reduction in salary when she went to the private school. She said she had to draw from her savings every month that year to meet her basic living expenses. She planned to get a summer job when school was out.

Chris was frustrated about her low salary ($13,400) because she compared herself to friends who were not teachers, had less education, and often made twice as much money as she did. Part of Chris's motivation to leave teaching was to be able to live more comfortably. She did not want to worry for the rest of her life about whether she would make it through each month.

Leisure Activities

Chris's financial condition limited her choice of leisure activities. Often her social life consisted of going to friends' homes to talk and have drinks. Occasionally Chris went out to dinner or, when dating, to places to dance and have drinks. She took her first vacation in six years during the summer of 1981 and spent a week at a lake resort, fishing. She worried about whether she could afford it but shared expenses with the person she dated and so had a relaxing week.

Chris also drove to her parents' farm for weekends and, while there, floated down the river in a boat, fished, and drank beer with friends.

Health

Although Chris's weight was in the normal range, her nutritional habits were poor. During times of stress, she became thin because she had only coffee for breakfast, sometimes skipped lunch, and also skipped dinner. Instead of eating, she smoked and drank, stayed up late at night talking to friends or because she had insomnia, and then did not feel well at school the next day. Although Chris's habits made her susceptible to colds and flu, her most serious health problems were the result of personal stress. For example, when she began teaching in the city, her mother became ill and the person she was living with ended their relationship. The feelings of sorrow, anger, and depression described earlier made her appetite non-existent, her sleeping habits erratic, and her cigarette and alcohol consumption increase.

> Diary entry, November 19, 1980: I am very tired today since we returned home late last night from visiting my mother, who is ill. The tensions of the past few months are beginning to take their toll on my health. Besides the personal problems, the students' lack of consideration and apathy adds to the anxiety and stress.

> Diary entry, January 21, 1981: School has been fairly well okay lately. Students seem to be more settled and accepting, but the home front has been a battleground. My emotional stability is slipping again. I can't sleep, eat, and think effectively. Most of the time alone, I drink coffee and smoke. Definitely self-destructive behavior.

> Diary entry, August 1981: This without any exception has been the worst year of my life, both in teaching and in my personal life. Part of the problem of writing in the journal was the fact of trying to escape. I wanted to be as far removed from my life as possible. I drank heavily this year and for the first time in my life I was drinking alone, which I had never done before. I came very close to going over the brink.

Chris was in counseling for a short period of time, and when she felt close to "going over the brink," she considered having her therapist hospitalize her. But she knew her mother needed her then and she did not want the person who left her to know how upset she was. Despite the turmoil in Chris's personal life at that time, she continued to go to school every day and teach. She worried about breaking down and crying in front of her students but found that they usually did something to make her angry so that she forgot about crying.

The next year, in a more positive teaching situation and with her new relationship growing, Chris's health habits changed. Although she continued to smoke, she drank less, ate more nutritionally and regularly, slept better, and found her mental health to be "quite a bit better."

CONCLUSIONS: OVERLAP OF HOME AND SCHOOL

There was a complex relationship between the personal and occupational areas of Chris's life. Her experiences with and perceptions of ninth-grade students versus high school students have been described in detail to explain her dissatisfaction and later increased satisfaction with teaching. However, her personal life often became predominant and influenced her classroom behavior in observable ways. When personal problems were particularly stressful, her enthusiasm in the classroom was low and she lacked motivation to interact with students or help them learn. Her affect was flat and her facial expression and bodily posture exhibited exhaustion and depression. Chris reflected on the interrelationship between her personal life and school life on several occasions and was cognizant of the negative effects one could have on the other.

> Diary entry, September 24, 1980: I am beginning to hate my position as a teacher. I am sure a great deal of my malcontent is due to other factors besides teaching. My personal life has always affected my occupational feelings more than what is proper, quote "proper."

> Diary entry, November 21, 1980: I think I actually may have been able to teach a little while in each of my classes. I feel part of it has to do with my personal life beginning to be a bit more stable. This weekend I will not be making the four-hour drive home because it is only a three-day week this week and I will have Thanksgiving at home. I am having a very difficult time handling my mother's illness. We are so very close and I feel so deeply for her. I have faith that she can beat this thing, but it will take faith and much positive

thought. Thinking about these problems does affect my teaching, but often I am able to throw myself into the work that needs to be done and, for a few fleeting moments, forget the garbage, but life can be a bitch.

Diary entry, August 1981: When I look back at this school year, I am not pleased with my performance at all. First of all, I failed in my personal life and then I failed at doing what I like most. I could not open up with those kids. I know one of my basic problems was that I did not like myself. They must have sensed that too, because I would never divulge to anyone some of the things that they said and did. I would get up in the mornings and cry because I did not want to go to school. It did get somewhat better, but I did a shit job, and I never did relax and become myself in the classroom. Frankly, all I wanted to do was survive.

Things did get better at home and school, as previously described. Her enthusiasm, motivation, and affect in the classroom all improved, as did her regard for students.

There were as many examples of the effects of Chris's school life on her home life as there were effects of home on school. Her dissatisfaction with ninth-grade students clearly permeated her thoughts while at home and motivated her to spend time outside school seeking alternatives to teaching. During the chaotic early days at the private school, Chris's time outside the school day was taken up with meetings, phone calls, and worry about the fate of the school and her job. In her second position, time outside school was also required because she had so many different subjects to prepare (as compared to only one per day in the junior high). She had new books to read, lesson plans to write, tests to construct, and papers to grade. However, those everyday requirements of teaching and the actual teaching did not bother Chris because she liked the students in that school. It was the continued instability of the job that was unsettling to her because of her financial situation. Thoughts of school were always present in Chris's life outside school, particularly every time she had to go to the bank to withdraw money from her savings account to meet basic living expenses.

Chris's home life and school life were inseparable; the interconnections were complicated. While it was clear what factors influenced her preferences, attitudes, and experiences in different schools and with different types and ages of students, it was difficult to determine to what extent she recognized those factors. She came to understand that to be a more effective teacher she needed to like herself and choose relationships that were constructive rather than destructive. At the same time, she recognized the need to separate school problems from her personal life so she could ensure that constructive relationships endured.

Epilogue

In 1984 Chris's school closed. Utility bills were exorbitant and enrollments were declining, so even increased tuition costs could not meet operating expenses. There was also a serious rift between the board and teachers, which resulted in the resignation of several teachers, including Chris, prior to the announcement that the school would close. By working 16-hour days, the teachers organized into a corporation in a relatively short period of time; they found a new facility and opened a new school based on the philosophy to which they were all committed in their former situation. The teachers would be able to test many of the contradictions discussed in Chapter 1. For example, if there were no divisions of power between administrators and teachers (as well as no males) and all staff participated in making decisions, would teachers be more satisfied? Or, if all teachers were committed to a philosophy of teaching that allowed them informality with students, would it hamper their effectiveness? For Chris, the situation presented all the dynamics she embraced as a teacher. She was energized and enthusiastic—quite a different person from the one who unhappily taught ninth-graders in a junior high school a few years before.

In her personal life, Chris maintained the stability she found with her spouse and celebrated her third wedding anniversary in 1984. She gave some thought to returning to her parents' farm because her father had died.

4

Marie: A Married Elementary School Teacher with No Children

Marie was a 41-year-old woman who taught gifted elementary school children in a medium-sized school district in the Midwest. Marie's background was quite different from Lee's and Chris's, because she grew up in an upper-middle-class home in a large urban area. However, her reasons for choosing teaching as a career were quite similar to Chris's—she was encouraged by her parents to teach because it was a good job for a woman, it fit in best with having children and family life. A teaching degree was seen as a kind of "insurance policy" to be used if "something ever happened" to her husband. Marie's desire to please her parents and fear of failure in a male-dominated profession (medicine), particularly in the early 1960s, led her into teaching.

Marie's case shows the positive effects of a good teaching situation. The gifted children in her classes were highly motivated, her classes were quite small, she taught in a good facility, and she was freer from administrative control than other teachers. Her situation also shows the difference in life-style created because Marie had no children and had a husband who earned a large salary, shared the housework, and with whom Marie experienced no conflict.

TYPICAL DAY

Marie and her husband woke up at 6:00 A.M., made their bed, dressed, and ate breakfast. As usual, they had orange juice, a cheeseburger, coffee, and fruit, which would stave off their hunger until their dinner that evening. Skipping lunch had kept Marie's weight at exactly 100 pounds, an amount somewhat underweight for her 5 feet 2 inches. The two cleaned up the breakfast dishes and checked their two-story house to make sure everything was in place; then Marie got into her white Corvette, her husband into his new Volkswagen, and they each drove to work across the small city from their suburban house.

Marie arrived at her modern open school an hour early so she could prepare for the day. She walked down the carpeted hallways into a large area partially partitioned from the school's library-media center. After checking over the room's well-stocked supplies of books, materials, and equipment, Marie opened new boxes of books and games she had ordered from state funds provided for gifted programs. She thought of ways she might integrate the new materials into the day's plans.

At 8:30 A.M., students arrived by bus, quietly filed into the classroom, hung up their coats, and sat in a circular arrangement of chairs in the center of the room. Today was one of Marie's favorite classes—the second grade. There were only eight students, so Marie would be able to give them individualized instruction before they traveled back to their schools at 2:00 P.M.

Marie began an informal discussion to give each child an opportunity to introduce a new word to the others, share stories and objects from home, and comment on the others' presentations. As new words came up, she had students find their meaning in the encyclopedia. A discussion developed on the meaning of *iron curtain* and students used reference books and maps from the media center to clarify it. After the discussion, Marie took the students to the library, where she helped them select reference books for science projects they were to prepare on alternate energy sources. Students worked quietly yet enthusiastically and shared their discoveries with the other students. Some students had checked out several fictional books and exchanged them for other books.

When they returned to the room, Marie reviewed Bloom's taxonomy with them before they began work on their science projects. Students who were finished with their projects used the microcomputer or built electronic gadgets with materials Marie provided. Those working on projects asked numerous questions but Marie did not answer them. Instead, she led the students through a series of logical inferences that allowed them either to figure out the answers for themselves or to deduce where they might go to find the answers in the library. She often reminded them about the level of Bloom's taxonomy they ought to be using in their thought processes and problem analyses.

At lunchtime, the children ate in the cafeteria at tables separate from the middle school children in a large, noisy open room. Eating no lunch, Marie sometimes sat with the children and sometimes with the other teachers. After lunch, Marie allowed the children some exercise time, while reminding them that they were at the middle school and should therefore play quietly so as not to disturb the seventh-grade English class next to their class. A few students peeked between the bulletin boards that partitioned them from what they viewed as the "big kids."

After the break, the remainder of the afternoon was spent talking about Greek mythology and the children's projects, which were to focus on a particular character. Some were writing plays, making masks, and drawing scenery; some were making diagrams and writing reports; and some planned speeches in which they portrayed the character they chose. Marie helped each child individually.

After the children left the school, she began a series of parent conferences, discussing each child's progress with his or her parents and helping them think of ways to help their child at home. Marie was concerned about the parents who had an overinflated notion of their child's abilities and worried about the pressures they might place on the child.

At 4:00 p.m., Marie left school, ran some errands—paid bills, took books to the library, and went to the grocery—and arrived home at 5:00 p.m. Her husband arrived soon after and together they cooked dinner and then cleaned the kitchen. They retired to their den, where they watched a television show on the Public Broadcasting System and at 9:00 p.m. settled down to read. Marie caught up on recent issues of teachers' magazines and her husband read magazines related to his computer work. They also read each other's magazines so they could discuss the contents together. Marie began a novel to relax before falling to sleep at 10:30 p.m. and slept soundly through the night.

PERSONAL HISTORY

Growing Up

Marie was raised in an upper-middle-class home in an Irish Catholic neighborhood in a large city. Her father was a banker who had a law degree, and her mother was a teacher who left teaching to raise her children but participated in extensive volunteer work. Her parents were in their forties when Marie was born, and when she was 10, her brother left home to begin college. After he left, Marie was treated like an only child. Although in some ways Marie liked her parents' indulgent treatment, she was relieved when her mother went back into teaching.

> Interview, July 8, 1980.
> MARIE: I noticed a definite difference when she went full time and had all the planning and preparation, grading and everything. It was a relief to me [laughter].

Marie's parents were quiet people who worked hard, read a lot, and believed that education was the most important means of achieving upward mobility. In the evenings, her mother worked at one table, her father at another, and Marie and her brother each worked at desks in their rooms. The focus on education and hard work was reflected in Marie's parents' attitude that being sick was simply a way some people got out of work. Marie did not remember her parents ever being sick until they were in their eighties, which was shortly before their deaths.

Interview, November 13, 1981.

MARIE: It was not that they [her parents] didn't believe in being sick, but they just didn't believe in missing work. You were either dead or at work.

Although Marie's parents were permissive in some ways, they were very strict in others and told Marie what she could and could not do. Because Marie was an obedient child, she never argued with them; she commented, "I didn't know there was a choice. I never doubted that even if I didn't agree with my parents, they were doing things for my best interests." Marie's parents also never argued with each other, and she said she never saw her mother cry. She was told that her mother cried at her graduation but added, "I missed it." The only time she remembered her father being upset was when he saw a photograph in the newspaper that showed some black soldiers sitting on a curb eating while the men they were escorting, Nazi prisoners, were eating inside a nice restaurant. Marie's father's emotional outburst was so rare that she said the incident became legend in her family.

Marie never remembered arguing with her brother during the 10 years of her life that he was only living at home. After finishing high school, her brother joined a Jesuit group for 10 years, then left to work on a doctorate in experimental psychology and to work as an administrator in the laboratories of a large corporation. Marie had infrequent contact with her brother and that contact was usually over the phone.

Diary entry, December 21, 1980: I spoke to my brother and his family on the phone this week. My sister-in-law pointed out that we now constitute the "senior partners in the firm," since none of us has a surviving parent. I don't feel mature enought to be the older generation. I wonder if anyone ever does.

Education

Marie attended Catholic schools through her first two years in college. She began school in an order of particularly strict nuns, but because she became upset about the nuns' yelling at other students, her parents transferred her to another school. Marie said she was never yelled at but "I felt like I was." When she was in the first grade, Marie developed polio or spinal meningitis (she could not remember which) and ran a high temperature for several days. Although she recovered, her doctors were not sure what she had had and one thought she probably suffered some brain damage. Her parents took the word of that doctor and had Marie put in a special education class. When teachers saw that Marie had no problem with learning, they took her out of special education. However, Marie found that the class had been more fun because there were special materials and more interesting activities than in the regular classroom, where students had to sit all day and do work sheets. Marie was unhappy when she was moved out of the class and thought that the reason she was moved was that she did not look like the other children, who, she later deduced, had Down's syndrome.

Marie loved school, made excellent grades, and was always the top student in her classes. Nevertheless, her parents' expectations for her academic performance appeared to be indelibly influenced by her label as brain damaged. Marie remembered her parents saying that her brother was the smart one and she was the sensible one. She said they thought he learned by osmosis and that she learned by hard work. The double standard of expectations for Marie and her brother continued throughout their lives. They told her brother he did well because school was easy for him and that he was naturally intelligent and encouraged him to complete a doctorate. In contrast, her parents were relieved when she obtained a teaching certificate and could not understand why she wanted a master's degree.

It was not until Marie was in college and took an IQ test that she realized that she was indeed bright. However, she adopted her parents expectations for her performance. She had an opportunity to be in an honor's program in college and majored in chemistry—in the hope of going to medical school—and in education—to please her mother. But, Marie claimed, "There turned out to be too much lab work," and when her schedule became too demanding, she gave up chemistry for education. It was not until she had married, left home, and finished her degree that she decided she did indeed want to be a teacher. Although her mother had been disappointed when Marie left college to marry, Marie's getting a teaching degree put her back in her mother's good graces.

Personal Relationships

Marie's husband, Jim, was raised in her neighborhood, had gone to Catholic schools, and shared the same values as Marie. They knew each other most of their lives, began dating at age 15, started "going steady" the week he graduated from high school, and were engaged the week he graduated from college (when Marie was a college sophomore). They married, to the chagrin of her parents because Marie had not finished college; Jim joined the Air Force, and they began to move whenever he was transferred. During Jim's first assignment in the northeastern part of the United States, Marie finished her college degree.

For a short period, Marie felt obligated to be a good officer's wife, but quickly became bored and devoted her time to her teaching career.

Diary entry, June 1980: Then there was the Officers' Wives' Club. During the first year or so, while Jim was in flight training and we moved every few months, I joined the Wives' Club activities with some enthusiasm. By the end of the first year, however, the thought occurred to me with increasing regularity, that although this extended vacation was great fun for me right then, I did not want to wake up one morning, when I was 40, and find that I spent my life at swimming pools, golf courses, bridge luncheons, and tea tables. (Now, at 41, I find it comical that I thought my life would be "spent" by the time I was 40. But 20 years ago that was exactly what I said to myself.)

During the ensuing 19 years, I limited my OWC activities to the minimum possible. The first few times other members called to suggest I take a day off to pour, teach, or present/receive a silver tray at a luncheon, I found it difficult not to laugh. However, upon reflection, I'm glad they considered their activities more important than teaching, just as I considered teaching more important than social functions. I'm sure it worked out best for everyone concerned.

Marie considered her husband her best friend and could think of no sources of problems and conflicts between them.

Interview, June 3, 1981.

> INTERVIEWER: What would be some sources of problems at home?
>
> MARIE: [Long pause]
>
> INTERVIEWER: There must not be a lot.
>
> MARIE: [laughing] Nope. Better turn off that [tape recorder] for a while while I think. If you mean long term ... that sounds unbelievable. What do we snap at each other about? I think maybe because we're tired or something. I don't know. I can remember unpleasant tones of voice but not [laughing] what they were about. That is strange.

Marie thought about the question and wrote the following in her diary.

Diary entry, June 7, 1981: I asked my husband if he could name any sources of continuing conflicts in our home life. When he finished laughing (that took a while), he suggested it might be easier to list the topics we have not debated. However, he assumed if he thought of such a subject and suggested it out loud, we would immediately take opposite points of view on it and thereby eliminate its relevance.

I think your question pertained to negative emotional responses. Probably, though, Jim's supposition that conflict resides in the cognitive domain is the answer to why I couldn't think of any examples in the affective area. Our mutual grounding in Jesuitical debate convinced us that resorting to ad hominem tactics proves the weakness of your point of view or your powers of reasoning. So, any time we reach that unfortunate point, we begin to laugh at ourselves. It is difficult to sustain negative feelings when you're laughing.

The intellectualization of conflict and its relegation to the cognitive domain made a phenomenon such as divorce incomprehensible to Marie and her husband.

Interview, June 3, 1981.

MARIE: No matter how difficult the situation, I don't think either one of us would ever consider separation or divorce one of the possible solutions. I mean just because of the way we were brought up. Your parents are your parents and that's it and your husband is your husband and that's it. There's no sense nurturing long-range conflicts; you may as well find a solution.

Throughout their marriage, Marie had been able to live as comfortable a life-style as she had growing up. For her whole life, all her needs had been met. After her husband retired from the Air Force, he worked in a social service job, then taught computer science at a college. His salary plus retirement payments and Marie's income allowed them to live a comfortable life-style.

Work

Marie's work history was based on her husband's transfers to various parts of the United States and Southeast Asia. She had taught in the Northeast, the Southwest, the South, and the Midwest. She usually had to leave partway through a school year but thought that had been acceptable because of the broader societal consensus that if a man is transferred, his wife follows him. She thought she had been lucky to find jobs quickly in each new place they lived.

Interview, June 3, 1981.

MARIE: There was always a job. I was amazed because in the late 1960s and early 70s, I kept reading in every magazine we'd pick up that an overabundance of teachers couldn't find jobs and especially if you had a master's you were just out of luck. Nobody would hire you because they had to pay you more. But we didn't have any problem. There was always, immediately, the first week we got there, a job. The only thing I can figure out is that I was willing to do whatever was available, as long as it was teaching.

When Marie's husband retired from the military, they decided to settle in the Midwest for a few years. Marie taught fourth grade for five years and then decided to apply for a position as director of a newly formed gifted program. Her teaching position is described in the section on School Life.

Marie originally decided to become a teacher to please her mother but also said that at the time she grew up, being a teacher was something women could do and something that would fit in with raising a family. Although Marie had no children, she discovered that she loved teaching, regardless of her vagueness about her reasons for entering the field. In fact, she could not imagine anyone staying in teaching if they did not like it. Marie was happy with herself and with her work most of the time.

> Diary entry, June 16, 1980: In school, my favorite neighbors are classes that laugh a lot. Laughter is so contagious it makes you feel like laughing yourself, even if you don't know what the joke is.

> Diary entry, November 22, 1980: I love the holidays. I usually feel like I'm smiling inside, but this time of year I feel like I'm laughing. Maybe it's an overload of sugar from the holiday goodies. Whatever it is, I like it.

> Diary entry, November 30, 1980: If I composed a list of things I'm grateful for, I'm sure it would be the standard one usually seen or heard—Maslow's hierarchy in various translations. The first 10 items on my list would not have changed much over the years, but which one was the most important would have. While I lived overseas and for a few years after returning to this country, being an American would definitely have been number one. However, at most other times in my life the thing I'm most grateful for would be tomorrow.

> Diary entry, January 24, 1981: Tuesday, the central office administration sent out the annual survey forms to ask if teachers want to keep the same jobs they have this year. I restrained myself and wrote a simple "yes" in the appropriate blank. What I wanted to write was, "The only thing I would like better than doing this job 9 months a year is doing it 11 months a year."

Marie's only concerns with her teaching program were the effects on students of labeling them as gifted, the selection process and its impact on students who did not meet the criteria, and the possibility that state guidelines might be imposed that would limit enrollments and thus force some students to be dropped from the program.

> Diary entry, May 9, 1981: I feel increasingly discouraged about the possibility of ensuring justice in the identification of intellectually gifted students. Having the same psychometrist give all the WISC-R tests used for entrance requirements has certainly improved the fairness of the procedure. However, it seems as though every day this week some new problem or grievance came to light.
> There are several students who, according to every teacher who ever worked with them, other school personnel, parents, peers, and my own common sense, obviously belong in the gifted program. Unfortunately, according to the required test scores, they do not. Who appointed the test makers the high priests?

Marie and her husband sat down periodically and planned 10-year and 20-year goals. Marie planned to retire early, and she and Jim would work on doctoral degrees as a way of enjoying their retirement years.

SCHOOL LIFE

Cultural Setting

Marie's classroom was located in a middle school that housed 100 teachers and over 1000 students in the sixth, seventh, and eighth grades, in a city with a population of less than 25,000 people. The midwestern city had a stable population, a number of small industries, a couple of shopping centers, and many fast-food restaurants and churches. It was a conservative, religious, and traditional community with a preference for Country-Western music.

The community had defeated numerous bond issues so the school buildings, except for the middle school where Marie taught, were old and in poor repair. Because of declining enrollment in the schools, two of them had been closed. In a reorganization of the elementary schools, either the first, second, and third grades or the fourth and fifth grades were housed in each of the elementary school buildings. This forced some teachers to be relocated, which caused a disruptive period for personnel, but after one year, most teachers wanted to keep the new organization.

During the first two years of the screening process for the gifted program, children from less affluent parts of the city were underrepresented. Efforts were made to improve testing procedures so that children from all socioeconomic strata would be represented. By the third year, IQ scores for first-graders showed equal representation from all socioeconomic classes.

School Administration

The school was headed by a principal and two assistants. Although Marie saw them on a regular basis, her interactions with them were brief. The superintendent was a strong advocate of the program, was instrumental in getting it started, and hired Marie. Therefore, he was supportive of her although they had little contact. In turn, Marie was supportive of him and all her other administrators in the district and took their decisions and advice seriously and with enthusiasm.

> Diary entry, August 15, 1980: This year, instead of hiring a guest speaker, our central office administrators spoke to us. I thought that was an excellent idea, especially since two of the three are fairly new (two or three years) to this district and brand new (six weeks) to their present jobs.
>
> I was delighted with what they said. All three of them stressed that they wanted each of us to be the best teacher we possibly could be. Each of the administrators invited us to speak to them about any way they could help us in particular or the school system in general. I feel these were very sincere offers. I'm sure they would discuss and consider any request or suggestion from a staff member.

The new superintendent spoke to us about the characteristics of the ideal teacher, such as a sense of mission, empathy, organization, dedication. He said that he had decided to work on being a better listener this year. I thought it sounded like a good idea to pick one area to try to improve on. I decided to work on being better organized.

Throughout Marie's teaching experiences she had been satisfied with all her administrators. She thought they made the best decisions possible no matter how they affected her working conditions. This view was strongly influenced by her mother's opinion of administrators.

Diary entry, March 14, 1981: Whenever I ponder the motivations of administrators, I remember one of just two pieces of advice my mother, herself a teacher, ever gave me about teaching. "Don't waste any time or energy being upset with administrators for being two-faced. That's just part of their job." The more years I spend in schools, the more I understand what she meant. All of the world's champion complainers—whether they are students, parents, teachers, staff, neighborhood residents, or people whose only discernable connection with the school is the indignation they are expressing concerning something they perceive to be connected with the school—all bring their grievances to administrators. One way to survive such a job is to placate everyone.

School Facility

Marie's school was a 10-year-old open-plan building with a swimming pool, a large central cafeteria area, and a media center. Built when open schools were popular, there were no interior walls. Then, when open schools fell into disfavor, architects discovered that walls could not be constructed to separate the classrooms. Although the teachers built visual barriers around their classroom space with bookcases and bulletin boards, unfortunately, those barriers did not block out noise. It was possible simultaneously to hear English, social studies, science, and math classes. The result was that teachers had to talk loudly to be heard in their own space—which further increased the noise level. Because Marie had a soft voice, she often talked to students in small groups or individually in order to be heard.

Sixth-, seventh-, and eighth-grade classrooms were usually separate wings of the school. There was little interaction between students in the three grade levels. Marie's students arrived before the middle school began and left before it ended so they were completely separated from the middle school students. Their only contact was in the cafeteria, and there they did not eat at the same tables.

The middle school was colorful, carpeted, air conditioned, and well kept. Its problems were the high noise level and a claustrophobic atmosphere, because there were no windows. However, Marie was pleased with the location of her classes because of the accessibility of the media center.

Teacher Morale

Marie's attitudes about teachers were as positive as those about administrators. She once commented that she enjoyed being around teachers more than other people because she thought most teachers were like her —happy.

> Diary entry, May 1980: One of the things I have enjoyed most about my job this year is being able to work with so many different teachers in the district. Their cooperation has been great!

> Diary entry, August 14, 1980: We went back to work this week—two days of teachers' meetings and classroom preparation. It was such fun to see everyone again and chat! For me, that is one of the most enjoyable bonuses of teaching—the camaraderie among the staff members. Even though many employees changed buildings this year, we have an instant feeling of community, since we know our basic goal is always shared—to do the best and the most we possibly can to help each student.

Students

Marie taught 50 students in the second through sixth grades and for 15 seventh-grade students, she met with their English and reading teacher to coordinate special projects. Students qualified for the program if they were nominated by teachers or other school personnel (such as counselors) and scored above the 95th percentile on IQ and standardized achievement tests. Students from each grade level were bused to the middle school one day a week, so Marie taught a different grade level each day.

Marie had frequent contact with the parents of the children who were in the program. Some called her at night and she estimated that she averaged at least one call per night from parents or from students; sometimes there were more and some calls lasted for two hours. But Marie encouraged the calls, because she thought they helped her maintain contact with the children since she saw them only once a week. She had a conference with each child's parents once a semester and invited the child to be present for half the conference, but the children never attended. Her main concern with parents was about their misunderstanding or exaggeration of their child's having been labeled *gifted*.

> Diary entry, May 30, 1981: The longer I work with gifted students and their parents, however, the more aware I become of the possible dangers of labeling and the probable perils of mislabeling. We were dealing mainly with first-graders at Wednesday's meeting. The younger the children, the more potential for excessive pressure I perceive.
>
> The term *gifted* raises the expectation levels of some parents inordinately. When performance does not readily and rapidly fulfill these unrealistic projections, the younger the child, the more devastating the effect.
>
> Like all students, gifted children gradually reach the realization that they cannot possibly please everyone. If they can honestly assure themselves that

they have done their best, they must be satisfied with that. If some other person—such as a parent—is not satisfied, that is that other person's problem. Primary-age children, though, do not seem to be capable of such detachment. If an authority figure is disappointed, the young child feels rejected and dejected.

Although the students enjoyed the excitement of coming to the middle school and being treated special, Marie was not sure what the children's perceptions were of having been labeled *gifted*.

> Diary entry, September 21, 1980: Monday we had 15 second-graders, 11 boys and 4 girls. This will be a lively, vocal group—hooray! One young man in this class is obviously well organized. He brought his supplies in a bag which he had carefully labeled, "For Gift Did Class." That certainly exemplifies synthesis-level thinking—two words he already knew neatly combined into a new one he heard. I wonder if he figured a *gift* for taking standardized tests *did* place him in this particular class? I'll have to attempt to draw him out on the subject of what *gifted* means.

Marie was worried about the possible elitism that could occur among the children in the program. Although she knew that some teachers singled the children out when they returned to their classrooms and had them tell the rest of the class about what they did in gifted class, neither Marie nor the school district had studied the effects of having been labeled *gifted* on the children's peer-group relationships.

Classes

Marie had to plan lessons each week that could be completed within the time the students were in her classroom because of the difficulty of sustaining thought and motivation from week to week and because there was not enough space to store 50 children's projects in the room. At times, she would introduce a unit or subject one week and ask the children to prepare something for the next week. She always kept her plans flexible, however, so that if an opportunity arose to have a field trip or invite a guest speaker she could alter them accordingly.

Marie's classes were exceptionally well organized; in fact, she could easily be viewed as Kounin's (1970) ideal type of classroom manager. She never raised her voice or became angry, yet students were attentive and knew exactly what they should be doing at all times. She never had to punish a child because none of them had a moment to consider misbehaving. Part of her success was due to her ability always to appear under control. Even when things did not go on schedule, she quickly made alterations that avoided disruption. Marie's high degree of orderliness and total yet subtle control gave an atmosphere of formality to her classrooms. Students treated her with respect and totally enjoyed their classes, although they never touched, hugged, or kissed her—nor she, them.

She truly listened to her students and treated each one with equal respect. In fact, she talked with students in the same tone of voice, manner, and language as she did with adults. What was transmitted was a mutual trust and enjoyment. Marie described a day she found particularly enjoyable. Her definition of fun in the classroom was that students exhibited creative thinking.

> Diary entry, December 7, 1980: This was a great week! The students began to identify the topics they wanted to use for their independent study projects. We spent a large proportion of each day brainstorming the possible topics. I can't remember ever having more fun in a classroom.
>
> I feel certain that for most of every class period, most of the people in the room were really thinking, sharing ideas enthusiastically, and thoroughly enjoying the whole process. That's hard to beat for fun or sheer satisfaction.
>
> Some of the children were so full of ideas they had difficulty containing themselves. As soon as one of them finished and the next person began his or her turn, the previous fluent thinker would think of something else and bounce up and down or wave a hand frantically. A few inventive ones even thought of moving around the circle in order to increase the frequency of their contributions.

It was tempting to attribute Marie's teaching effectiveness to the fact that she had an ideal situation—small groups of the brightest students in a large room filled with materials and equipment. However, having observed Marie in her traditional fourth-grade classroom with children of all abilities in an old school building, we found that her teaching techniques were consistent over time, students, and classrooms.

HOME LIFE

Marie and her husband lived in a two-story home in a middle- to upper-class neighborhood. The house was well furnished and the lawn well kept. Most of their time was spent in a den, which had a couch, two comfortable chairs, two floor-to-ceiling bookcases, a television set, and a fireplace. It was here that they talked, read, or watched television. In warm months, they sat on their patio, barbecued their dinner, admired their yard, and visited with neighbors.

As pointed out earlier, Marie and her husband were best friends. They never argued, merely debated issues. Their lives at home were well ordered, and they tended to look on personal situations analytically and intellectually rather than in affective terms. The consistency of their marital stability, seemingly conflict-free, was a stabilizing force they took for granted.

Household Duties

Marie and her husband shared household duties. Since they had no children or animals, their house tended to stay clean and free of clutter. In fact, they were able to install black carpeting across the floor and counter in a bathroom—which stayed clean. Cleaning the house was not a major source of concern for either of them, merely something that had to be done to get to more important things, like reading.

> Interview, June 3, 1981:
> INTERVIEWER: How do you decide who does what?
> MARIE: If something is bothering me, I do it. If something is bothering him, he does it. Usually, we pretty much split it. Now that we have two lawnmowers, we split the mowing and then split the inside. He likes to vacuum better than I do, and he doesn't like dusting. But generally he seems to end up vacuuming and dusting also [laughter].
> INTERVIEWER: Who does the cooking?
> MARIE: Whoever gets hungry [laughter].

Marie and her husband wished they had a housekeeper so that neither one of them would have to be bothered with housework, but they had not been able to find someone. Therefore, they grudgingly gave their time to the tasks.

> Diary entry, September 6, 1980: Since this weekend consists of a scant two days, I'm afraid I'll be forced to employ some self-discipline in how I spend my time and energy on Saturday and Sunday. We always fall back on our old tried-and-true system—"want-to-do" and "should-do" lists from which to choose activities for each day. Sometimes we decide no one would be seriously injured if we skipped the "should-do" list that weekend, so we feel free to proceed with uninterrupted wish fulfillment. However, the first weekend of the school year seems a bit early to celebrate the joys of irresponsibility, so we'll dutifully if grudgingly mow grass and clean rooms along with our current choices from the "want-to" list.

Financial Conditions

Given Marie's husband's military retirement pay, his social service job, and, later, college teaching income and Marie's teaching salary (about $20,000 in 1982), there were no financial problems. The only period in which Marie expressed any concern at all about their economic situation was when President Reagan's budgetary cutbacks included funding for the agency in which her husband worked. However, Jim's background in computer technology enabled him to get a job in a computer center at a small college near their town.

Leisure Activities

Marie's strong financial status allowed her and her husband to enjoy a wide range of leisure activities. They did everything together and had no desire to spend time apart even though they sometimes did things with another couple.

> Diary entry, December 28, 1980: They very best part of this very fine week has been that my husband and I have had more time to spend together than we usually have. I wish he did not have to go back to work tomorrow.

During the work week, Marie's leisure time was spent watching special television shows that were either dramatic performances on public television or political programs, reading, or talking to her husband. On the weekends, she and Jim went to nearby parks for picnics, to a large city for dinner, dancing, or museum visits, or to other spots of interest that were potential sites for a gifted-class field trip. In the summer, they went on vacations to scenic places where they could enjoy classical music, read books, think, and be near relatives. Most of their leisure activities focused on relaxing, yet intellectually stimulating, experiences. Even staying at home provided these experiences.

> Diary entry, January 4, 1981: This has been a luxurious week. Among the luxuries I enjoyed were reading whole magazines or several chapters of books or watching whole television shows without interruptions or simultaneous chores. The best luxury of all, of course, was the opportunity to obey my biological clock instead of my alarm clock.

> Diary entry, August 15, 1981: This week, with the appearances of back-to-school advertisements, the realization did impinge upon my consciousness that certain limitations circumscribe my leisure. So, typically, I concentrated on lolling in luxuries—sleeping late on a rainy morning, ignoring the calories while I consumed carbohydrates, disregarding the clock while I read.

Health

Marie was in excellent health, was slightly underweight but observed good eating habits, was rarely sick, and coped with stress well. Although her eating habits were somewhat unorthodox (cheeseburgers for breakfast), her filling breakfast sustained her through the day. She said she never got hungry at lunch nor during the afternoon. Her only health problem was allergies, which required taking antihistamines. The side effects of the antihistamines affected her teaching.

> Diary entry, February 7, 1981: When I asked myself "What happened this week?" myself's reply was "Beats me," followed by an abstract depiction —blur in motion. I suppose that was a result of the antihistamines I have ingested this week in a mostly futile struggle with my allergies. After prolonged concentration, I did perceive a few clear scenes in that blur.

Marie thought stress was controllable, that rather than stress causing illness, that illness could cause people to be "moody and grouchy." She also thought that stress emanated from inside individuals rather than from external sources, such as working conditions. Even in the most stressful situations, Marie was under control.

> Diary entry, June 1980: The most serious disadvantage to our 20 years as transients was that we were not able to spend enough time with our parents. We didn't realize the gravity of that disadvantage until we were in Southeast Asia and our parents were here, facing crises—debilitating strokes, terminal cancer, widowhood, etc. When we returned to America, we were able to arrange to be stationed close enough so that I could visit them most weekends. The time spent there certainly cut down on preparation time for school. However, in one way, I think these visits helped me as a teacher. Observing our parents' deteriorating health and realizing there was no realistic hope for improvement made some of these weekends very frustrating experiences. During the school week, I would be so determined not to take these frustrations out on my students that I probably manifested more patience and ended up with better rapport than I would have under less stressful circumstances.

CONCLUSIONS: OVERLAP OF HOME AND SCHOOL

Marie was able to compartmentalize her roles as teacher and wife. There was no overlap of Marie's personal life into her school life, unless her husband attended a school function with her during the evening, and little overlap of her school life into her home life, except when students or their parents called her. Marie had an enormous amount of paperwork, but she was able to complete it while at school.

Although Marie usually reviewed her day with her husband, the fact that she loved her job, had no problem students, had no papers to grade at home, was not involved in school or school district politics, and took her principal's authority and decisions for granted, made those reviews pleasant accounts rather than disruptive occasions or sources of stress.

At home, especially after her and her husband's parents had died, there were also no sources of stress. Her husband shared the household duties, they enjoyed each other's company more than anyone else's even after over 20 years of marriage, and their joint incomes provided sufficient economic stability to afford a comfortable life-style.

> Interview, June 3, 1981.
> MARIE: I guess I do compartmentalize a lot. When I get to school I totally forget about everything else till school's over.... Gee, I can't imagine being able to worry about problems. There are so many demands on your attention.

Epilogue

In 1984, Marie continued to teach gifted children and live in the life-style described in this chapter, including a trip to Europe.

5

Sylvia: A Married Secondary School Teacher with No Children

Sylvia was a 32-year-old married woman who taught secondary English classes in a medium-sized city in the Southwest. She and her husband, who was in the military, had no children. As was true of several of the teachers described in these chapters, Sylvia chose teaching as a career to fulfill her parents' wishes. Also, teaching was one of the few easy options for women in the 1960s and Sylvia feared failure in more competitive, male-oriented occupations.

Sylvia's case illustrates the problems of teachers who take jobs because their husbands move to a different geographic region. They usually take whatever job is available rather than one they would choose. When Sylvia switched from a middle school in a medium-sized midwestern town to a large high school in the Southwest, she went through a difficult period of adjustment. While suited to and happy with teaching in the first situation, she was unhappy and even intimidated by the second situation. A bright, sensitive, creative woman and teacher, Sylvia's confidence was undermined. Unhappiness at work combined with marital problems negatively affected Sylvia's health, both physically and mentally.

TYPICAL DAY

Sylvia's alarm clock rang at 5:30 A.M. She turned it off and wondered why she had even thought she could jump out of bed and into her jogging clothes and run three miles before getting ready for school. She carefully got up so she would not wake her husband, put on her jogging clothes, laid down on the couch, and went back to sleep. At 7:00 A.M. her husband woke her and she quickly drank two cups of coffee and waited for the surge of energy the caffeine would give her. She gathered up the large stack of students' research papers she had begun to grade the night before and drove to her school, which was a few miles outside the military base where they lived.

Sylvia arrived at her large, sprawling high school 30 minutes before the 2000 students who attended the school. She checked her mail in the main office and walked down the carpeted hallway to her office, which she shared with all the other teachers in the English department. Her space in the office had a desk, file cabinet, and chair and was at the back of the room because she was one of the newer teachers. Her colleagues were drinking coffee and enjoying a cake someone had brought from home. The teacher who had the desk next to Sylvia's teased her about taking papers home to grade. Sylvia felt confused and thought to herself, as she had many times before, "Is it me? Am I that bad a teacher? Or is it them? Am I a better teacher for taking work home?" The conflict in her mind remained unresolved so she shrugged and smiled at the other teacher, gathered her plans for the day, and went to her classroom.

She looked around the room and straightened papers and hung up a new poster. She could hear the teacher in the next room talking loudly to an early student. Sylvia wished for solid walls rather than the movable partitions that divided the once open classrooms. At least, she thought to herself, it was not so bad as the school she taught in that had no walls at all. Still, she wondered what it would be like to teach in a school that had walls and was quiet.

At 8:30 A.M., a bell rang and students rushed in, banging lockers, yelling, joking, and shoving their way into classrooms. Sylvia knew that little would be accomplished academically that day because it was Homecoming Day and students' minds were on the upcoming football game and dance. There was an air of excitement and students were on good behavior because they were wearing dresses or suits in honor of the occasion. Sylvia was amused at the large corsages, which were decorated with ribbons and bells, that some of the girls wore. They were gifts from boyfriends or parents. The cacophony of sound was more deadening than usual, particularly from those girls who had on more than one corsage.

Sylvia's classroom filled with 30 students. She called roll and then began a discussion of a story in their eleventh-grade literature book. She had each student read a few paragraphs, stopping them from time to time to ask questions and define the meanings of words. In the back of the room, two students were jabbing each other, as unobtrusively as possible, until movements attracted Sylvia's attention. She reprimanded them but kept her voice in the same quiet tone as when discussing the story.

After 30 minutes Sylvia was aware of the students' increasing restlessness; she had them close their books and gave them a lesson she had prepared for a day such as homecoming. Each student started writing a short story, continuing until Sylvia stopped them. They then passed their papers to the next student, who continued the story. After all students in a row had written something on each page, Sylvia had someone read the completed stories. She had warned them before starting not to write anything obscene so she held her breath as the stories proceeded. The repeated theme of the stories had to do with what most of the students did in their spare time—drink beer.

Sylvia decided that her first class had gone well so she followed the same plan in her other classes. At lunchtime she walked to the large open area that served as a student lounge and cafeteria. All 2000 students ate in only two shifts but the room seemed uncrowded, because many students were outside eating at picnic tables. The warm climate allowed the students to go outside much of the time. Sylvia stood beside one of the lines going into the food areas, where students could choose between hot lunches and snacks. She had been on lunch duty for a week, which meant standing for 30 minutes to make sure there were no problems in the line. Because there never were, Sylvia felt foolish standing there like a prison guard.

After lunch Sylvia went back to her room to record some grades. Although she needed to go to her desk in the English office, she hesitated to do so because she was not in the mood to listen to more complaints from her colleague. She finally succumbed, however, because she wanted a cup of coffee.

Sylvia followed the same lesson plan in the afternoon as in the morning but became increasingly disturbed at the students' behavior as they became more restless. She wondered how many times she had asked them to be quiet and whether or not other teachers were having as much difficulty keeping control. She was relieved when the students were allowed to go to the gymnasium to spur the football team on to victory.

Sylvia filed in with the other teachers, crawled ungracefully up the bleachers, and tried to fix an enthusiastic, school-spirited look on her face. She gritted her teeth, however, when the school band played at full volume, the noise reverberating off the unsoundproof gym walls. As the cheerleaders cheered, the football players tried to look appropriately macho-humble, and the flag corps waved their banners in elaborate whirls, Sylvia reminded herself that things could be worse. After all, she had sponsored the whirling flag girls the year before.

The students left, corsages wilting, and the teachers crawled down out of the bleachers to their classrooms. Since it was Friday, Sylvia took a particularly large stack of papers home and hoped the other teachers would not comment. She was optimistic that she would get caught up at last with her paper work—at least *maybe* she would.

On her way home Sylvia planned dinner, stopped at the grocery, and drove to her three-bedroom, standard-military-style home. The cat greeted her and she talked to it while getting out its food and putting away the groceries. She tried to clean the kitchen from the morning's mess before her husband got home so he would not be angry. She wanted the weekend to go well and hoped they could do something relaxing. Yet the stack of papers she brought from school nagged at her thoughts and began to depress her.

Her husband arrived home, took off his uniform, and the two of them had a drink while Sylvia prepared dinner. Her husband seemed quiet but did not say—and probably would not—what was bothering him, so Sylvia rethought the prospects of a good weekend. After dinner Sylvia cleaned up and joined her husband in front of the television. She fell asleep during a sporting event, later woke up and watched a movie, then went to bed. Before dropping off to sleep, Sylvia once again thought of the stack of school papers and decided that she would set her alarm, get up early, and get the grading over.

PERSONAL HISTORY

Growing Up

Sylvia grew up on a small farm in the Midwest, where her parents raised livestock. She remembered a peaceful childhood of going barefoot, going to the corner drugstore, making clover chains, and playing the piano. But she also remembered that her family was poor or, as she described them, "medium poor, not poor poor." They never had a car, so she and her sister sat in kitchen chairs in the back of a pickup truck when they went anywhere as a family. She also remembered that her mother was haggard and thin from overwork and that her father had an explosive temper and frequently went into rages. Sylvia and her sister were afraid of their father, even though he was not physically abusive nor did he call them abusive names. Instead, he became extremely critical. Sylvia's sister cried and hid in her room at those times but Sylvia said she became stoic. She felt that this impassiveness when dealing with conflict had negative effects on her adult life. She was fearful, for example, whenever her husband became angry and could not express anger herself.

Sylvia's mother and father decided to make use of the teaching degrees they had earned prior to farming; they sold the farm and began teaching in a nearby city. The fact that they were teachers influenced Sylvia's occupational decision.

Interview, June 1980.

SYLVIA: I loved my subjects. Now I was raised in a teaching family and I didn't really stop to consider other fields. I guess I took it for granted. At first I was going to teach art, but I wasn't good enough in art, and then I was going to do special education, but I didn't get along that well with slow students. Then I went into English and all you can do with English is teach, or that's what I thought. So I guess the reason is that I fell into it.

Sylvia's mother was her role model as a child and throughout some of her adult life. She thought her mother was the perfect working woman, that she could handle extraordinary amounts of work, could cope with her husband's rages, and knew how women should treat their husbands. She believed her mother was a living example of the ideal woman depicted in women's magazines of the 1950s (like June Cleaver or Harriet Nelson). By going to the same college as her mother, becoming a teacher, and trying to be the best homemaker possible, Sylvia hoped to follow in her mother's footsteps. When she was 31 years old, she discovered the fallacy in her imagery.

Interview, December 27, 1980.

SYLVIA: My mother told me never to tell your husband you're depressed because he'll think it's him and you don't want that. And I know that's a bunch of bullshit but it's in here [pointing to her head] that my mother knows best. I can't help it, but every time I think about what she said; Mother's advice.

Personal Relationships

While in high school Sylvia met her first husband, also a teacher, and dated him throughout college, then married him after they began teaching in the same school district. After six years, they both became dissatisfied and decided to divorce. The two stayed in contact, had an amicable relationship, and even considered remarriage because each felt insecure outside their long-term relationship. After Sylvia decided not to marry this man again, she felt guilty and worried about what people would think about her change of mind. So she went to a counselor, who told her, "You can tell people you changed your mind." However, she continued to give emotional support to her ex-husband until he finally started dating someone else.

Sylvia finished her master's degree during this period, then returned to the same school system where she had begun her career. She dated several men before she decided to marry her second husband. Jason, who had also been married previously, was in the military and was stationed temporarily in the town where Sylvia taught. When they married, they moved into a small house near his office. After two years, he was transferred to a base in the Southwest and promoted. Jason was a quiet man who was serious about his work but rarely talked about it with Sylvia. She thought he did not talk about it because he was committed to a strict military code that classified his work as secret.

Sylvia felt her marriage was in a rut and wondered whether she had married a boring person, she was boring, or her expectations for marriage were too high. She sometimes thought that if she were more exciting, happier, and less boring, her husband would be also; at other times, she thought their problems would be solved if they did not watch so much television, did not have to worry about housework, or ate proper diets. As Sylvia expressed it, something was out of "sync" but she did not know what.

Through counseling, Sylvia's self-image changed; she learned to deal with conflict more effectively, and the quality of her marriage improved. Sylvia realized she needed to be able to do things for herself without feeling guilty or without shifting blame to her husband for feeling guilty.

An informal interview with Jason (when Sylvia was absent) concerned his upcoming transfer to Europe. He would have an important and time-consuming command and he worried about the huge responsibilities that faced him, but he had not discussed his fears with Sylvia. He said he wanted Sylvia to enjoy Europe even though he would not be able to travel with her. As the commander's wife, Sylvia would be expected to participate in a wide range of social activities, but Jason stressed his desire for her to enjoy living in Europe—with or without his company.

Work

Sylvia's work history included over eight years in the district where she began teaching and two-and-a-half years in the school in the Southwest. In her first job, she taught seventh-grade English in a junior high school with over 800 students. She enjoyed teaching seventh-graders and found them pleasant and fun. She had no discipline problems and got good evaluations from her principals. She said that at times she felt she was in a rut staying in the same school for so many years, but that her dissatisfaction was based not on her relationship with the students but on her feelings that her potential was not being fulfilled. Sylvia had close relationships with several other teachers, all of whom took their work seriously and had difficulty understanding teachers who did not or who did not take school work home. Moving to a new state, school, and grade level was disorienting, and Sylvia had a difficult time adjusting. After a year in the Southwest, she reflected on her difficult transition.

> Diary entry, July 15, 1980: It was basically an unhappy school year, and I never found a completely satisfactory sounding board so I tried to sort out what bothered me. It would have helped to get it all down on paper and off my chest.
>
> Actually I didn't have a bad year but there was always an underlying sense of unhappiness. There was no single reason but a whole combination of ingredients. For one thing, I was in a new school system in a new state. For eight-and-a-half years, I had taught in the same system (the only one I had taught in) and had been very secure and accustomed to routine, personnel, and

procedures. Suddenly I was thrown into this new environment in which things were really different. I hope to gain some perspective soon to determine whether this school system is a good one or not.

Another thing I fought all year was a constantly negative attitude in the English office. Almost everybody in the office openly and loudly criticized the administration, policies, other teachers, etc. Whatever there was to bitch about, they bitched about it. I'm used to doing my criticizing privately with one or two trusted friends. I found myself uncomfortable around this public discussion.

When I applied for a job here, I asked for high school even though I had spent the last eight-and-a-half years at a junior high level. I don't think I adjusted very fast. The high school age threw me for a loop at first. They were mature in some ways but were mainly noisy and unruly and sometimes rude. I didn't know how to handle them. I didn't want to use junior high methods of discipline but the adult approach didn't work either.

Sylvia also said she had no permanent classroom so moved from room to room throughout the day, had to sponsor the group of girls who did flag routines, and had to comply with strict curriculum guidelines and testing programs. She missed her first school, with its familiar surroundings, and teachers with whom she felt comfortable and who were not critical and where she had her own classroom space and more flexibility for planning classroom activities.

Sylvia's negative experience with high school students (her school life there is discussed in detail in the next section) led to an increased dissatisfaction with teaching, but she was not sure of the exact source of the dissatisfaction.

Interview, December 27, 1980.

SYLVIA: I might just be sick of teaching. It might have been just with me, being run down and tired or malnutritioned. No, I think I've got a problem with some personality characteristics that led to this low-grade chronic depression that I have to work on before it gets out of hand. I'm too self-effacing. I worry about what other people think and I worry about how happy everybody is before I'm happy. And that's sick, sick, sick. So I want to get that straightened out before it really becomes a problem.

I don't know which came first, the chicken or the egg. I guess it doesn't really matter how much teaching has contributed or working under pressures has caused my tendency to depression or if it's the other way around. It's time for me to get out and find something else.

I don't know. I'm willing to take wagers on how much longer I stay and I think one day, "Oh, I think I'll stay in and teach a little longer." Next day I'd say, "Well, I've about had it. Why do I need to teach?" The next week I'd say, "It's okay. I've had some successes and it's going to be a good year after all." Just schizophrenic all the time. It's probably normal.

Sylvia's loss of enthusiasm for teaching continued throughout the school year, her second in the high school. After she began counseling, she thought of alternatives to teaching and whether she wanted to commit herself to another year in the high school. Sylvia considered alternative careers in social work, counseling, and library science, and alternately thought about working on a Ph.D. in English. In each case, she considered her future in relation to her husband's career. When Jason told her he had been assigned to a command in Europe, Sylvia stopped considering plans for herself because she knew she would be expected to perform social functions as the commander's wife. Her decision became a nondecision until she found out whether her husband would retire in three years at the end of his European assignment. His retirement, a topic of discussion in their marriage since its beginning, would also determine Sylvia's future. Where they would live and what they would do were vague and undecided.

Sylvia was then faced with deciding what to do in the intervening months until they moved to Europe. With her counselor she came to realize that she did have alternatives to teaching but worried that her husband might be angry because they had depended on her teaching salary. When she finally mentioned her feelings to him he told her if she wanted to quit she should. But the better Sylvia began to feel about herself, the better she felt about teaching.

> Diary entry, May 31, 1981: I've been mulling and mulling about teaching next year. With all my good feeling, I want to teach next year.

Sylvia explained that there were several reasons why she went back to teaching, most important of which was that she had faced most of her problems in counseling. She also said that it would have been difficult to tell her principal she was not coming back, that it was easier to go back than not, that she had been given advanced students for the next year, that she could mandate a good year and plan her life to help her cope (such as hiring help with the housework), and that she did not want to give up her paycheck. She also knew she would leave before the school year was over, when her husband was transferred. Sylvia's experiences during her last year at the school are discussed in the latter part of the next section.

SCHOOL LIFE

Cultural Setting

Sylvia's high school was one of two in an area that included a medium-sized city and a large military base. The city was increasing in population because same of the military personnel who lived outside the base decided to stay after leaving military duty. There were several new shopping centers and a small expansion of housing subdivisions in outlying areas, and numerous small businesses (pawnshops, massage parlors, etc.) were opened to attract military personnel. However, the military base was self-contained and personnel could live and shop on the base. Most did so because it was significantly less expensive to buy gas, see a movie, go to a bank, or, if an officer, eat and drink in a private club. The city and base existed in a symbiotic relationship with frequent movement and interaction between both groups.

In the high school, students were often socially segregated according to city versus military, although Sylvia observed that conflicts rarely occurred between the groups. Conflicts were more likely to occur along racial lines. Because of the social diversity among military personnel and the large Mexican-American population of the southwestern state, many races and cultures were represented in the student body. The most serious rivalries were between blacks and Mexican-Americans. There was some fighting at school, and knives and a gun had been confiscated from students and their lockers.

The transient nature of the military population made teaching, particularly record keeping, more difficult; students continually dropped out and new students enrolled throughout the school year. It was also difficult because the new students had different academic backgrounds and had worked at different paces and in different texts in past schools; the teachers had to spend time introducing them to new sets of expectations and new materials.

Parents who were native to the area tended to be traditional and conservative ("red necks") and worked in the city or were ranchers. The military personnel ranged from the lowest to the highest ranks. With the exception of open houses at school, Sylvia had very little contact with parents. When problems occurred, it was the administrators who discussed them with parents.

School Administration

Because of the large size of the school, principals (one head principal and three assistants) stayed in the central office most of the time. Teachers notified the assistant in charge of their area about any discipline problems. Sylvia was satisfied with the principals' procedures for handling discipline problems and she was bothered by the other teachers' constant criticism. They criticized the principals for being weak and ineffective and thought the principals were poor disciplinarians.

> Diary entry, August 22, 1980: I must confess that last year I acted like an innocent with virgin ears. I was disturbed at the amount of negative comments about the principals and tended to defend them all the time (at least in my own

mind). I'm going to try to have a more objective mind but continue to keep my mouth closed.

During Sylvia's second year at the school, principals began to require lesson plans of new teachers, a policy with which Sylvia and the other teachers disagreed. The principals checked their plans and advised them when they did not follow required curriculum guides. When the other teachers found out the principals' specific criticisms, their remarks had a ripple effect.

Diary entry, October 7, 1980: Last year I felt stifled and too married to the curriculum guide, and I decided that vocabulary would allow for more creativity this year. I'm upset about our being told not only what to teach but what we can't teach. Where is professional independence or judgment? I'm not the only one upset—several of us are giving vocabulary or spelling. Any day now I guess we'll get called on the carpet. I'm beginning to understand why there is a morale problem in the school.

Sylvia never did make negative comments about the principals or about their actions or comments. She was bothered more about the comments they did not make. She felt they did not notice her and did not give her positive reinforcement.

Diary entry, October 26, 1980: I've also been feeling very anonymous. I need to think of some way to honk my own horn. I don't have a reputation as being either a good teacher or a bad teacher; I simply have no reputation. I want some positive feedback. I want to be noticed.

The only time Sylvia knew the principals had noticed her was when they came into her classroom to complete their evaluation forms.

Diary entry, January 28, 1981: I *hate* the observation process. I always feel insecure, nervous, and paranoid about the whole thing. I wish there were some other way to get evaluated. To base a teacher's perfromance on one visit to the classroom seems unfair. I'm not sure what a better solution would be. Perhaps more frequent and shorter informal visits—something like "How's everything going today?" or "What are you covering now?" "I just want to stop and say hello." I do think principals need to get a closer relationship with teachers. It doesn't have to be a buddy-buddy setup. But somehow, there needs to be more interaction. I haven't had a compliment (or a reprimand) all year.

Ironically, Sylvia finally got a pat on the back from her principal—after she knew she would be leaving the school.

Diary entry, October 29, 1981: My principal observed me and she was very complimentary about the lesson and the classroom and really everything. Then we got into a personal sincere conversation about how much happier I seemed this year, how my face had lost its stress, what a good year I was having. She asked what happened and I told her about the counseling. She said it obviously helped and that she definitely considered me as a master teacher and how she would give me a good recommendation. And would I be interested in doing in-service next year with self-image? I told her I wouldn't be here. It was a terrific shot in the arm and I think she felt on a similar wavelength. It was the kind of talk I'd been needing ever since I've been here.

School Facility

As described before, Sylvia's school was immense. Only a few years old, it was in good repair, painted colorfully, and carpeted. Classrooms on each floor in each wing were departmentalized so the teachers closest to Sylvia were also English teachers. Many of the interior walls were made of synthetic folding material so they could be opened to form larger open areas. The walls were rarely opened, however, and were irritating to teachers because students would move them or punch them and because they did not keep out noise from adjoining classrooms.

Each department had a large office in which a desk and a file cabinet were assigned to each teacher. Although the office space provided a place to work outside the classrooms, the desks were so close together that privacy was impossible. Each teacher had decorated his or her work space with posters, family photos, cartoons, and other personal memorabilia. Coffee, sometimes food, and equipment were also in the office.

The central core of the building was an open area where students could sit and talk and where the cafeteria was located. Half the area was sometimes used as a stage for concerts. Students ate at tables in the open area or went outside to eat at picnic tables. Teachers had a separate dining area adjacent to the students' dining room.

Sylvia's classroom had little in it except for 30 students' desks. They were lined up facing the chalk board and a round table, on which were stacked magazines, books, and papers. Other materials were stacked on the floor because there were no bookcases. Sylvia had hung up a few posters of attractive scenes with lines of poetry beneath them.

Teacher Morale

Given the vast size of Sylvia's school building and the grouping of teachers by departments, little opportunity existed to interact with the nearly 120 faculty members in the school. Sylvia felt isolated.

Interview, May 4, 1981.

SYLVIA: A month ago we filled out our feelings about school. We were asked to respond to the statement, "There is little backbiting and gossip." I said, "No," and suggested the administration try to halt it. I don't know what to do. There's a low morale and nothing is done. We're all truncated by departments and the administration is in an ivory tower. The unhappy people are those who stay in. They gripe the most. The ones who think it's better elsewhere get out. I tried to

stay out of it a long time, but I was ostracized. When I do do
it, I feel guilty, but it helps to relieve it.

Sylvia thought there were social barriers between teachers based on
whether or not their husbands were in the military and, if so, whether or
not they were officers. She said that teachers not associated with the
military often saw themselves as more committed because they thought
military wives would leave when their husbands were transferred. They
thought this showed a lack of commitment to the school and to students.
Nonmilitary wives also saw officers' wives as "rich and snotty" and thought
that after school they went to teas and other social gatherings rather than
working at home.

Diary entry, July 15, 1980: A sociogram of the English office would be
fascinating. There were strange cliques and alliances and feuds. The first day of
school a woman asked me to come to her room and proceeded to give me a
30-minute briefing about the good guys and the bad guys, whom to trust and
not trust, etc. As it turned out, this woman was one of the worst about feuding
and being negative. She was the one who told a friend of mine that the reason I
was so pushy was because I was an officer's wife. Me pushy??

Because of Sylvia's isolation from other teachers, she had misconcep-
tions about them and developed unrealistic expectations of her own
behavior as a teacher.

Interview, December 27, 1980.
SYLVIA: During this period I was looking at myself as a poor teacher
          and thought everybody else was organized and efficient and
          had exquisitely quiet classrooms. I was the only one who had
          any problems and I know why I thought this. It started in my
          brain and kept working and working and took some convinc-
          ing that I wasn't that poor and other people have problems,
          too.

Diary entry, September 17, 1980: I get jealous, envious, or frustrated
when I compare myself with teachers who don't take schoolwork home. What
do they do that I don't do? Are they superefficient or do they not give as much
work? Am I patting myself on the back because I do take work home? Am I
deluding myself? I know that everybody is different and that I shouldn't
compare myself with others, but how do I keep from doing it?
Maybe I'm defensive because there have been several teachers in this
school who are adamant about not taking work home and who look with
disdain at those of us who do.

By the end of Sylvia's second year at the school she had made some
friends—though not in the English department. By the beginning of the
third year she was able to look forward to the beginning of school. She
made careful plans to meet her friends on the first day school began so she
would not feel overwhelmed or isolated in the crowd of teachers.

Diary entry, August 21, 1981: It was a good feeling to be back in school again. I probably say this every year but every year I mean it. It's good to see friends again, to talk to people I haven't seen in three months.

I met three friends and we were like four sisters all day. One seemed very glad to see me, in fact, we hugged each other. We ate lunch at a Chinese restaurant and caught up on all the scuttlebutt. It was a very good day.

Students

The population from which Sylvia's students came was different from most populations because of its racial, cultural, and socioeconomic diversity. The students of military parents had traveled all over the world or throughout the United States. While this diversity made a varied student body, the transiency was disruptive. Record keeping was more complicated and routines and procedures more diverse than in high schools with a stable student population. Sylvia thought the students who had traveled were bored more easily because of their varied experiences. She thought that accounted for some of their restlessness and disruptive behavior. On the other hand, she acknowledged the difficulties she had in adjusting to high school students. She was not sure how much of the students' behavior was due to being military children and how much was simply normal for high school students.

Interview, December 27, 1980.

SYLVIA: I've decided that if I stay in teaching, I might go back to the middle school where they're not so negative and everybody likes school, or seemingly likes it, and they aren't out to get the teacher. In high school, they are. They can't wait to trip you up and make you look like an ass, and they want to set up this adversary relationship. I don't know if it's down there or if it's all over.

Sylvia also worried about the students' apathy and complaints about homework. Many made it clear that they would rather be "partying" than at school.

Interview, December 27, 1980.

SYLVIA: No wonder they don't like school. When they are out "partying," which is their euphemism for getting drunk or whatever, they're free and nobody is telling them what to do. They're old enough to get drunk and whatever else they do and then they come to school and here is this diminutive person telling them what they have to do, making them study boring stuff.

Sylvia's assessment of students' boredom, resentment about homework, and preference for "partying" may have been on target, according to the comments of some of her students. Sylvia asked them what they thought about their classes, how their English class was different from their other classes, and what they did when they were not in school. Of the 60 students who gave written answers, the most frequent response to what they thought about their classes was "boring." They also added that they thought they had too much homework.

STUDENT A: What are your classes like? Stupid and Boring!!!
How is your English class different from the others? Just as Bad !!![1]

STUDENT B: What are your classes like? The classes are usually boring! Teachers usually teach and never let you have a day off, which I think we deserve once in a while.
How is your English class different from the others? More discussing, reading, work! Never a day off! In others we at least have one day off, but I don't think I've had one yet in English this year.

STUDENT C: What are your classes like? Big time boring.
How is your English class different from the others? Just as boring except sometimes you get to sleep like during filmstrips.

Other students commented that they liked Sylvia but not English as a subject.

STUDENT D: What are your classes like? All the classes I go to are very dull. As far as I'm concerned, when I graduate, school is through for me—college is definitely not on the agenda. Who cares about Science, History, and English besides teachers and college brats. Don't get me wrong, I agree you should have enough education to get along in life, but everything I have done in school now, I did in 6th grade.
How is your English class different from the others? This class is allright. I like the teacher and the people, but the subject stinks. It's all a repeat of 6th grade.

STUDENT E: What are your classes like? Well they're the usual. My first hour is boring, but only because I don't get into English but the teacher is pretty cool. My other classes are about the same. It is ok.
How is English class different from the others? I don't know about the others but mine is ok. I'm not doing good in it but I enjoy the teacher. She likes to joke around. She gives homework left and right, but she's still ok.

STUDENT F: What are your classes like? I really like my class when the teacher talks every day conversations with his or her class but at the same time teaching us.

How is your English class different from the others? My teacher does just that above. My English class makes me have a Good-day start even though I might sit there and look dumb, bored, and whatever the case may be. There's a lot of conversations and I listen.

Sylvia was also accurate about what students did outside of school, using the same group as a sample; they "partied," a few worked, and fewer did homework.

STUDENT G: Party! Party! If we study it is about 5 minutes. Open and Close book.

STUDENT H: I go to a party, go get drunk. Go get HIGH! Go to the lake, have fun. And don't worry about SCHOOL!

STUDENT I: Get Bombed, Boozed and Busted and into trouble. PARTY!!!!

Classes

Sylvia usually had 125 to 150 students among her five English classes. The first year at the school, she taught all eleventh-grade students. The second year she found out—on the first day of school—that she would have two ninth-grade and three eleventh-grade classes. She had one conference period and an hour for lunch but frequently, in that time period, was assigned to lunchroom or hall supervision. Teachers were expected to make sure students either stayed in the lunch line properly and cleaned their tables or did not enter certain halls in the building during lunchtime.

The plan and content of Sylvia's classes were determined by curriculum guides constructed by the state's Department of Education. There were huge volumes given every high school English teacher so that every student graduated in the state would have had the same substance in their English classes. At first, Sylvia found the guides cumbersome and awesome and worried that she was behind schedule (literature, grammar, etc., were to be covered during specific periods of time). As she adjusted her daily plans to those of the guides, she became more flexible. However, she quickly stopped her alternate plans when she found out that new teachers were sanctioned for not following the guides exactly. Sylvia felt a loss of autonomy over her classroom. The curriculum guides were confining and inhibited her creativity. But fearing sanctions, she stuck to them.

Although she used the curriculum guides to plan her classes, Sylvia did not write down detailed lesson plans for her classes, e.g., her objectives or the questions she asked. In fact, she said she taught on "whim."

Interview, May 4, 1981.

INTERVIEWER: Do you plan each thing you do?

SYLVIA: No. There are three general parts. I do this and this and the third thing if there's time. Things take care of themselves. It's natural. I've always done it that way. Even with sketchy plans they have always worked, but I'm always anxious about the next day. But once I start out, it's okay. It's always worked. The general plan is in my head. The first hour is my guinea pig.

So Sylvia had both a highly structured curriculum guide to follow and her daily plans were nebulous and difficult to articulate. She relied on years of experience to determine the timing of activities and level of difficulty of her questions.

In the classroom, Sylvia was soft-spoken and pleasant to the students. However, she never waited until they were totally quiet to begin class or make transitions from one activity to another. She continued to talk until the noise level was unreasonable and then asked them to "quiet down" but began again before they had all stopped talking. This pattern continued throughout her classes unless students were reading. In that case, eventually they all were quiet. Sylvia was disturbed by their interruptions but did not seem aware of the pattern she had created.

Also, the students did not take turns during question-and-answer sessions or general discussion periods. This, too, created opportunities for disruptive behavior. When Sylvia asked a question, students did not wait to be called on—whichever student called out first or was the loudest caught her attention and was allowed to continue. This created a problem because several students usually answered simultaneously and some students sat passively throughout the class and never volunteered an answer. Some of these students even did their homework assignments for other classes during the English lesson.

Sylvia's inconsistent momentum also created opportunities for disturbances. Part of her lessons went smoothly and quickly whereas others dragged and left gaps of time when students were unsure about what to do. Instructions or questions had to be repeated and, because the momentum was lost, students were disruptive.

Although Sylvia did not attribute classroom problems to her philosophy of teaching on "whim," she did acknowledge and express concern about her lack of assertiveness and her inability to control high school-aged students. She preferred to smile and talk in pleasant tones rather than be firm or stern. Sylvia's affect complicated her problems of control. As noted in her personal history, she felt quite depressed throughout the first two years she was teaching in the high school. Her smiles changed to strained expressions when students misbehaved. Her nonverbal behavior gave cues to students and contributed to their disruptive behavior.

Sylvia's attitudes about her classes and her ability to control them changed considerably her third year. Counseling gave her the self-confidence to deal with students more assertively yet feel more relaxed.

> Diary entry, September 2, 1981: I'm human this time in starting the year. Usually I put on this strict, phony front and convince the kids I am strict. This year, I allowed myself to smile and be myself, and yet I was firm. Not mean, but firm. It's worked fine but also I have a better bunch of kids this year. It's hard to tell if this approach is working because of the approach or because of the students I have.

Interview, October 22, 1981.

SYLVIA: I'm more assertive and act firm. I feel much better, more in power. I'm looser and I'm enjoying myself. They're quiet and attentive. Kids can criticize you, complain, and talk about you, and I've had 9 or 10 years of that. But if you have a good self-concept, you can accept things better.

Sylvia's positive year was reflected in her principal's comments (cited earlier). She was told how much she had changed in her teaching style and even in her facial expressions and that she was a master teacher.

Leaving School

Sylvia commented that she was glad she had taught another year—"I have proved to myself that I'm a good teacher." She was undecided, however, about whether she would teach in the future, particularly while she would have social responsibilities associated with her husband's work in Europe.

HOME LIFE

Sylvia and Jason lived in officers' housing on the military base. Their house was a prefab structure that looked similar to all the other houses in the area. The lawn, trees, and flowers were well kept. There was a large living-dining area that opened onto a patio and the backyard, a small kitchen and pantry area where the washer, dryer, and freezer were located, three bedrooms, and two bathrooms. The house was more than adequate for the two of them and they were able to use the extra bedrooms for offices and storage.

The living room furniture was arranged to face a television and an elaborate stereo system Jason had built. Some of the antiques they had begun to collect were hung on the walls or were in the bookcases. The floors were covered with light-colored linoleum tiles that were difficult to clean. Evidences of Sylvia and Jason's hobbies were found in different rooms—a banjo, an easel and a partially finished painting, a chair in which they were putting a new cane seat, some quilting supplies, and parts of several antique clocks.

As mentioned in the discussion of Sylvia's personal history, she and Jason tended to worry about their work when at home. This had a negative influence on their relationship and contributed to Sylvia's depression. Although their marriage strengthened after Sylvia completed her counseling sessions, problems in the other areas of her life (household duties, financial conditions, leisure activities, and health) that contributed to and were affected by her decision to go into counseling were not all solved. Some things were improved, some did not change.

Household Duties

Sylvia set unrealistic expectations for herself at home. She thought the house should be immaculate, that meals should be nutritional yet different, and that she should be a loving, attentive wife. However, because Sylvia rarely had the time or energy to realize all these goals, she often felt frustrated and overcome by what she perceived to be a dirty house. Her frustration and guilt increased if Jason became angry and complained about some aspect of the housework. Later, he usually offered to help or assured her that he really did not mind a messy house. This cycle of behavior—Sylvia's perfectionism, her limited time and energy, and Jason's inconsistent attitudes and help with the housework—is illustrated in the following excerpts.

The perfect housewife:

> Diary entry, August 28, 1980: I haven't mentioned much about meals. I was doing pretty well until today. I've done several crock-pot meals. Tonight we had odds and ends. Jason is extremely easy to please and keeps insisting I go to too much trouble. He wants to lose weight anyway. Consequently, I'm not a very inventive cook during most of the school year. I don't feel guilty. I just wish we put more emphasis on gourmet, elegant meals. It would be nice. But sometimes I go in spells where we do eat out of *Bon Appetit.*

The reality of time and energy:

> Diary-entry, August 26, 1980: I'm restless and tired tonight. I came home from school and was greeted by a kitchen looking _____. I was half hoping a good fairy would clean it up while I was at school. Anyway, I was a little depressed but cleaned it up right away to get it over with and then fixed supper.

Jason's inconsistency—anger:

> Diary entry, February 18, 1981: It started around 9:30 or 10:00 P.M. last night when Jason got mad about the way everything in the study was all stacked up, unsorted, piled up, and neglected. He had been hunting for some papers and was getting pretty upset because he couldn't find them. On another occasion, I might have tried to ignore it or I would have at least coped with the anger. But last night something clicked and I started crying and crying and

crying—not because I felt stepped on but because the incident triggered all that had been churning inside me.

Jason's inconsistency—helping out:

> Diary entry, September 28, 1980: It was a good weekend. I worked like a dog Saturday morning to get most of the housework out of the way. Jason helped me some, too. I'm getting a little more assertive about that.

Jason's inconsistency—ignoring the mess:

> Diary entry, September 9, 1980: I've lost interest in keeping the house orderly. Do you suppose I can adjust or will I keep knocking my head against the wall? I know the answer to that. Because Jason doesn't seem to care what the house looks like and because he encourages me to relax and not worry about the house, I tend to do that. Maybe when I get back some of my energy, I'll rearrange my priorities.

This cycle repeated itself throughout Sylvia's diary.

Financial Conditions

Sylvia and Jason's combined income allowed them a comfortable economic situation and a sizable savings account. As an officer, Jason had free housing, including utilities, and their groceries and clothes were purchased on the base at reduced prices. Medical and dental care was also free, as were Sylvia's counseling fees, and their cars were already paid for. Their only major expense was income taxes, because they had no deductible expenses.

Because their financial situation was so stable, Sylvia considered leaving teaching. During the period she was undecided, she worried about not earning an income, despite the fact that Jason assured her he would support them if she decided to quit.

> Diary entry, May 14, 1981: I'm wondering about money—I'm so spoiled about bringing a paycheck home. The paycheck represents security for one thing. I don't worry about the bank account. And to some extent the paycheck gives me freedom. I can justify buying things because I work. However, I'm timid about buying things for myself partly because I myself am stingy and partly because Jason wants us to save as much as we can. So—it's going to be hard to go without the paycheck and without the feeling of contributing.

Sylvia did save some checks and spent them totally on herself—the checks she received for writing the diary for this study. She hoarded them for special things she normally would not have bought.

Leisure Activities

Because Sylvia and Jason were usually tired when they got home from work, their leisure activities were limited. They were also limited by the inordinate amount of schoolwork that Sylvia brought home on weekends. Most of the time they watched television, napped, or read. Each also had hobbies and they sometimes worked together on projects such as re-finishing an antique or going to an antique store. Sylvia painted in oils, made quilts, and researched genealogical history when she had time —usually only in the summer.

Sylvia and Jason visited their parents once or twice a year and took a one-week vacation, their first in three years. They sometimes went to social gatherings with friends or had dinner at the officers' club. However, outings, time for hobbies, and social engagements were infrequent and Sylvia felt bored.

> Diary entry, November 11, 1980: Another reason for my depression (and it really hurts to admit it) is that I get preoccupied about how routine my life is. I guess it's self-pity. There are plenty of things to do—reading, movies, nightclubs, exciting things. What I'm trying to say by beating around the bush is that Jason and I have opposite ideas of what is fun. Not opposite exactly because I like to do both things. It's just that I have a difficult time getting him out of the house. He would rather stay home than go out. And when I do suggest doing something and he's not interested, I take a nose dive. It's a vicious cycle. I need to get it out of my system or it's going to get worse.

Syvlia was concerned about the prospect of not working, moving to Europe, and assuming the social duties of a commander's wife; she was also concerned that Jason would not have leisure time to spend with her. She hoped to be able to gain the independence needed to socialize and travel alone or with a friend.

Health

Sylvia's dissatisfaction with teaching after moving to the Southwest and her unresolved problems in her marriage resulted in a cycle of stress that included sporadic eating habits and exercise routines, exhaustion, and depression. She blamed her depressions on a variety of causes in addition to teaching. She blamed her bio-rhythms, her diet ("Sunday, I mixed up a big batch of Adele Davis's special recipe, and I've been taking vitamins. Part of my problem could be diet related"), coffee ("Maybe, just maybe, I've discovered why I've been so tired. I think it was because I cut down on coffee. I may be forced to go back full force to my addiction"), or the lack of exercise ("I haven't run since the weekend and the kids are beginning to get on my nerves. I think a good run would flush out my irritability").

Although Sylvia did indeed feel better when she jogged regularly and ate nutritionally, she was inconsistent in her habits because she was too tired or depressed to carry them out.

> Diary entry, September 9, 1980: I was tired when I got home from school. I'm tired of being tired. Tell me everybody gets tired and that it's just not me. Anyway, I put leftovers on the stove, we ate, and both of us fell asleep watch-

ing the local news. I always feel better after a nap, but it's a vicious cycle. Now I'll probably stay up later than I should and then be tired tomorrow evening.

Sylvia finally got so tired of being depressed that she went to a counselor. ("I had been afraid before to talk about depression. It sounds like a dirty word—nothing I would ever catch, not old optimistic me.") After less than six months of counseling, she said she felt "80 percent better" but planned to keep "working on herself," particularly to keep telling herself she was a good teacher and "to hell with what the other teachers think. They'll talk about me anyway." She also tried to have more compassion for herself, to be positive, and to take responsibility for her life. Counseling had also given her courage to correct a long-term dental problem, get a new hair style, and lose some weight. As noted earlier, her new psychological and physical self-image increased her ability to deal with her marriage and had positive effects on her relationship with Jason.

CONCLUSIONS: OVERLAP OF HOME AND SCHOOL

The overlap of Sylvia's home and school life was so extensive it was difficult to consider one without simultaneously considering the other. While Sylvia had to compartmentalize in order to get through her classes, this was sometimes difficult for her, as was seen in her facial expressions, her tone of voice, and her hesitancy when disciplining students.

Sylvia's move to the Southwest began a period of dissatisfaction that lasted two years. She had difficulty adjusting to a new school, new state requirements, a new faculty that she found critical, high school students (rather than junior high students), a sense of isolation in the large building, no friends, no contact with principals, and a loss of autonomy in her classroom because of required curriculum guides. These factors, combined with a never-ending supply of students' papers that needed grading and recording, permeated Sylvia's home life. She felt overworked, tired, depressed, and unappreciated.

Sylvia once stayed home from school for a day to get caught up with schoolwork. She felt guilty calling in sick but could think of no other way to get ahead. She often said she wanted to stop bringing so much work home, but later diary entries showed she did not succeed. School life dominated her home life.

While at school Sylvia felt tired from working late the night before on grades, from getting up at 5:00 A.M. to catch up on paperwork, and from all the housework. The vague long-term depression she felt about teaching, her home life, and herself affected her teaching because she never felt totally in control of her classes or her work. She felt tense and humorless. One time when she and Jason had an argument before school her home life became predominant while she was in the classroom. Jason had been angry because Sylvia had not cleaned up the kitchen from the previous night's baking activities and he could find no place to eat his breakfast. After they argued, Sylvia "had a good, noisy cry," cleaned the kitchen instead of going to a faculty Christmas breakfast, and managed to keep up a "cheerful front" through the beginning of her second class.

> Diary entry, December 20, 1980: One of my students kept asking me why me eyes were red and then, "Why are you crying? Why are you crying?" All this attention got me started crying in earnest, and I had to leave the room. On my way into the restroom I ran into a teacher who asked what was wrong, and I just went ahead and told her the truth. Meanwhile, the inquistive student had followed me to the restroom to find out what was wrong. All this was embarrassing!

Sylvia returned to the room and assured her class it was nothing they had done that caused her to cry, but she found it difficult to cope the rest of the day. She had tears in her eyes and people asked her what was wrong all day. She concluded the following:

> On many other occasions, home concerns or problems have bothered me at school, but I was able to hide them more successfully. It was a combination of stress, Christmas, and its being my birthday (self-pity).

During Sylvia's third year at the school (after counseling), she felt better about herself and worked to balance her home and work lives. She still did most of the housework but tried to bring less schoolwork home to allow more time and strength for leisure activities.

Epilogue

During Sylvia's first year in Europe she taught as a substitute in an American school on the military base. The second year (1983–1984), she stayed at home with their new baby son. In 1984 they returned to the United States and Jason reenlisted. Once again, Sylvia was alone most of the time with her son. She did not know when or if she would return to teaching.

NOTE

1. Sylvia instructed students not to write their names on their papers. She collected them, then gave them to me after the students left the classroom. She took only a perfunctory glance at the papers and never asked me what they said. Direct quotes are unedited.

6

Phyllis: A Married Elementary School Teacher with Children

Phyllis was a 31-year-old married woman who taught first grade in a medium-sized school district in the Midwest. She and her husband, an agriculture teacher at a community college, had two sons, aged 7 and 4. Phyllis was quite traditional, both in her reasons for teaching and in her roles as wife, mother, and teacher. She went back to college to complete the requirements for teacher certification after her sons were several years old, and when she began teaching, she continued total care for her house and her sons, as she had before she worked outside the home. She grew tired of multiple-role responsibilities; at the same time, she was faced with the inconsistencies between her ideal of teaching and its reality. The strain caused conflicts with her husband and health problems. As Phyllis struggled for assertiveness at home and at school, she never lost her desire to be with children. She maintained high standards in her classroom and warm relationships with students.

TYPICAL DAY

Phyllis got up, showered, put on Western-style boots, polyester slacks, and a matching blouse, woke up her two sons, helped them wash and dress, and then fixed their breakfast. Her husband, John, had gone to work at 6:00 A.M. to check some equipment used in an agricultural experiment that took all his spare time. Her older son went to a neighbor's house to wait for the school bus and Phyllis took her younger son to nursery school in their van.

    Phyllis drove from the city along narrow, winding, blacktopped roads to her small elementary school. The school resembled an enlarged one-room schoolhouse more than the modern school buildings located within the city, even though it was in the same school district. Phyllis was careful not to park in the principal's space but had plenty of other spaces to choose from because she was the first teacher to arrive.

She walked into her room apprehensively, wondering if vandals had struck again, leaving her room a mess. She vividly remembered the acrid smell from the fire extinguisher that had been sprayed around the room and did not look forward to cleaning up such a mess again. The lack of action by police and school officials after a dozen break-ins was puzzling but she knew teachers had little power to question the officials' behavior.

The room was in order and Phyllis began organizing worksheets for the morning's activities. She made copies of the worksheets she would use to introduce a unit on life among the Eskimos and hung some pictures of Eskimos and polar bears she had found in her files. Shortly after she returned to her room, other teachers arrived; they spoke to her briefly but did not stop to talk. Phyllis wondered if she would ever be a part of the friendship network among the teachers but was glad they were being civil. It was several weeks since they had been openly critical of her innovative art projects. All the other teachers did the same projects, but Phyllis broke with tradition and planned her classroom individualistically. She thought it was worth being excluded if the other teachers did not have the motivation to plan unusual projects.

When the first school buses arrived, Phyllis put on her coat and went out to supervise the children before school began. Some of the children ran around to keep warm while others stood bundled in groups, shivering. Phyllis buttoned some of their coats and asked others why they had no hats on. She knew some would have earaches or catch the flu that was going around the school. As she hugged one of her first-graders, she wondered how soon she herself would get the flu.

When all the children had arrived, Phyllis rang a large bell. The children lined up and filed into the building. Her students hung up their coats, put up their lunch boxes, looked at various things around the room, and talked quietly or sat down. Phyllis passed tissues to those who had colds and reminded them to cover their mouths when they sneezed. She admired a student's new pants and shirt and then asked everyone to sit down.

The 22 students sat at their desks in groups of 4 or 5 and Phyllis took lunch money from those who planned to eat in the cafeteria. Then she explained the directions for each of the four worksheets to be completed independently that morning while she worked with the reading groups. She called the first group to the reading corner where they sat on the carpeted floor near the charts that had their new words painted on them. The other children got their worksheets and began marking or coloring in the answers.

As the children finished their worksheets, some went to a table that had several sets of headphones. One child carefully put on a record and they listened to the exercise on improving work skills.

Throughout the morning the children worked quietly and stayed with their tasks. After a recess, reading continued and Phyllis rewarded each child with a sticker that had words such as *super* or *great* printed on it. At lunch time, the child designated as leader for the day stood in front of the door; when the whole class was in line, they filed to the restrooms and then to the cafeteria. In the cafeteria, Phyllis could relax her supervision somewhat because another teacher and an aide were in charge of the cafeteria every day. Phyllis was anxious, however, when she saw that the principal was also watching the children go into the cafeteria and hoped her children would behave. The principal whacked the hands of those who did not with a ruler.

Phyllis was feeling the aftereffects of stomach flu and just ate a bowl of cottage cheese at the teachers' table, which was separated from those for the children by a low bookcase. She tried to enter into the other teachers' conversations but worried they would not respond or would become critical. So she quietly ate her lunch and returned to her room to wait for her children.

Phyllis enjoyed this part of the day because it was reserved for sharing. Children brought things from home and told about them, and Phyllis showed them some books about Eskimos and let them choose one for her to read to them. The children enjoyed her voice inflections and facial expressions and smiled and laughed with the characters in the story.

During the afternoon Phyllis presented spelling and math. After recess, the art teacher came into the room. Phyllis left and used the time to grade the morning worksheets. She was able to finish grading all four sets in 20 minutes, writing "Great work" or "Good job" or putting a "happy face" on them.

It was unreasonably hot in her classroom when Phyllis returned, so she opened some windows to let the cold air in. At 3:30 the children put on their coats, gathered their papers, lined up, and went to their buses, some hugging Phyllis as they left. Phyllis stayed for another 30 minutes to put a new decoration on her door. She liked to keep a theme for each month that was not organized around holidays. She taped penguins the children had made to the door to follow through with her Eskimo theme. As she made the final touches, the principal came by and told her not to work so hard. All the other teachers had left shortly after the students.

Phyllis picked up her sons at a babysitter's home, went home, and fixed dinner. She listened to her sons talk about their day's activities while she made her way through the morning's breakfast mess. John called and said he would be home late, which meant after midnight, so Phyllis and the boys ate and then went downstairs to their den to watch television. Phyllis washed a couple of loads of laundry and, after putting the boys to bed, cleaned the living room and cut out some letters for a bulletin board she planned to put up in her room the next day.

She went to bed and wondered when she would see John. She asked herself if her sons were getting cheated by not spending much time with their father but could think of no way to stop her husband's workaholic habits. As she turned over in bed, she felt stabs of pain in her back and feared her physical problems were not totally cured. She decided she would have to live with the pain, because her doctor could not find the source and John had ordered her either to get well or stay sick enough to provide the doctor with "real" evidence.

PERSONAL HISTORY

Growing Up

Phyllis was born and raised in a large city in the Midwest. Her mother was a teacher but had quit teaching before Phyllis was born and never returned. Her father was a salesman in an auto parts business and Phyllis grew up in a working-class or lower-middle-class way of life. Her parents still lived in the house where she was raised, although the neighborhood had changed from working-class whites to working-class blacks.

> Interview, September 29, 1981.
> PHYLLIS: It [her life-style] was conservative. I had everything I wanted. Dad is still wearing to this day clothes that he wore 30 years ago. But as to rich or frivolous—we've never had that.

Phyllis was an only child and said her mother waited on her and did everything for her until she left home to go to college. Despite her mother's attentiveness, Phyllis never felt close to her or thought she could talk to her about her feelings, because her mother gave advice and criticism rather than support. The same pattern continued in Phyllis's adulthood, so even though she saw her mother frequently, she never confided in her; she knew her mother would be critical.

> Interview, September 29, 1981.
> PHYLLIS: She [her mother] did everything for me and she didn't want me to have it as rough as she had had it. Her mom died when she was 6 years old of TB and she was raised by maiden aunts and a stepmother. But as to being able to sit down and discuss the nitty-gritty, Mom and I were never able to.

> Interview, June 4, 1981.
> PHYLLIS: Mom takes everything personally. It's hard to bounce

things off her. I got very upset when I tried to fill her in on what I'd gone through at school and she came back and said it was my fault that the problems happened. Mom feels that if too much dust clutters the house or my laundry is not all done or I have clothes stacked in the hall for a garage sale, that it's affecting my marriage.

Phyllis described her mother as nervous and insecure. She said she had never had a nervous breakdown but that she made everyone around her nervous because she got so upset about things. Therefore, they never had family gatherings at their house.

Phyllis described her father as unemotional and said she rarely talked to him while growing up, yet she felt at times that she was still his "little girl."

Diary entry, September 19, 1980: My dad's birthday. Memories. I'm a wife, a mom, a teacher, I'm still my dad's "little girl." You want to grow up; then again there's a little yearning to be freed of some of the decisions and responsibilities that come with adulthood, family, and career.

Phyllis saw her parents two weekends a month because her husband had National Guard meetings in the city where they lived. Although Phyllis did not enjoy talking about problems, it was the only opportunity she had to get away from home and out of town, and to be freed temporarily from some of the responsibilities of home and family.

Education

In junior high school, Phyllis was recommended for an accelerated language class. A teacher talked to her and told her she had great potential but would have to work harder so her grades would reflect her intelligence. In tears, Phyllis told her she would do her best, but she became extremely nervous when taking the entrance test and did not qualify. Instead, she did so poorly she was placed in a slow learners' class. Her mother went to school to protest, so they took Phyllis out of the class and put her in a college preparatory class. By the end of high school she was in an honor society. However, she never felt she was as smart as the others in her classes, so she studied hard and dated infrequently, in order to keep up her grades.

After high school, she became more liberated from her parents and dated a lot while living at home and attending a university in the city. When she transferred to another university to major in child development, she made her break from home. While in college she met her husband; she finished her degree but did not work in a formal setting for the following 10 years. After a period of depression, Phyllis went back to school to earn a teaching certificate so she could go to work.

Interview, September 29, 1981.

    PHYLLIS: I feel I worked through my own bit of depression before I finally picked myself up and went back to school and got recognition. I think I'd been wallowing in depression. I spent four years getting a degree and sat back while John furthered himself in the military. I could never get a job because they wouldn't hire women who were married to military people because they left in the middle of the school year. Then I didn't start on my degree because we didn't have enough money. It was more important for him to get a master's degree and get his job and I just sat there. I was really depressed. I think that's why I would sit in front of the TV and not lift a finger all day and just take care of the kids.

Personal Relationships

Phyllis's husband had been born and raised on a farm; he never dated, was active in church work, and was a workaholic. After his experience in the military, he remained on active duty on weekends and in the summers, wore his hair in a short military style, and was very traditional in his sex-role attitudes. The more liberated Phyllis became after she got her degree and went back to work, the more threatened John felt. This resulted in marital problems that were never resolved during the time of the study (see the Home Life section for further discussion). Phyllis looked back on her idealism at the time they married.

Interview, September 29, 1981.

    PHYLLIS: You were supposed to be stable and settled and secure with not a problem in the world.

    INTERVIEWER: Live happily ever after?

    PHYLLIS: [laughing] Yeah. Like Cinderella. Guess I'm finding out late in life that things aren't that cut and dried. Just because you do your best doesn't mean that everything is going to turn out all right. I guess I'm really a slow learner.

She also commented on the effects of her increasing independence.

Interview, June 4, 1981.

    PHYLLIS: For so many years he [John] made me feel that I was wrong all the time, that my opinion was the wrong opinion. He sees that when I went back to school, our problems got worse. I became independent. Then I started speaking out and putting my foot down, because I could not be wrong all the time. Every time I come up with something that's different from what he believes, I have to have all my ammunition ready. He makes it a challenge all the time.

Work

Phyllis was extremely enthusiastic about the prospect of beginning a teaching career. She had a good student teaching experience and had taught a few months in a school that had a principal who exhibited ideal characteristics—he was warm, supportive, and visible, yet took care of all the things teachers had no time for in their classrooms. Phyllis was transferred to another school where she began her first year.

> Diary entry, August 5, 1980: They rearranged school so things are in an uproar but my room is cozy. Real windows. My first room that is all mine! This is what I worked for. Even the dust on the books looks inviting.

Phyllis's ideals quickly dissolved as she met the reality of teaching, as discussed in the next section.

SCHOOL LIFE

Cultural Setting

Phyllis's school was located in a midwestern city with a population of over 25,000. Her elementary school was the smallest of the five in the district. Declining enrollments had caused some schools to close, and although Phyllis's school was supposed to be one of those, it was kept open because of parental protests. Parents regarded the school as rural, traditional, cohesive, and familial in atmosphere. They liked the idea of their children being educated in a cloistered environment rather than in a large school, which they viewed as impersonal and cold. Phyllis found the atmosphere to be quite the opposite of warm and cohesive, but parents continued to have that perception.

Phyllis's students were from rural, working-class or lower-middle-class families, although there were a few more affluent families. Most children rode the school bus, a few walked, and a few parents drove their children to school. Families were conservative, traditional, and religious and favored a strong basic education with no "frills." The children were of all ability levels; they ranged from those who scored above the 99th percentile on standardized tests to those who were behaviorally disordered or had learning disabilities.

School Administration

During Phyllis's first weeks of teaching, much of her enthusiasm was dampened by the ineffectiveness of her principal, who was in her last year before retirement. She had been in poor health and had taken sick leave for part of the previous year. The principal was sometimes ill and often tired throughout the year; and she treated teachers in an infantile manner, fluctuating between being unreasonably strict and unreasonably negligent. At times she monitored the teachers' behavior closely and at other times left the building for hours to have her hair styled or to lie down and sleep in the back of her car.

> Diary entry, August 14, 1980: Our first staff meeting! The "do's and don'ts" came down. You do not run the ditto machine by yourself—and other petty things and very little on curriculum. Things that seemed so natural and flowed so smoothly at the other school are made into drudgery for all. We are not treated as professionals but as "things" to be watchdogged for the first false move. I feel spied upon by my principal, not consulted or cooperated with.

To Phyllis's chagrin, the principal made her her "pet," giving her preferential treatment at times, while at other times treating her as unreasonably as the other teachers (e.g., grading their plan books). Her occasional preferential treatment had extremely negative effects on Phyllis's rapport with the other teachers. There were only eight teachers in the school and Phyllis was the only newcomer. Their long-time cliques allowed no opportunity for including Phyllis after they observed the principal's behavior. This problem persisted throughout the year, which distressed Phyllis and led to her considerable loss of enthusiasm about the working conditions of teaching. Nevertheless, she continued to be quite positive about being in the classroom with children.

The principal's loss of control produced negative behavior among the teachers. When the principal left the building, the teachers passed around a green piece of paper to signal that she had gone. They left their classrooms and gathered in the hall or engaged in other informal behavior normally prohibited. When the teacher nearest the parking lot saw the principal return, a red piece of paper was circulated to denote that informal behavior should stop.

Phyllis, who was a religious person, felt sorry for the principal despite the numerous points of disagreement they had. For example, she volunteered to buy the principal's Christmas gift from the faculty because no one else would do it. She chose an assortment of cheeses displayed attractively on a cheese board; but the first thing the principal said when she opened the present was "I don't like cheese."

After the principal retired, a new principal was assigned to the building. He was also the principal of another, larger school and was more often there than in Phyllis's school. He was assisted by a "head teacher," a person without administrative certification who handled discipline and other procedural-organizational problems that arose during the principal's absence. In addition, the head teacher taught a full classroom schedule.

The new principal established order in the school, which Phyllis suspected was the result of orders from the administrator, who knew there were serious problems under the former principal's leadership. The new principal observed teachers more frequently and for longer periods of time and came into their classrooms as often as possible to see if anything was needed. As a result, the old informal networks collapsed to some extent, because opportunities for slacking off were eliminated. The principal also used funds the other principal had not touched and purchased much-needed supplies for the teachers. He treated children warmly and set up a reward system for their attendance records. When Phyllis had to leave school for family emergencies or meetings in other schools, the principal took over her class. Phyllis thought the principal had restored a good atmosphere in the school and felt she was being treated as an adult once again. However, this principal left the district at the end of the year to take a higher administrative position in another district. So Phyllis had a third principal in her third year of teaching.

School Facility

As described previously, Phyllis's school was a small school within a large district. It was located in a wooded area and had a large grassy space that was used for a playground. Originally, it had been built as a temporary solution to a large increase in enrollment and was therefore constructed with prefabricated materials. Later, it had been renovated somewhat because parts were unsafe. There were six classrooms, an office, a playroom, and a cafeteria. The walls had wood paneling and the class-rooms were all carpeted.

During the first months of Phyllis's first year, vandals broke into the building about a dozen times. Each time they stole food from the freezer, once smearing hamburger meat all over the cafeteria, turned teachers' desk drawers upside down, took books and materials from the bookcases and threw them around the rooms, and sprayed a fire extinguisher around several rooms. On the morning after these incidents occurred, the police were not brought in. Instead, teachers were expected to clean up the mess quickly before students came. Parents became alarmed and volunteered to guard the building. Although the incidents eventually stopped, Phyllis and the other teachers were never told why the police were not called, what the administrators' reactions were, or if the vandals had been caught. Phyllis found it a frightening time, which did not contribute to her enthusiasm for her job.

Phyllis's classroom contained 22 tables and chairs for her students, a teacher's desk, a couple of large round tables, bookcases, a variety of materials including books, records, and games, and several bulletin boards filled with pictures, posters, children's papers, and projects. In fact, every square inch was filled with materials or equipment children could use in a learning activity, either visually or manually.

Teacher Morale

Phyllis's principal had the strongest negative effect on morale. Her poor leadership encouraged negative behavior patterns among the teachers, including their exclusion of Phyllis. Their strong friendship groups, resentment of the principal's preferential treatment of Phyllis, and resentment of Phyllis's creative projects and lessons resulted in inflexible patterns that existed the whole school year. The other teachers were critical of Phyllis behind her back and often to her face. They thought she was a rate buster and was trying to show them up. Phyllis often cried when she got home from school.

> Diary entry, May 3, 1981: I don't know if I'm stubborn or what. One minute I feel like I should leave because I can't take the pressure anymore and the next minute I feel like a "group" should not be forcing me to do something that I really don't want to do. Because I really love the atmosphere, the small school, the play yard, the grass, the swings, and the parents at the school. I just hope I can find some way to cope with it.

She tried a number of different ways to cope. She tried to be friendly; she stayed to herself; she offered help; she prayed. All these techniques failed, and the problem was as serious at the end of the year as it was at the beginning. Finally she gathered enough courage to talk to the principal about being transferred, but the principal told her she was needed in the school and should stay. She also told Phyllis not to talk to the superintendent and that the superintendent also wanted her to stay in the school, but Phyllis never knew the details of their conversation. She suspected that the principal, a few weeks away from retirement, did not tell the superintendent about the morale problems in the school. They would have reflected negatively on her leadership.

During the second year, some of the cliques of the first year were broken up. Although Phyllis never became totally comfortable around the teachers who had been critical of her the previous year, she found that former patterns of persecution were absent. She no longer cried every night.

Students

There were approximately 150 children in Phyllis's school in the primary grades. There were two first-, two second-, and two third-grade classes. Phyllis's first-graders were from all ability levels because the students were distributed equally between her and the other first-grade teacher. On some occasions, she had students who qualified for the behaviorally disordered or learning disabled classrooms. If those classes were filled, she had to keep these children in her classroom. Although these children were not discipline problems, Phyllis had difficulty finding enough time to give them the individual attention they needed. She gained a reputation for dealing with problem children, however, and one child who had been expelled from several different schools was put in her classroom. This boy was older than the other children, much larger, and physically unattractive. Although Phyllis had to monitor his behavior very closely, she was able to control it and help him develop new social skills so he was accepted by the other children.

Phyllis often exhibited "mothering" behavior with her students. She hugged and patted them, gave them frequent positive reinforcement, straightened their clothes, made sure they were warmly dressed in inclement weather, took care of them when they were sick, helped them in the bathroom, reminded them of good manners, and scolded them when they misbehaved. In fact, she treated them like she did her own children, although more formally because she expected them to pay attention all day and not be disruptive. Her behavior when with students matched her philosophy of teaching.

Interview, September 29, 1981.

PHYLLIS: I really strive to help my students have a good attitude about life. I guess it's mostly attitudes. The attitude to want to learn and the attitude to give everybody a chance to learn, to show other people the respect they deserve. I know a lot of highly educated people that are very rude. I'd rather have them come out of my class with a good moral attitude and willingness to listen to other people. I want to help prepare them for life. A lot of life is not facts, it's getting along with others. A good attitude about others will make them better citizens. I try to take the time with them to show the concern I do feel for them. It's like I've got 22 [says her own sons' names] and I can't get mad at them. I can just hope that when they become adults, they've developed into good people.

Classes

All the teachers in the school followed the same basic schedule, reading in the morning, and spelling and math in the afternoon, because they had to coordinate recess and lunch schedules. Some students went to other classrooms for reading, depending on which teachers had groups that best fit their reading levels.

Phyllis spent the first days of school teaching children their schedule so they were clear about what they should be doing at any given time. This allowed several overlapping activities to take place at the same time. Observation showed that she achieved her goal, because children never asked where they should be or what activity should be taking place. Phyllis was able to work with reading groups without having to monitor the behavior of the rest of the class, because they followed her directions, worked quietly, and when finished with their work, selected a game or book to occupy themselves.

During whole-class activities such as math lessons, Phyllis monitored the children's work very closely. She walked around their desks and checked their work as they completed answers so she could give immediate feedback. She kept them alert by asking questions and held them accountable for listening and responding. The children paid attention, kept to the task, and did not interrupt other children.

Transitions from one activity to another were smooth. Phyllis kept up a constant narrative during transitional periods, telling students exactly what they should be doing and what was going to take place next. She did so in normal tones of voice. Even when reprimanding a student, she did not raise her voice.

Phyllis's discipline style was firm. She expected children to sit up in their chairs, do their work, not bother other children, and wait for their turn and to be called on before talking. She used quiet, well-behaved children as models for those who were not behaving properly. She discouraged tattling, although a few children habitually monitored the behaviors of others.[1]

Although a strong disciplinarian, Phyllis generated enthusiasm. Children's responses, facial expressions, and affectionate gestures toward her showed that they enjoyed her and her class. She planned a variety of activities such as art projects and social studies or science units to keep up their enthusiasm.

> Diary entry, September 23, 1980: Pecos Bill is the center of my social studies unit today. He's quite a character. We've an activity sheet to discuss and then take home. Print, print, print—the alphabet is becoming our master. It pushed the children and myself to exactness.

> Diary entry, February 23, 1981: It's international friendship week and so we stressed how we can share ourselves with other people. On Tuesday we looked at good words that we can use about ourselves because we have to like ourselves, too. And we used this little exercise, "Here is a good word I made up myself," and I had them write two sentences of their own words to tell something good about themselves.[2]

HOME LIFE

Phyllis lived with her husband and sons in a working-class neighborhood on the outskirts of the city—their block faced open fields. The house was small and had three bedrooms; it also had a basement den where the boys watched television and played. A carport housed their van, an old car, and the children's tricycles and toys. There was a small front yard and a larger back yard—neither had trees.

Phyllis's living room furniture was arranged to face the fireplace. On the mantel were photographs of the children and crafts Phyllis had made. The walls were also covered with photographs and craft items. The living room opened into the dining and kitchen areas, which were heavily trafficked because the back door was used as a main entrance.

The house was often cluttered with books and papers and the kitchen with dishes, pop bottles, and cereal boxes. Phyllis worried about the clutter but had little time or energy for housecleaning and there was not adequate storage space for all their things.

One of the children was in a gifted program and the other had difficulty in preschool. Phyllis often compared the two and worried about her youngest son's not working up to his age level. Most of her time outside of school was spent with her children—reading to them, playing with them, watching television with them, and taking them to church activities, cub scout meetings, or soccer games. She had total responsibility for them because her husband, John, was rarely home in the evenings. His absence was a constant source of irritation and frustration to Phyllis. She felt he had unfairly thrust her into the stereotypical housewife role.

Interview, July 9, 1980.
PHYLLIS: I feel like he still falls back to the traditional, more stereotyped idea—that the wife is going to make more consolidations than the husband.

And a year later.

Interview, June 4, 1981.
PHYLLIS: I seem to be able to make more of a conscious effort to spend time at home [than he does]. I'll just go back to the old roles—the wife is supposed to do this or that. It does seem we're not balancing out as much as I would like in that respect.

Over time, Phyllis became increasingly dissatisfied with her marriage because of John's absences from home and his lack of interest in helping her with household duties and child care.

Diary entry, June 20, 1980: I'm just plain tired of John's project at the college and how it is cheating me out of a husband and the boys out of a dad. What pleasure is it bringing us as a family?

Interview, July 9, 1980.
PHYLLIS: He is so engulfed in his projects that one of these days he's going to turn around and say, "What memorable things have I done with my kids?"

Phyllis had difficulty considering divorce because she thought their problems could be resolved if John would realize that his family was as important as his work. She tried to talk him into going to a minister to discuss their problems but John thought he could change without anyone's help. However, he did not change his behavior so Phyllis talked to his parents and some of his colleagues. They all agreed that John should spend more time at home, but John continued to justify his long hours as necessary to do a good job.

A year after the above comments were written or discussed, Phyllis had gained a considerable amount of confidence in herself and became more assertive. The more assertive she became, the more threatened John felt. He did begin to stay home more, but Phyllis found it a never-ending battle to get him to do so. She thought it was worth the effort because she felt much better about herself.

> Interview, February 12, 1982.
> PHYLLIS: For years I've settled for just making it through. But now I think I want more than that. I want it to be good sometimes, too.

Household Duties

Phyllis did all the housework. She cooked, cleaned, washed and ironed, shopped, and paid the bills. As indicated in the previous section, she did all the work because John was rarely home, and, when he was there, his traditional attitudes inhibited him from sharing the work. In fact, he told Phyllis that she knew she would still be a wife and mother when she chose to go back to work and that therefore, she should expect to do all the jobs she had always done.

Phyllis had a long argument/discussion with her husband about the fact that their jobs outside their home were comparable but that the distribution of tasks at home was inequitable. She said nothing was resolved but that he did start "pitching in" more or "picking up the slack."

Financial Conditions

Phyllis and John's joint income, including John's income from his National Guard duties, was approximately $25,000 a year. Phyllis had a higher salary than John but said he did not mind because he said he was working because he loved his work not because he wanted to make a lot of money. They had been able to pay all their bills and start a savings account. It was their first account because they never had enough money until Phyllis began working. They also spent very little on leisure activities, clothes, or travel and simply spent their incomes on basic necessities.

John had been offered several jobs paying twice his current salary but had refused them because he was afraid to move far away from a rural area. To him, their city of 25,000 was large after having been raised on a farm. The only reason John would consider leaving his job would be to go back and run to his parents' farm. Phyllis was quite resistant to the idea because she did not want her children to go to school in a small, rural area. Also she was not sure she could adapt to rural life after having been raised in the city or that she could cope with seeing John's parents daily.

Leisure Activities

Phyllis and John had few leisure activities. The primary inhibiting factor was that John never took time off from work. They never took vacations, went out to dinner or a movie, played sports, or anything else that might have been relaxing or different from work.

John had no hobbies and because Phyllis took total responsibility for their home, she had almost no time for herself and, therefore, no time for hobbies. Her children were her constant companions. On rare occasions on a Saturday she hired a baby-sitter so she could have her hair cut and styled, but she felt guilty being away from home and spending money on a baby-sitter.

Phyllis and John's only outings were to church or to see their parents. They were very active in a small church and sponsored a youth group for several years. As soon as school was over, Phyllis taught summer Bible classes for a week and volunteered for other activities when extra help was needed.

Two weekends a month Phyllis and John drove to the city where her parents lived. She and her sons stayed at her parents' home while John went to National Guard meetings. When they visited John's parents, John worked around the farm. Therefore, Phyllis was left by herself with both sets of parents. According to Phyllis, being away from home was just like being home, because she was always alone and had the responsibility of her sons.

Health

One of the more disruptive factors in Phyllis's life was her children's illnesses. She stayed up all night with them if necessary and had to take sick leave to be with them. She had always stayed with them when they were sick and continued to do so during her first year of teaching, but in her second year, she insisted that John take some of the responsibility also. He did and she was considerably relieved.

Phyllis's health deteriorated during her two years of teaching. Being excluded by the other teachers, working under an ineffective principal, and worrying about her marital problems produced stress and physical ailments associated with stress—compulsive eating, exhaustion, and pains in various parts of her body.

Interview, October 14, 1980.

PHYLLIS: I feel it's making me more nervous and I am reverting back to some of my compulsive eating habits. I have been craving chocolate and eating things that I had the will power before to resist. I feel I'm using up all my will power just coping at school. I'm always in my room grading papers and setting up a learning station or something like that, or going to the bathroom or getting a drink, to stay away from food. The whole situation is making me so nervous I've gained 7 pounds.

A few months after her second year began she developed a low-grade infection but waited four weeks, until the pain was unbearable, to see a doctor. She recuperated during Christmas vacation but during January often felt nauseated and had diarrhea. The doctor could not discover the source of her problem but gave her antinausea medication. Phyllis continued to feel sick and was in pain. John was unsympathetic and told her, "either get really sick or really well." As Phyllis's pain increased, the doctor put her in the hospital for tests and she missed a few days of school. The tests revealed no organic problem so she went back to school despite her pain. Because the doctors told Phyllis that nothing was organically wrong, her husband told her she ought to feel fine and continued to be annoyed when she complained. Phyllis was frustrated at John's lack of sympathy and upset with her doctor because he could not identify the source of the pain. Having no alternative, Phyllis returned to teaching and doing all the housework; she eventually regained her strength but continued to have periodic pain.

CONCLUSIONS: OVERLAP OF HOME AND SCHOOL

Phyllis's home life and school life often overlapped. The surprise, bewilderment, and sadness of not being treated kindly, or at least professionally, by other teachers and the realization that her principal was unreasonable and incompetent led to a loss of idealism about teaching that Phyllis found depressing. She brought school problems home, cried about them, and tried to figure out ways she could change or help make things better.

At home, she had come to the realization that her marriage was not ideal either. In fact, she questioned whether she had a marriage at all. She felt depressed about her husband's lack of involvement with their family and dealt with the situation in the same way she did with school problems—she tried to figure out ways she could change or help make things better.

Phyllis also described herself as trying to be a "supermom" but found that as a working woman she could not do all the things she had done for her children when she was not working. She often felt guilty.

Diary entry, May 16, 1981: I started working on grades and also on trying to get some housecleaning done and sometimes I feel like I neglect my home and I spend too much time preparing for school. I don't want my kids to have to suffer because of it and I try not to. Therefore, I spend more time with them and just forget the house—as I have to decide what priorities are going to rule my life and what priorities aren't.

The problems Phyllis brought home from school were related to her job of teaching rather than to teaching per se. Regardless of how difficult her working conditions were, she had positive remarks about her students. She had to bring their papers home occasionally and also worked on lesson plans or projects. However, her husband was critical of her when she brought papers home; he pointed out that she nagged him about his working in the evenings and, therefore, she should not bring work home. So Phyllis saved her paperwork for the evenings her husband was gone—which were frequent.

The effect of home life on school life was particularly strong when the children were sick. For example, her son once became ill while at the baby-sitter's house. Because Phyllis was unable to leave school, she called John to pick him up and take him to the doctor. The doctor said he had bronchitis, and when John tried to return him to the baby-sitter she refused to allow him to stay because he might be contagious to the other children. John called Phyllis and told her she would have to come home. She felt guilty for having left her sick son and frustrated at having to deal with another problem, so she sat in her classroom while her students were at recess and cried for a long time. When the children returned, she tried to continue teaching but finally had to tell the principal the problem and ask if she could leave. Her principal took over her class and she hurried out but did not explain to her students what the problem was. They were curious and upset because Phyllis was normally smiling and consistent in her behavior.

Whether at home or at school, Phyllis tended to blame herself for problems. She thought if she changed her own behavior in some way that situations would change. Playing the eternal victim, however, had negative effects on her health and self-esteem. Although she began to want things to "be good sometimes" and discovered she was not wrong all the time, despite what her husband had led her to believe, she was uncertain about how to change herself or situations.

Epilogue

Through 1984, Phyllis stayed in the same school and in her marriage.

NOTES

1. Phyllis once left me in the classroom while she went to the principal's office. The children started talking and as the noise level rose, I began to feel more nervous. (As a nonparticipant observer I had assumed an inactive role and did not want to be regarded as an authority figure.) I was saved by a girl who came to me and said, "You're supposed to turn off the lights when we're noisy." I did and they were immediately quiet. After a few moments in the darkness the girl said, "You're supposed to turn them back on when we're quiet." I did and the room was quiet when Phyllis returned.

2. Phyllis wrote in her diary and talked with me about class projects on the same language level she used with her first-grade students.

7

Julie: A Married Secondary School Teacher with Children

Julie was a 37-year-old home economics teacher who taught in a rural school in the Midwest. She was married and had two daughters. One was 5 years old and one was born during the study. Julie's husband was a vocational agriculture teacher in a high school in the area near their home. He commuted in one direction each morning while Julie commuted in the other.

Julie chose teaching as a career at a time when women had few other choices (during the early 1960s). Her parents, teachers, and even she expected her to be "feminine" and incapable of dealing with work that was difficult and strenuous, despite the fact that she was a bright, attractive, strong woman. She chose teaching because it was suitable work for a woman, particularly for one who majored in home economics, sewed, and liked children.

A traditional wife, Julie changed jobs whenever her husband's work necessitated that they move. Her career history showed the detrimental effects of this pattern on her salary. Accepting whatever job was available often meant a significant decrease of income. It also meant that Julie worked under adverse conditions, particularly in small rural schools, because she had no other choices of jobs and had to contribute to the family income. To find a job with satisfactory conditions and a livable salary would take a considerable amount of time and income.

TYPICAL DAY

Julie's day began at 6:30 A.M. after a night interrupted several times by her baby. These nightly interruptions continued throughout the baby's first year and thus Julie arose every morning feeling tired. She showered, dressed, curled her thick auburn hair, and then woke her husband and daughter. She fixed their breakfast while feeding and entertaining the baby, who sat in a high chair amid toys, cereal, and toast. Her older daughter chattered as she ate and was prompted numerous times to get herself dressed.

Julie's husband, Bob, emerged from the bathroom and helped dress their daughter but had to leave quickly because his school day began earlier than Julie's. Julie checked the baby's diaper, packed a diaper bag full of paraphernalia, wrapped both children in coats, and left her house carrying the baby, a babyseat, the diaper bag, a bag of school materials, and her purse. After settling both children in the car she began the 15-mile drive to her school.

Part way on the winding, mountainous drive, she stopped at her baby-sitter's farm, where she left her daughters. To avoid being late to school she then drove 55 MPH on the curvy road marked 35 MPH and arrived shortly before the bell for the beginning of school. As she walked the short distance from her car to her classroom, many of the school's small student body greeted her warmly, some calling her "mom" and others hugging her.

As students came into her classes, they chatted briefly about ball games or dates and then quickly settled into their work. One class made cookies and took them to the kindergarten in another part of the building, other classes baked cakes, and others sewed garments. Students shared machines, equipment, and space in the overcrowded room and opened and closed windows throughout the day to try to adjust to the poor ventilation and inadequate, uneven heating system.

Classes were often interrupted by students and faculty who came in to get ice out of the refrigerator, fix iced tea, sew, or use the washer and dryer. One teacher asked about altering a pair of slacks and another about getting a spot out of a dress, both of whom Julie accommodated while teaching her classes.

At noon, Julie had "detention duty." She sat in a small room with broken furniture and large puddles of water on the floor (from a structural leak), to watch a few students who were being punished. The students were not supposed to talk and therefore sat and stared or tried unobtrusively to entertain one another. Julie ate lunch in the remaining time; she grabbed a tray, climbed over a cafeteria bench at a "teachers' table" in the midst of the students, ate a sticky clump of spaghetti and a peach cobbler that resembled paste, dumped the remains in a garbage pail, and returned to her classroom.

Afternoon classes were disrupted because students were absent from class to rehearse a talent show. Systematic lesson plans were difficult to implement, and Julie had to alter her plans at the last minute because teachers were not given adequate notification of activities.

At 3:10 P.M. students left the building and boarded school buses. At 3:12 P.M., as Julie straightened her room and organized materials, the superintendent, principal, and several teachers left in an old Army-surplus station wagon in which they commuted together to save gas costs.

Julie drove back the winding road to her baby-sitter's home, picked up her children, and arrived home around 4:00 P.M. For the next hour, she played with her children and prepared supper, because her husband expected to eat at 5:00 P.M.

Julie had removed a package of beef that morning from their freezer, which was well stocked with food from her in-laws' farm; she fried meat and potatoes to go with the home-canned vegetables and homemade bread her mother-in-law had given them. Bob ate hurriedly, played briefly with the children, changed his clothes, and went deer hunting for two hours before changing again to return to his school for an extracurricular activity.

Julie cleaned the kitchen and began getting the baby's supplies ready for the next day. She scrubbed bottles, boiled nipples, and washed clothes, then straightened the house, talked to her oldest daughter, and held the baby when she cried. The phone rang several times and, while holding the baby and folding clothes, she talked to her mother, her mother-in-law, and a student who wanted to discuss problems about her boyfriend.

Julie bathed and prepared her older daughter for bed, read her a story, tucked her in, and got her a drink. After a few additional firm words about "getting right to sleep," her daughter was quiet. Meanwhile the baby was still wide awake and crying from time to time. Julie discovered she had a temperature, gave her aspirin, and put her to sleep, although she knew she would now be up frequently during the night.

Julie lay on the couch at 10:00 P.M. and watched TV until Bob came home. Together, they had cake and ice cream and then went to bed. At midnight the baby awakened and Julie got up to begin a night-long vigil.

PERSONAL HISTORY

Growing Up

Julie lived in several locations, from rural to urban, while growing up. Although she described her childhood life-style as middle class, she also said there were "rough times," because her father changed jobs before each move and the jobs varied in status: a restaurant owner in a small town, the manager of a drug store in a large city, a construction worker in a medium-sized city, and a social worker in a small town. Her mother worked through all these variations and eventually became her father's boss when she was promoted as a social worker.

Julie does not remember ever observing her parents argue but said she hated her father and asked her mother to divorce him when she was 12 or 13 years old. She said her father was not physically abusive, because he only spanked her with a belt, but that he was extremely verbally abusive. He criticized her constantly and told her repeatedly that she should not try to do anything with herself because she would only fail.

Interview, November 19, 1981.

JULIE: Daddy always told me, "I don't know why you're going to college. You'll never finish. Nobody's going to hire you. Just stay home."

Julie's mother now says she was unaware that Julie felt so strongly about her father. She told Julie that he treated her as he did through ignorance and that he wanted to protect her from trying anything at which she might fail. But Julie recalled his sometimes overt and crude and sometimes subtle criticisms and punishments. When she was a teenager he once pulled open the front of her bathing suit to see how she was "developing," and another time he grounded her for five days for coming home five minutes late from a date.

Julie's brother, two years older than she, also tore down her ego in a way that Julie considered damaging to her self-image but the "normal thing" for an older brother. For example, he often told her she was fat and that she was adopted. Her brother got along with their father and, like Julie's mother, did not understand Julie's negative memories of their father.

In recent years, after her father developed a degenerative disease and was placed in a nursing home, Julie became closer to him. They communicated for a while but later he was incapable, physiologically, of speaking.

During her adult years, Julie became quite close to her mother and frequently took her two daughters to spend the weekend at her mother's home. Her mother supported Julie emotionally and helped out financially by buying clothes and toys for the children and luxury items for Julie.

Education

During her school years, Julie was a good student and often made straight As; she was beautiful, popular, and active in music and drama. She and her grandmother were very close but she felt that the time she spent with her grandmother and on the housekeeping left her little time to study.

Julie said that no teacher during her school years influenced her toward teaching but that her high school home economics teacher "pushed" her into home economics. Then, because the college she attended was primarily a teacher-training institution, to get a degree in home economics meant she would get a degree in education. Thus, she ended up in teaching.

Work

Julie felt insecure when she finished college and did not know how to apply for a job; therefore, she never did.

> Interview, November 19, 1981.
> JULIE: No one ever told me how to do it. I didn't know who to call and yet I didn't want to admit it. I was scared to death and never did apply.

Julie got her first job as a teacher in a head-start program in a small town because a college instructor told her about the job and arranged an interview. She and a college friend moved to the town together.

Marriage and Family

The next seven years of Julie's life were spent in the small town where she first worked, then married, and later took a job in the local school system as a home economics teacher. The years there were particularly tumultuous because of her husband's personality.

Many years older than Julie, her husband was a somewhat successful businessman, but had only a sixth-grade education, was unable to have children, and was an alcoholic. Julie described him, when he was sober, as loving, affectionate, and thoughtful. But when drunk, he was verbally and sometimes physically abusive. In his anger, he was critical of Julie, ridiculed her education, and, at times, became violent and threatened to shoot her. Julie stayed in the marriage for six years because she loved the sober side of his personality and was fearful of the drunk side.

During their marriage, in addition to her regular teaching job, Julie taught two night courses for extra money, helped in her husband's business ventures, and shared a farm operation with him. She drove farm machinery, helped build a house and barn, built fences, trained horses, raised calves, and fed cattle before and after the school day. In addition, she did 100 percent of the housework.

Julie finally escaped from the marriage, got a divorce, quit her teaching job, and moved to a university town, where she began work on her master's degree. Shortly after she began her graduate classes, she met her second husband, a graduate student at another university. He was a few years younger than she, but he immediately appealed to her because he was the opposite of her former husband. He was young, educated, did not drink or curse, and was able to have children. They married soon after; she moved to his apartment while he finished his degree and took a job in a social service agency.

After they married, Julie discovered that although he was not like her first husband, some of his other traits made her equally unhappy. He was uncommunicative and went for long periods of time without talking, refused to discuss marital problems, did no housework, and was rarely home after he took a coaching and teaching job at a high school in another town. When they moved, Julie commuted 60 miles a day to a social service agency where she earned more than her husband.

After the birth of their daughter, her husband took another coaching position and they moved again. Julie returned to teaching for two years until they divorced and she moved to her mother's home. A bitter legal battle had continued since their divorce over visitation rights.

While living with her mother, Julie worked in a furniture store and then began selling insurance. She was highly successful and had a good income working only a few days a week. She was also dating her current husband, whom she had met in her most recent teaching job.

Bob, a vocational agriculture teacher, was a large, warm, balding man 10 years younger than Julie. He was born and raised in the rural area where they taught and therefore knew (or was related to) most of the people who lived there. A gregarious, friendly person, he was active in community activities and hunted and fished with many of the local men.

Although Julie was hesitant about a third marriage and was concerned that he was so much younger than she, she thought he would give her the affectionate and loving relationship she had not found in her other marriages. They married and moved into his home.

Julie stopped selling insurance because Bob was unhappy that she traveled a lot and came home late at night. Despite her good salary, he insisted she quit because he worried about her and thought her place was at home. Although Julie did not agree with him when she first discussed her reasons for quitting, she later changed her position.

Interview, November 19, 1981.

JULIE: If we're both as dedicated to our jobs as he [her husband], we'd suffer and our children would suffer. One reason I had to quit selling insurance was that he had so much he did, it didn't do for me to come home at 10:00 or 11:00 P.M. He wanted me to quit long before I did. It's one thing to say to your wife, "I want you to have your identity and freedom," but it doesn't work if the man's job is really demanding. I think that when I get older I'll have the time to be committed to my job. I don't think I'll be over the hill.

After quitting her insurance job, Julie began teaching in the rural school described in the following section.

SCHOOL LIFE

Cultural Setting

Julie's school was located in an isolated mountainous area of a national forest. The school was the central point of a town consisting of 100 persons, a grocery, a couple of garages for automotive repairs, and a few modern houses. The school drew its population of 200 students from a wide geographic area, which had once had only one-room schoolhouses.

Since the earliest settlers, the inhabitants had been farmers. Most had come to the area in poverty and felt that land of their own, even though it was unsuitable for farming, was preferable to starvation. Owning land was a source of deep pride. However, in recent years the small farmers had not been able to compete in the marketplace with large farm owners and felt the press of modernization and change through the development of a heavy tourist trade in the area. Most depended on their farms to provide their families with garden vegetables and beef or hogs but worked for large businesses such as the telephone or electric company. The men typically worked as construction workers and the women as waitresses or maids in motels.

Most inhabitants were born and raised in the area and had attended the school where Julie now taught. Parents expected their children to go to school as long as possible. Whether or not they graduated from high school was not important because they knew the jobs they would get would not require a diploma. Before and after the school day, most students had heavy responsibilities toward helping with the farm work or housework; they saw that their lives would be little different whether they quit school or continued until graduation. However, the traditional values of the area determined that children obey their parents and so they both worked and went to school.

The cultural values were heavily influenced by religion (primarily Baptist, which supported the work ethic), family (including obedience to parents), and fear of "city ways." Dances were not allowed at school, and meetings were not scheduled on nights when church services were held.

School Administration

The school system consisted of one school, which housed all grades, K–12. It was governed by a six-member (all male) school board and a superintendent who had been in the district many years. The superintendent had managed to keep the school out of debt despite serious financial problems and thus was highly regarded by people outside the school system, according to a state inspector's comments to Julie. Keeping out of debt was partially accomplished, however, by having a starting salary for teachers of under $7200 per year.

Julie's first principal, who dressed in a leisure suit with a brass belt buckle that said "Jesus Saves," spent little time in the school because he planned early in the year to move on to another job. When in school, he avoided teachers, disciplined students, or lifted weights in his office.

The second principal also lasted only a year and was seen as weak and ineffective by the teachers. Although Julie thought he was sensitive to the needs of teachers and students, other teachers thought he was too lenient and somewhat effeminate. He became the butt of teachers' jokes and they sabotaged his authority by criticizing him openly in their classes. Teachers excluded Julie because she refused to criticize the principal and would not discuss him with students.

> Diary entry, November 12, 1980: He [the principal] is so nice and seems to be so helpful. Already, though, I hear the other teachers tearing him down. This is his first year as principal and I'm sure he has lots to learn. But it's so refreshing to have an administrator who is so friendly and nice. I think I can see why they become callous and temperamental. They become paranoid from the teachers' knifing them in the back. I don't think that talking behind someone's back gets anything accomplished and it does tear down the morale of a school so badly.

The teachers were also highly critical of the superintendent and there was a negative atmosphere in the school. The building was in terrible disrepair, the morale among the teachers was low, and the turnover rate was high. Moreover, there was a lack of trust among the teachers and between the teachers and administrators, which resulted in frequent critical remarks or "back stabbing."

School Facility

The school building was about 50 years old and had had few renovations since it was built. The only observable sign of renovation was in the superintendent's and principal's offices; they were paneled and contained more modern furniture than the rest of the building. The halls were narrow and poorly lighted and the wood floors were nearly black from use. The teachers' lounge and the cafeteria were at the end of a steep, narrow stairway—at the bottom of which ran a small stream of water that smelled like sewage.

The lounge door was made of boards nailed together unevenly. Inside, there was no ceiling, only a maze of wires hanging from rafters. It was a small room crowded with old books, pieces of equipment, discarded junk, an inoperable refrigerator, a soft drink machine, a table with a mimeograph machine, two couches and a chair with horse heads stitched on them, and a toilet stool with an out-of-order sign on it.

The cafeteria had enough folding tables with benches to allow everyone in the high school to eat at the same time. Teachers ate together at one table, although the room was small enough for students to talk to the teachers from across the room. After the meal, everyone scraped his or her leftover food into two garbage pails placed between the serving line and the teachers' table. Although Julie thought the food was the worst she had ever eaten in a school, she said nothing because two of the cooks were related to members of the school board.

The boiler in the school was old and frequently broke down. When this happened school was dismissed and the janitor was expected to make necessary repairs. When operating, the boiler caused vibrations and loud noises in the classrooms above it.

Julie's classroom was in the worst repair in the school because of a number of leaks. The roof leaked and caused extensive water damage to the ceiling. A steam leak caused the hardwood floor to buckle, forming a triangle three inches high at intervals across the room. Julie was told it could not be repaired until summer, so she wore flat, rubber-soled shoes to keep from tripping. She also brought a large piece of plywood to cover an area that had broken through. Julie worried that a student would trip or fall through the holes in the floor and she did not think the school's insurance would cover the injuries.

Teacher Morale

The low salaries and poor building condition contributed to the teachers' lack of trust and low morale. The teachers felt distant from the principal and superintendent—despite their physical proximity—and worried about losing their jobs. The administrators fired a number of teachers each year and hired inexperienced ones to keep teachers' salaries low. Their method of firing teachers was to call them out of their classes, tell them they would not be getting contracts, and then have them go back into their classes and resume teaching. Teachers discussed these procedures over lunch, criticized the administrators, and expressed concern that they might be the next fired. One teacher questioned her dismissal and the superintendent told her that their (his and the school board's) main concern was that her last name was not the same as her husband's. The school board had asked the superintendent to find out if she was really married but he refused. However, his conversation with her indicated that he did indeed want to know if she was married to the man with whom she was living. There were other instances of overt sexism and sex discrimination from the two male administrators. Julie, who was buxom, provided this example.

> Diary entry, April 28, 1980: When I got into the carpool this morning, everyone was laughing. Mr. [the superintendent] had commented that I looked like Dolly [Parton] as I walked to the car. I asked if it was my long blonde hair. There was no comment (since my hair is short and brown). That comment didn't set well with me and my whole day seemed off to a poor start. There was nothing to do but laugh it off, but I kept thinking what I could have done to give him the impression that I would even appreciate a comment like that. I took it as lack of respect for women. I would certainly not comment on the size of his testicles.

Students

Because of the small size of the school, its informal atmosphere, and the fact that several teachers discussed school problems in their classrooms, students were well aware of most personnel problems and everyday situations involving the administrators and teachers. They empathized strongly with the teachers, as is clear in the following interview with a student.

INTERVIEWER: What do you think it's like to teach here?

BARBARA (twelfth-grade student):   I think the reason we don't keep teachers but one year is because it's cheaper. They take the first-year teachers right out of college and it's really rough on them. And it's rough on the students because it takes a while to get used to a job. And that's a lot of the problem—inexperienced teachers. If they'd pay a little more, the students would learn.

I do feel sorry for the poor teachers who come here. They're treated awful by the administration. The rooms are cruddy, cruddy study materials, you know, it's not fit to work here.

Really, teaching is not worth it. I mean it's one of the worst professions you can go into unless you're just wanting to do it for the kids. Yeah, I can see why a teacher would if they liked kids, but for the money—no. I work as a maid and I get treated better than they do.

Students liked the small size of the student body and the informal, relaxed atmosphere of the school. In fact, there were few cliques, and students tended to support one another.

SHEILA (eleventh-grade student who transferred from a large city in the West):   Coming to school here isn't like coming to school; it's like coming to a party. The only reason I don't like to stay home from school is cause I have to go a whole day without seeing everybody. And I don't dread Mondays anymore. You know, I'm always glad when Monday comes because Saturday and Sunday I go without seeing anybody.

TANYA (twelfth-grade student):   The senior group are just my best friends and as in any school and with any friends you're going to have your troubles. We have our troubles but we're all real close and we just get it worked out real fast.

Although students enjoyed the social atmosphere of the school, they were also aware of its academic weaknesses and worried about the effects on their future.

BARBARA (twelfth-grade student):   Going to school here is like you're protected, and then when you go out to other places you're kind of scared. It's really hard the first time going out and getting a job in a large place. I've worked ever since I was 14. But it scares me a bit to go to the city. I know lots of kids don't even go. I force myself to go to some other city and stay at least for a week in the summer.

You don't learn the way you should because when a kid comes down here from another school, they're a lot smarter than the kids that have gone to school here. I don't think it's because we're stupid. We're not stupid.

INTERVIEWER: How do you feel about the relaxed atmosphere, compared with your other school where things were stricter and you worked every period?

SHEILA (eleventh-grade student): Oh, it's nice, I mean, I love it [laughs]. I'm lazy, but I know it's hurting the students, too. It'd be hard if someone was going to college.

I know there are several people who started college and flunked out because it was too hard. It'll be real hard for me to get back in the habit of studying every night. I never study for a test. Here, I never study.

INTERVIEWER: Do you take anything home at all?

SHEILA: Yeah, half the time I don't to it. It don't matter. Turn it in late. Who cares?

INTERVIEWER: What kind of grades do you make?

SHEILA: Straight As.

Shelia also worried because she realized she no longer used proper English but felt helpless to change because everyone used improper English. Other students made fun of her for wanting to go to college and she slowly changed her goals.

SHEILA: Oh, this has had an effect on me. Who cares, if you go to high school?

After graduation, most students would work on farms, in factories, or as construction workers (like their parents) and marry young. Until that time, they worked, went to school as a social activity, and on weekends sat in a group in the little community where the school was located, drank beer, and drove up and down the highway, drag racing.

Classes

During the school year, Julie taught 10 home economics classes, several of which were one semester courses. For most of the classes (the largest had 12 students), there were no materials, so Julie had to develop her own and xerox copies for students. In sewing classes, two or three students had to share one sewing machine; and in cooking classes, eight or ten students had to share two stoves. There were few cooking utensils, so students brought pans and skillets from home when necessary.

Because students had a heavy work load at home, had little money, and lacked transportation, Julie drove to discount stores to find fabric and sewing materials for them. Although some stores where she shopped were

50 miles away, she was not reimbursed for the traveling. She also brought materials from home to give students or to use as the basis for projects.

Julie organized her classes around the needs of her students. She knew that most either were already responsible for the household duties or would marry young and assume those duties and that they would never have the money to buy clothes or some kinds of food. Students were taught to sew with the idea that they would probably always sew their own and their families' clothes. Child development was taught with considerable classroom discussion about parent-child relations, because many students had suffered child abuse or were responsible for baby-sitting with younger siblings and a few already had babies of their own.

Because of the constant disruption in the classroom caused by students and faculty stopping by and activities that took many students out of class, Julie continually had to adapt her plans and schedules. Although occasionally irritated, she was not disturbed by the disruptions but accepted them as part of the normal routine of the school. This was consistent with her teaching philosophy, which was based on flexibility and student input and feedback.

Interview, February 3, 1981.

JULIE: I like to include my students in some of the planning of what we do in class. I see that we cover it—what they would like to do to carry some of our objectives through. I think that doing that really helps them to feel involved and even more responsible for the class because they are in on the planning stages. I like to be flexible. If I see something that they would enjoy more and still reach our objectives, I don't care to change horses in the middle of the stream, if we can do it with a good transition that's not real disruptive to them.

Building good rapport with students was as important to Julie as teaching the substantive parts of her courses. Students were responsive to her concerns and affection for them and shared their problems with her. Julie felt deep sympathy for many, because they had been raised in foster homes and bore psychological scars. One girl, for example, shared with Julie that she had been in 14 foster homes, had been molested by a foster father, and had been burned with cigarettes and beaten.

In a discussion of parent-child relationships in a child development class, Julie was able to integrate the points of her lesson with personal comments students shared about their lives. The fact that some of the discussion was quite intimate indicated students' trust in Julie. Students discussed their concern for a fellow student who had been beaten by her boyfriend. They confided that the girl was afraid to break up with the boy because they had been having sex. The discussion centered on ways they could give the girl support when she returned to school, because they knew she was embarrassed and afraid.

Although Julie occasionally became frustrated in dealing with teen-agers, such as when they did not help during fundraising activities or left messes for her to clean up, she considered this behavior normal for the age and focused on students' positive qualities. She found good qualities even in those students who had the most problems and whom other teachers found the most problematic. The effect of her positive expectations for all students, regardless of the labels other teachers had given them, was a mutual respect between her and her students.

Interview, February 3, 1981.

JULIE: You just have to treat students like they're human beings. I think teachers lose sight of that sometimes. But they're human.

When Julie returned to school after the birth of her baby, she thought the comments of a student made the low pay, poor facilities, and daily problems worthwhile.

STUDENT: You've got to be the most loved teacher in this school. I don't even have you for a class and I'm glad to see you back!

Leaving School

At the end of the school year, Julie quit her job. Her husband told her she was not to go back to school because the cost of their baby-sitter and the gas for commuting left only $200 from her paycheck. He thought that amount was not worth the effort it took her to go to work every day and that she needed more time at home. Although Julie had mixed feelings about his directive ("I suppose if I pitched a fit, he would let me come back"), she knew that her take-home pay the following year would be even less because she would need two baby-sitters—one for the baby and one for her older child, who would be in kindergarten for half a day.

The next year, Julie substituted for teachers in schools close to her home and earned enough money to pay for emergencies, such as new glasses for herself. She was able to stay home with her children but had mixed feelings about not working after over 20 years of continuous work.

Interview, November 19, 1981.

JULIE: I think it's a woman's responsibility to be home with kids. For a child to be secure they need one parental figure. If the father has extra duties at work, it can't be him.

I probably haven't changed my opinions but circum-stances have changed. I guess I always thought it would be neat to have kids and stay home but I enjoyed the career and would like to go back to it. If I had lots of money and didn't have to work I'd be happy to stay home and to paint. I've always found lots to do at home.

Many women who stay at home are so depressed. They think it's so glamorous to work. They think it's great. But they don't know, maybe you had company late or were sick, or the laundry doesn't get done and you have to drag yourself out.

The grass is always greener. Since this is my first time at home, I love it, but I don't want to do it forever. I thrive on people and I think most healthy people do.

HOME LIFE

Household Duties

Julie had major responsibility for household chores and child care while she was working and total responsibility when she left teaching. Bob sometimes helped with cooking and dishes and often helped to bathe or dress their 5-year-old. But his help was sporadic because he often had to be at school in the evenings or on weekends. Thus, Julie did all the work, which reinforced the situation; Bob was rarely required to help because Julie had already finished the work.

A similar circular pattern occurred with their baby. Julie was home with the baby for several weeks and was the one who got up with her during the night. The baby cried when her father held her. After several months, Julie took total care of the baby rather than listen to her cry—and the baby continued to cry when her father held her because he rarely did. Thus, patterns of child care and housekeeping developed that shifted the burden to Julie, but both she and her husband contributed to this inequality.

Julie's acceptance of household duties and her attitude that her husband's work and activities took precedence over hers were reflected in several diary entries.

Diary entry, May 4, 1980: With Bob also being a teacher and especially at another school, it nearly doubles my duty to attend. Somehow he doesn't feel the need so much to attend *my* school functions. Old syndrome of "wife" follows "husband."

Diary entry, May 20, 1980: I went back to school to finish inventory and clean my room. [My daughter] went with me. I still had interruptions from people coming and talking. We left at 4:00. I was very tired but went to Bob's ball game [softball]. It poured rain, but we sat under an umbrella and [her daughter] sat more quietly than ever before. Bob's team won.

Diary entry, May 21, 1980: Cleaned house, took nap, did laundry. Bob fished.

Diary entry, May 22, 1980: Cleaned house and cooked for company. They came about 2:00 P.M. Bob and [friend] went fishing.

Diary entry, December 6, 1980: Cleaned the house and did laundry all day. Bob went fishing until noon.

Diary entry, January 14, 1981: Bob was home with a side pain. It's worse. He still can't hold the baby [four months old]. It's sure hard to get anything done with such little help.

Diary entry, November 7, 1981: Bob got up early to fish. I did housework, sewing, and laundry and did some planning for Christmas. Supper ready when [in-laws] dropped by and ate with us. Visited awhile and went home. Bob didn't catch one fish.

Despite the fact that Julie would have liked more help, particularly when she was substitute teaching several days a week, she accepted the responsibility. She felt lucky to have a good marriage after two divorces and felt that doing all the housework was a small price to pay for having an affectionate husband.

Interview, November 19, 1981.

JULIE: When you're not getting along well in marriage, you're not happy about doing their dirty clothes. But now I enjoy that. I don't resent a lot I do alone. I don't like him gone, but I don't resent it. I would just like to be with him more.

Financial Conditions

Finances were a constant concern in Julie and Bob's life. After Julie quit teaching they had difficulty buying food at the end of each month and relied heavily on food frozen from the past summer's garden, beef given them by Bob's parents, and animals shot on Bob's hunting trips or fish caught on fishing trips. Julie made most of her children's clothes as well as her own and made Bob his only suit.

At one point they considered buying a gas station to increase their income. Julie would have had to run the station if the deal had gone through. However, such investments were not truly feasible because they lacked savings. Moving out of the area was also not feasible because Bob had been born and raised in the area, was deeply committed to his parents and their farm, and did not like cities. Therefore, the four of them lived on Bob's salary of about $16,000 per year (in 1982 for a twelve-month contract, with a master's degree).

Leisure Activities

Financial conditions and problems also affected the family's leisure time and social activities. Most evenings they watched television or visited relatives; both liked to fish and hunt deer, but Julie rarely went because of child-care duties. These activities were not particularly costly and were central parts of their lives. Rare treats were driving to a city, eating at

McDonald's, and seeing a movie. They traveled farther away only for conventions and stayed with relatives to cut costs.

A major focus of Julie and Bob's lives were their families—Julie's mother and Bob's many relatives who lived in the area. They either talked on the telephone, visited, or ate with a relative every day. Julie often took her daughters to her mother's home for a weekend while Bob stayed home and fished or worked at a school activity. Julie was able to rest somewhat while there and was glad Bob could have time to do what he wanted rather than become bored at her mother's home.

Bob's parents were farmers; although in their seventies, they still worked hard and had considerable wealth in land and other assets. They were kind and loving to Julie and were quite traditional in their attitudes and values. Julie and Bob adopted these values, including very clear sex-role behavior when they visited. The men sat in one room discussing farming or hunting while the women worked in the kitchen preparing dinner. Bob's mother, an excellent cook who produced a wide variety of homemade foods, directed the activities. A typical meal was ham, salad, corn, green beans, sauerkraut, pickles, pickled beets, potato salad, bread, and jellies, plus two kinds of pies or homemade ice cream for desert. The men were called in and sat down on one side of the table; they ate and then left without comment. While the women cleaned up and washed the dishes, the men began playing cards. After the dishes, the women sat talking or playing with the children. Often, Julie was quite tired but could not leave until Bob finished the card game. After sitting through this ritual many times, Julie decided to break tradition and started playing cards with the men.

Health

As a result of numerous large meals, most of the people in Bob's family, including Bob and Julie, were overweight. Eating was both a cultural and a social activity. Traditionally, huge quantities of food were eaten to provide energy for the physical tasks required in farming. Although most of them did not still work at farming, or did so in a minimal way, they continued to eat in the same excessive manner. Meals were also times for family and friends to gather. Foods were shared, dishes were admired, and large quantities consumed as a way of showing close ties. Meals were occasions for sharing and socializing; rest was valued and few other social activities were possible.

Bob's parents continued these traditions and often invited their extended family for meals. Being overweight was the norm and therefore not a stigma. In fact, Julie said that her own weight problem was closely linked to her husband's and his family. She rationalized that although she was overweight, she was considerably less so than her husband, and thus she reduced her concern about it.

During Julie's pregnancy and after the birth of her baby, she had difficulty sleeping. She suffered from numbness of her hands and arms, which caused pain; later, she simply woke up when the baby woke. The result was that she was tired throughout her workday at school.

Julie and her family were often sick, which increased her exhaustion. For example, her daughter caught walking pneumonia, her baby had a cold, and Julie had the flu—all within the six-week period Julie had taken off from school for the baby's birth. Four out of the six weeks were filled with family illness, during which time Julie often stayed up all night with a sick child. Excerpts from her diary during two time periods illustrate the illness cycle.

> Diary entry, December 21, 1980: I had an upset stomach last night and diarrhea.

> Diary entry, December 22, 1980: The state supervisor was here at school today. The superintendent said we had no demerits and made no suggestions. The supervisor visited my classroom and gave me a nice compliment. There was a chili supper and Christmas program, but I was too tired to go. I had diarrhea.

> Diary entry, December 23, 1980: Last day of school today. My in-laws and Bob were home when I got there. Bob was sick with chest and side pains. He stayed home and I had diarrhea.

> Diary entry, December 27, 1980: Stayed at in-laws' farm. Bob is not well and has a fever. His family had a reunion. Forty-six people were there.

> Diary entry, December 30, 1980: Did housework and took care of Bob. Up until 12:30 A.M. sewing [relatives] shirts. No New Year's Eve party.

> Diary entry, October 27, 1981: Substituted in the fourth grade. My throat swelled and got very sore. Also had a fever. Called the principal to say I wouldn't teach tomorrow. Went to bed early. Bob sick, too.

> Diary entry, October 28, 1981: I was supposed to go to the city for a meeting with the psychologist [the meeting concerned the legal suit with her ex-husband and the effect on her daughter] but was sick and not able to go. We all went to the doctor and I asked for a prescription for Bob too. Did the grocery shopping and the baby screamed all the time we were in the store.

> Diary entry, October 29, 1981: Allergic reaction to antibiotic—showed up on my face and neck.

> Diary entry, November 2, 1981: Felt bad most of the week.

CONCLUSIONS: OVERLAP OF HOME AND SCHOOL

Multiple responsibilities at home and at school left Julie tired, sometimes sick, and without free time. However, she had positive feelings about her roles as wife, mother, and teacher. For many years she had desperately sought a loving, affectionate husband with whom she could "be herself" and children on whom to focus her love and attention. She thought problems in daily life were to be expected and accepted.

Interview, February 25, 1981.

JULIE: The twelfth grade were taking tests, so I couldn't have some of my classes. There were club meetings during my conference period, so I couldn't work at school. Bob was gone several nights, so I didn't have much time at home to do anything for school. It was just mainly getting to school, getting my classes over with, coming home, and trying to take care of everything. Do what little laundry I could and fix supper. I wonder whether I'm just teribly disorganized, or if everybody with small children by themselves have that much work, or if it's just me?

Julie questioned her own capabilities for coping with multiple responsibilities, rather than blaming others, and continued to juggle multiple situations and activities. Home responsibilities and problems infringed on her teaching in both positive and negative ways. She found that going to school was a welcome respite from home.

Diary entry, November 11, 1980: I found myself less organized with getting two girls dressed and diaper bag and all. It's almost less tiring to be at school. Even though I enjoy holding the baby very much, it is very tiring to hold a baby and try to keep a near 5-year-old happy, fix lunch, bottles, etc.

Yet her lack of sleep and family illnesses influenced her effectiveness at school.

Interview, February 3, 1981.

JULIE: It is tiring. At school I missed things in the students' sewing. Yesterday there was a girl who sewed her lace on wrong. That's twice that she's sewn it on upside down. You would think that she would catch it by now, but yet that's my job. That's why I'm there, to catch those things, and I let her sew it on upside down because I didn't think to check. There have been some other mistakes that I've let go by that they've had to take out. It's just from being tired.

Family responsibilities also kept her from attending all the extracurricular activities that students would have liked her to attend. The club she sponsored took extra time, for which she received no extra pay. She often had to take her children to these functions and on trips to buy supplies, for which she was also not reimbursed.

The major factor that influenced conditions at school and at home was finances. As described earlier, the school was in terrible condition, had inadequate facilities and materials, and paid teachers subsistence wages because of lack of funds. This created a negative atmosphere, one that Julie was not sorry to leave.

> Interview, February 25, 1981.
>
> JULIE: I will be really glad to leave. I'll miss the students but the general atmosphere at the school is just so dreary. Part of it is physical—the facility. And my room is the worst there is. That's real depressing to me. If it wasn't for the students, it'd be really bad.

Subsistence wages finally affected her home life to such an extent that she quit. Her low salary, dissatisfaction with many aspect of the school setting, and desire to be a good wife and mother strengthened and supported her husband's argument that she stay home.

> Interview, February 25, 1981.
>
> JULIE: It's almost double duty by the time I help Bob with his school activities. He's got a picnic coming up and a barbecue twice a year I always help with. It'll be so nice not to be doing my thing. Then I can work on his more.

Julie coped with the overlap between home and school because of her traditional values, which placed precedence on family and home. Yet she also worked throughout her three marriages, managing both school and home, because she saw no option for doing otherwise. She worked when and where she had to, depending on where her husband took a job and how badly they needed additional income.

> Interview, November 19, 1981.
>
> JULIE: I think I've done pretty good, after all I've been through. And I haven't been through all that much compared to others. Just through a couple of bad marriages and that's not the worst thing that could happen.

Julie had a strong belief in the power of positive thinking, strong religious beliefs from her childhood, and a good sense of humor, which helped her cope with most situations.

> Interview, November 19, 1981.
>
> JULIE: You are what you make of yourself. You *choose* to be lonely or depressed.
>
> INTERVIEWER: How do you cope?
>
> JULIE: I always said my mother taught me to make the most of situations. She said she couldn't take privileges away or send me to my room because I'd always find something to make me happy. I'm also dense. People

can be doing me in and I'll be smiling all the while. And later I'll realize how terrible they treated me.

A lot of my hang-ups have to do with being a Christian. Our church taught by guilt. I feel strongly about not tearing someone else down. Teaching in the church taught you to turn the other cheek and go the second mile, but never told you you didn't have to put up with the shit in between. God doesn't expect me to be trampled on. He sent Jesus to take care of that.

Epilogue

After a year at home, Julie and her husband found they needed her income. Bob could not support a family of four on under $17,000 a year, and Julie was ready to get out of the house. So she accepted a job in an elementary school for $10,000 a year, a $2000 increase from her previous job. Julie taught three elementary grades in a rural school even though she was neither certified nor experienced in those grades. Her older daughter was in school all day and she found a suitable baby-sitter for her younger daughter. Commuting remained a problem, however, and the following year she went back to college to earn credits toward elementary certification while substitute teaching to earn extra money. After completing certification, she found a job in the school district in which her husband taught (1984–1985). Nearly five years after Julie married, she finally found the job she wanted. It paid well compared to her previous jobs and was close to her home.

8

Valerie: A Divorced Elementary School Teacher with Children

Valerie was a 35-year-old black woman with two teenaged daughters. She taught reading in a parochial school in a large urban area (population over 500,000). Valerie grew up poor. Education was seen by her large family as a means of upward mobility. The more dissatisfied Valerie became with teaching, the more hours she accumulated toward degrees or teaching certifications—a common solution of teachers to try to change their frustration with teaching conditions. Not surprisingly, however, her accumulated college hours did nothing to change the conditions under which she taught nor her attitude toward those conditions. In fact, she found that when she looked for jobs outside teaching, her college hours worked against her—she was considered overqualified. Valerie's case illustrates conditions and experiences that lead some teachers to quit. Valerie's case also illustrates the difficult conditions under which divorced women with children live—if they do not receive child support nor have regular contact with their former spouse.

TYPICAL DAY

Valerie woke at 7:30 A.M. and within twenty minutes had bathed, dressed, and left her two-bedroom apartment. She dropped one daughter off at her parochial school and then traveled through heavy traffic toward the inner core of the city, where her school was located. She drove the last blocks without noticing the gutted buildings and the piles of rubble in vacant lots and parked her car near her classroom window so she could thwart any attempts at vandalism or theft. She rang a buzzer that signaled to the church's secretary that she had arrived. The door was unbolted then locked automatically after she entered. Valerie was 15 minutes late so she immediately began getting materials ready for her first reading class.

Throughout the morning, students of different grade levels came and left at 35-minute intervals. Because standardized reading materials were used, most of the students began working without assistance. Valerie spent a few moments at the beginning of each class greeting the children and then expected them to work quietly so that she was free to instruct or test individual children. She reprimanded students who did not comply with her rules and demanded that they address her as "ma'am." She thought they needed strong discipline and structure in the classroom because their parents did not provide it at home and that she was providing a good role model when she corrected a student's use of poor grammar.

At noon, after having taught five classes (29 children), she joined one of the five other teachers in the kitchen, where two women were preparing lunch. The long tables were set with bowls for soup and a piece of bread and peanut butter beside each bowl. There were not enough spoons for everyone so the cooks washed them as the children finished eating. Valerie took her soup back to her classroom. She and the other teacher turned on a TV (provided by Title I funds) and watched a soap opera. When the show was over, Valerie turned off the set and listened to her colleague's tale about a sixth-grade black student who had called her a "bitch." When the teacher, who was white, did not respond to this as the student thought she should, he called her what he though the ultimate insult—"Whitey." They talked further about the boy's problems and discussed the time he had set his sister's bed on fire—with her in it. Valerie and her colleague decided that his problems and those of other children should be blamed on their mothers. If mothers taught their children what they should, the children would not have problems, they reasoned.

Valerie taught her three afternoon classes (22 children) interspersed with three planning and conference periods. She had little to do during those three periods because her aide had graded all the tests and papers and had constructed a bulletin board. Therefore, at 3:10 P.M. (20 minutes before school was officially over), Valerie left with no work and great relief and thought to herself, "Another boring day." Her spirits lifted, however, when she thought of the freedom she would have for a few hours.

She went to her exercise class and hoped she worked off enough calories to lose some weight. Relaxed from the workout, she arrived home to find her daughters doing their homework while cooking dinner. Famished, Valerie ate heartily despite her earlier resolve to lose weight. After dinner, she left her daughters to finish their homework while she went to a night course at a small college. She was uncomfortable throughout the class because she thought the teacher was boring. She wished she could take courses at a large university in the city but the tuition was too expensive.

When Valerie arrived home, her daughters were already in bed so she decided to clean the house. At 10:00 P.M. she went to bed to read for a few hours before falling asleep. Her last thoughts were troubled, however. She wondered for the thousandth time how she could escape from teaching, where a new job might be found or what field she might choose, and also about her financial limitations, which might trap her in teaching forever.

PERSONAL HISTORY

Growing up

Valerie was born in the same city where she taught. In fact, her school was not far from the housing project where she lived with her mother, father, and 10 siblings. Her father was a steelworker and her mother a nurse but their incomes were not sufficient to keep them out of poverty.

Interview, September 1980.

VALERIE: I had a tough background. I used to pick pockets. I did a lot because I was hungry. I don't know when I started, but I stopped when I was 12 out of fear of going to jail. I never wanted to go to jail and I was hungry and I stole. I wanted something to eat. I ate off fruit trees, vines, you name it, and I've eaten it. And to this day I don't eat fruit hardly because I ate it all my life for breakfast, lunch, and dinner and I don't want any more. There are quite a few things I don't eat because of this reason.

INTERVIEWER: And what was your neighborhood like?

VALERIE: Looking at it now, it was rotten. It was a mess!

Valerie commented that all 11 children felt some resentment toward their mother but were "crazy about" their father. He was the central force in the family and kept them together, although because the children had a wide range of ages, some left home before the younger ones were grown. The poverty and hunger had negative effects on the childhood relationships among Valerie's siblings but they became closer during their adult lives.

Interview, September 1980.

VALERIE: Speaking in terms of me and my brothers and sisters, we were more or less going for self. See, we were hungry. I hate to harp on you that we were hungry, but *we were hungry*! We were going for self and sharing didn't enter the picture. This is one reason why I'm selfish and I know it. But I have good reason to be. I have some now, I know

better, but I can't control it [laughter]. But now we are
moderately close.

Despite their poverty, all Valerie's brothers and sisters became
professionals, most had graduated from college, some had graduate
degrees, and one was in medical school—even though neither of their
parents encouraged them to continue in school. Valerie thought they were
all motivated out of a desire never to be in the situation in which they grew
up.

Personal Relationships

When Valerie was 19, she married; during the four years of her marriage,
her two daughters were born. She separated from her husband shortly
before he was drafted and sent to Vietnam. She said she stayed married to
him during his three years in Vietnam so she could collect his military
support checks. During those three years she considered herself still
married and thought it would be immoral to date ("I was in my good
stage"). Later she regretted that decision because she had turned down
opportunities to be with men she thought would be good marital choices
—professional football and baseball players and one man with a Ph.D.

Valerie described her ex-husband as having no feelings at all but did
not think he was much different from other men. She commented, "Men
do not have feelings." She included the man she was currently dating. He
was a principal of a large school and she enjoyed his company, but she was
worried because he still lived with his parents and was "used to getting his
own way." She did not think she would ever marry him but hoped to
remarry someday so that she would be relieved of financial burdens.

Valerie's children saw their father nearly every weekend and he
indulged them in extravagances such as a color television set. However, he
stopped paying child support and Valerie had to hire a lawyer and go
through court to obtain payments. For a long period of time, she had
supported herself and her daughters on her salary of $16,000.

Education

Valerie began college after her divorce. At the time, she was a secretary
for the city's board of education, and she knew she did not want to be a
secretary for the rest of her life. "I wanted to do more for me and I wanted
to be more." While going to college, she worked at several jobs and then
began to substitute teach—although her degree was in social science rather
than in education. She decided she liked teaching so she began a graduate
degree in education that would also satisfy certification requirements.

Interview, September 1980.
VALERIE: I had an interest in children. After working with them as a
substitute, I wanted to try to further their progress—

education progress as far as possible and especially our black children who need it most.

Valerie claimed that she studied very little in college and, because she had little money, rarely bought books. She thought she had outsmarted the system by making it through with little study but continued to take courses beyond her master's degree, based on the belief that more education might help her advance in teaching or help her leave teaching. Despite the fact that this had not happened, she continued to take courses and earn degrees in attempts to change her life and improve economically.

Work

Valerie had taught in two schools during her seven years of teaching. Before working in the parochial school, she had taught primary grades for five years in a public elementary school in a middle-class black neighborhood where 100 percent of the students and 50 percent of the faculty were black. Although the building was only 20 years old, it was in poor repair. Valerie described falling plaster and a leaking roof.

Interview, September 1980.

VALERIE: One of the teachers was in her room and when she moved out of a spot when it was raining, the second she moved the ceiling fell on her spot. That's the kind of building it is—need I say more?

Valerie also said the school had an inadequate supply of books and materials so she had to bring her own or try to get them from friends.

Valerie was not given tenure in the school district and was quite bitter about the way her case was handled. She had been selected as head teacher (she was in charge of primary teachers and responsible to the principal) for four years and saw her problems beginning with the selection of a new principal, during her last year in the school. Valerie described him as a "buck" for the white female superintendent. She meant that the superintendent was very powerful and that teachers, principals, and school board members succumbed to her power. She thought her principal was overly deferential toward the superintendent and would do anything she asked —thus, Valerie called him a "buck." She thought he had been hired as a "hit man" to get the school through a financially difficult period when enrollments were declining.

The principal became critical of Valerie early in the school year, and, even though they had few contacts, he remained critical. Valerie never figured out the source of his criticism because she had no history of problems in the school. She thought his attitude may have been due to the fact that she had so many graduate hours that she was an expensive teacher to have around or that she had rejected sexual innuendos while in his office. She also recognized that during the year she became frustrated and was therefore defensive and even argumentative with him, which might have contributed to his negative evaluations. She described the following encounter.

> He [the principal] told me "somebody" said I was teaching on a college level. I looked at him and said, "Well, what do you want me to do? What are you telling me for?"
>
> He said, "I just thought I'd mention it."
>
> And I said, "For what reason?"
>
> He said, "I just thought you'd want to know."
>
> I said, "I'm not interested, but on the other hand, if I'm teaching on a college level and if these children are learning on a college level, they can go to college next year. And when they go to college next year, you tell their parents to all chip in and buy me a Mercedes, or a house, or send my kids to college. You do that for me." And then I said, "Is that all?"

Valerie also thought that the principal was critical of her because she was isolated from the other teachers and never sat in the teachers' lounge or was a part of teacher cliques. But Valerie thought she went to school to work and that conversations in the lounge were negative and a waste of time. She commented, "I've got a degree to teach, not to eat in the teachers' lounge. It's just not the thing I want to do, to sit in the teachers' lounge and run kids up and down."

Another dimension of Valerie's not mingling with other teachers was related to her conception of the differences between black and white teachers. A strong disciplinarian, Valerie saw white teachers as lax and permissive.

Interview, September 1980.

> VALERIE: There were a lot of discipline problems, and, it's really bad to say but it's true, that the discipline problems were in the white teachers' rooms. There were some white persons there that felt this is the way the black people act, so they didn't see anything wrong with kids jumping up and down and climbing on the walls and walking across the window sills. They actually believed that this is how these people are supposed to act. So you have a problem right there.

When Valerie's contract was not renewed, she contested the principal's decision and had two investigations done by outside groups. Both investigations revealed that there was no basis for criticism of Valerie's teaching or activities in the classroom and that the problem appeared to be a personality conflict between her and the principal. Because she was not tenured, however, state law gave Valerie no basis for a case; school systems had the right to fire untenured teachers because these teachers had no negotiative or bargaining powers. Because of the case, Valerie had difficulty finding another job. In fact, she could not find one in any public school; therefore, two weeks before school began, she took the job in the school described in the next section.

Interview, September 1980.

INTERVIEWER: You do not see a future in teaching?

VALERIE: There is none at all. Maybe somebody else does and if they do, I wish they would call me and let me know. But I sincerely doubt that there's a future in teaching for me. As soon as I can get out, I'm getting out.

INTERVIEWER: Why do you stay in teaching?

VALERIE: Because nobody will hire me to do anything else. Believe me, I have tried and I have been told that my qualifications exceed the limit. They say, "We don't have anything to suit your qualifications. We will call you. Don't call us." Nobody is hiring people with a master's degree plus 30 hours. I don't really care what I do as long as I can support the three of us and also have a little recreational money. I'm desperate at this point. One of the other reasons that I really haven't gotten out of teaching, and I guess this may be the number-one reason, is that I have my whole summer off. I have become addicted to the summers. You know, like a dope addict on dope, I'm addicted to the summer and I like it. I love not working in the summer.

When asked if there was anything at all in teaching that gave her satisfaction, Valerie first reponded, "No, I'm not sure there is. I can't think of anything at this point." After a moment of laughter, she said that the responses from children always gave her satisfaction.

Interview, September 1980.

VALERIE: I'm crazy about them [the children] and I want to help them. Because those children need help and anytime you find children that will ask you for help, then I will give it. So that's the number-one reason why it's really intriguing to me. I love it for that reason.

Valerie thought that teaching might be an enjoyable job if teachers received occasional pats on the back but said they never got them.

SCHOOL LIFE

Cultural Setting

Valerie's school was located next to the church that supported it in the inner core of a city with a population of over 500,000. Population shifts had created a migration from the inner city to the suburbs, although a reversed trend had started in which wealthy whites were buying city properties to convert the old apartment buildings into expensive condominiums. Renovation of the property had not begun, however, and the area was inhabited mostly by poor blacks and some whites who had lived there when it was more affluent. Some buildings had been razed and left in heaps of rubble, others were condemned, and others were inhabited. In general, the area, including the school grounds, looked like a war zone in World War II. Fortunately there was a park across the street from the school, and this was used for recess. It was also a meeting place for men who had conversations between cars and park benches while the children played.

The enrollment in Valerie's school had dropped from 200 to 100 in recent years because of the movement out of the neighborhood. Since the area had one of the highest murder rates in the country parents did not want to send their children to the school. Most of those who did attend lived in the neighborhood, walked to school accompanied by their parents, or were driven to school. They paid only $25 a month tuition. The only requirement for enrollment was attendance at the church with which the school was affiliated. The church did not want to accept students whose parents were trying to escape desegregation in the public schools. However, parents had to attend the church only a few times in order to qualify to enroll their children.

Valerie, her aide, and other teachers worried about the high rate of child abuse in the area. They described one family that consisted of two sisters who between them had 11 children. All of them lived in a small apartment, and when the police arrived, they found the children starving and lying in filth among rat droppings. Another child in Valerie's class frequently ran a high temperature and his mother thought the only way to get the temperature down was to allow him to run outside in his underwear during the winter.

Despite Valerie's own poor background, she always blamed parents for children's problems and had little sympathy for the poor. She was concerned that people on welfare did not really use the money for needed items and said that a friend of hers who owned a grocery said the only time you see Cadillacs was on the day the welfare checks came in. Valerie's animosity toward the poor reflected her own frustration at having to teach in a school not far from where she grew up—in the same cultural milieu.

School Facility

Valerie's school was in a deteriorated state because the church had little money for repairs, renovation, or redecoration and it was built over 40 years ago. The atmosphere was prison-like because of the locks on the doors, heavy wire mesh over the windows, and dimly lit corridors. The darkness was partially due to unusually high ceilings with only a few bulbs hanging down. The floors were dark with dirt and age, the walls were painted in haphazard colors, and electrical wires hung out of the ceiling and walls. The classrooms were huge and looked even larger because of the small enrollment. Each of the six teachers had a classroom and shared the first- through eighth-graders. The lunchroom was in the basement, next to the restrooms, and behind it was an unused bowling alley stacked with junk, some of which appeared to be flammable.

Valerie's classroom was smaller than the other rooms and was somewhat crowded because of all the reading materials she used from the Title I program. There were tables and chairs, individual work areas, a teacher's desk, several bulletin boards advising children to read, and a television set. One of Valerie's wire-covered windows faced the street where her car was parked and the other faced a brick wall.

Teacher Morale

Valerie's classroom was somewhat isolated from the rest of the classrooms. That, plus her strong negative feelings about teachers' cliques (there was no lounge to sit in, however) and the fact that she tended to arrive late and leave school early meant she had little contact with other teachers—with one exception. She and the special education teacher often had lunch together, and they talked about topics one would normally hear in a teachers' lounge. The other teacher was from a small town in the Midwest, was white, and was at the school because the church had supported her financially while she was in college. She looked to Valerie to help her to understand city life. Together they laughed about sliding through college, complained about college professors who were "educated dummies" because they had not taught in public school classrooms and did not know what they were like, and talked about students and parents and about their own social lives. These encounters were Valerie's only contact with other teachers. Underlying their talks was Valerie's insistence that she hated the school because it was terribly depressing, even though the pay was adequate and she enjoyed children. Valerie and her colleague knew there was little to be done about the depressing conditions under which they worked and, therefore, they just talked and joked about the situation.

Students

Ninety-five percent of the students in the school were black. Although most were poor, there was a wide range of dress. Some wore expensive dresses, jeans, and tennis shoes, while others wore clothes that were tied together or shoes that were losing their soles. Over 50 percent of the students qualified for the reading program. Because some had sporadic attendance, however, Valerie feared they would make little progress in their reading abilities by the time they left the eighth grade.

While Valerie worried about the children's home lives, child abuse, and parental neglect, she felt it was her duty to be a good role model for them, to show them how an educated black person should talk and behave. She often corrected their grammar and helped them pronounce words properly. In response to a student who said, "Do we 'pose to do this?" Valerie defined the word *pose* and the word *suppose* to the child and had her repeat it several times.

Valerie said she thought the younger children, in the first and second grades, were cuter and more enjoyable than the older students. She also said that as the day wore on, she wore out and that she had less tolerance for children in her afternoon classes.

Classes

Valerie taught all eight grades daily in 35-minute periods and her 52 students all had to be tested and their records kept for federal and state reports. She had an aide to grade most of the tests and help with the reports. Because the lessons were programmed, Valerie had no lesson plans to prepare and only had to make sure each child was moving ahead to his or her unit.

When students walked into the room, Valerie greeted them and expected them to go immediately to work. Valerie worked in a clinical, diagnostic style, either with the whole group or with individuals, by continually questioning, correcting, or testing. Her seven years of teaching served her well. She was completely familiar with the materials and could move the students along with little disruption.

At times, Valerie was animated and vivacious with students, and at others, strict and inflexible. She often called them "Baby" or "Honey," patted them or teased them, but if they interrupted her or talked to one another, they were strongly reprimanded. For example, when helping one student, she called him "Son" and laughed with him as he read a sheet entitled, "Happy birthday, Teddy"; then she had him sing a song to her. Some students came over and stood quietly until she acknowledged them and answered their queistions. (Questions were often about what the pictures on work sheets were supposed to be because students were asked to write the initial sounds. For example, a blob that looked something like a teapot was supposed to be a *k* sound for kettle.) But when a girl called her name out she reprimanded her.

Observation, February 19, 1981.

VALERIE: I told you never to call out my name, especially when I'm working with a student. We don't play in here. If you can't follow the rules, you'll be out of here. Do you hear me?

STUDENT (tearfully): Yes.

VALERIE: What?

STUDENT: Yes, ma'am.

This occurence was rare because Valerie made her rules for appropriate behavior clear to her classes at the beginning of the school year and expected students to remember them.

Interview, September 1980.

VALERIE: I never had any discipline problems. The first day of school I explain what I expect in my classroom, and I contact parents before school begins so I can tell them what I expect. I find out what they expect from me, and I let them know that under no circumstances is your child in here to play. I let Mom and Dad know that if little Sally or Henry does something that is not appropriate as far as the classroom is concerned, I'm going to become very angry. I don't ordinarily have problems because I work it from the before-school angle.

Valerie required students to address her as "ma'am" and could switch from warm to strict if they did not. Even in small groups (three to five students) when she was animatedly reading a story with which the children were delighted, she required them to raise their hands, take turns, and answer "Yes, ma'am."

The discipline in the school was similar to Valerie's classroom discipline. One interesting form of punishment was called "walking the corner." Students who talked in class were allowed to go outside during recess but had to walk in a straight line down the street to the corner, then turn around and come back, and repeat the pattern for the whole recess period. During one period, 16 children were walking the corner and only 3 were allowed to play on the playground.

Leaving School

Throughout the period of the study Valerie reiterated her dissatisfaction with teaching, applied for numerous jobs, and applied to graduate programs in other fields. As she pointed out, she was often overqualified for jobs, and some graduate programs did not want to take a student with a master's degree plus 30 graduate hours. Feeling stuck in a job she hated, Valerie had to teach another year at the parochial school because she had no alternaive and had to support her family.

HOME LIFE

Valerie lived in a two-bedroom apartment on the outer edge of a commercial district in the city. It was halfway between the inner city where she taught and the suburbs. The apartment was modest and simply kept. There were no portraits, stereo, or other such furnishings in the living room, just a collection of somewhat worn furniture.

Valerie shared the apartment with her two daughters. One was in the tenth grade in a public school and the other in the eighth grade in a parochial school. Valerie was proud of her daughters and was pleased that they did well in school.

> Diary entry, November 20, 1980: I went to pick up [her daughter's] report card this afternoon. She did a very good job. I am proud of them both. They are doing well in school.

Valerie was as strict with her daughters as she was with her students. She had made clear to them what she would and would not allow and stuck to the rules she made for their behavior.

Interview, September 1980.
VALERIE: I may be authoritarian, as most psychologists would look at it, but I really don't care. Since it's my house and all, I'll run it as I see fit, but I tell them, "When you become of age and out of my house, you can do as you please but will do as I say or there won't be any doing at all." We get along pretty well.

According to Valerie, she and her daughters had few conflicts.

Interview, September 1980.
VALERIE: They [her daughters] have not caused any undue, unnecessary heartache, which I don't anticipate even. And they're pretty clean little kids, you know. They each have their likes and dislikes. I have mine. But we get along. We stay out of each other's way when we don't want to be bothered but other than that, we're a wholesome little single-parent family.
　　　　　There are quite a few things we do together. We talk a lot. We usually sit up at the table and they tell me everything. We talk about their schoolwork. We sit up and do homework.

Valerie looked forward to the day when her daughters would be grown up and she would be single again but also worried that she would be terribly lonely without them.

Household Duties

Valerie and her daughters shared the housework. If she was not home, or was coming home late, her daughters were expected to do the housework and cook dinner. Because their apartment was small and three people helped clean it, housework did not consume much of Valerie's time nor did she have to spend much time worrying about it.

Financial Conditions

Valerie was constantly worried about her financial situation, which contributed to her desire to leave teaching. The costs of living in a city (rent, taxes, and so on), the costs of keeping a car, and the costs of raising two teenagers left little for extra expenses. The fact that she received no child support complicated her problems. However, Valerie was extremely frugal and despite these financial hardships, she had a small savings account. This enabled her to continue to take college courses and enjoy some forms of entertainment, but she knew she would never be able to buy a house. Her feeling of being trapped in her job was exacerbated by the inequality of her pay to her high level of education, but she could find no way out of teaching and, therefore, no way to improve her financial situation. She thought that marriage to the right person would be an alternative and would relieve her financial strain.

Leisure Activities

Valerie used the time after school to enjoy a wide range of activities. Although she enjoyed playing cards or watching television with her children, she also enjoyed getting out of the apartment with the man she was dating.

> Interview, September 1980.
> VALERIE: There's no telling what I'm going to be doing between the hours when I get out of school and 5 o'clock. I can sleep or I'll go shopping, to an art museum, or anywhere on earth. I like being outdoors. I would go and watch him fix a car for five or six hours and help and do whatever. I go bowling at 6 o'clock, or motorcycle riding. I relax doing anything that I enjoy and that could be cleaning up my house if I'm in the mood for it or riding a bike or motorcycle or swimming. I am just easy to please and it doesn't take a lot to relax me. If I can get away from school, then I'm relaxed. At 3 o'clock, I mean, I'm relaxed.

Any nonschool activity seemed to be relaxing to Valerie, and she liked to have a variety of activities to choose from. When she did not, she became bored and complained there was not enough for a person who neither smoked nor drank to do in the city where she lived.

> Diary entry, November 23, 1980: The girls and I went to help a friend's mother get ready for and serve a dinner at her church. I told her that I wasn't helping her again. I didn't like the "queers" that were there. The priests, other adults, and three children (between the ages of 9 and 11) drank more wine than I have ever seen in my life. I don't choose to be around drunks, so, hopefully, for her sake, she won't ask me again.

> Diary entry, November 24, 1980: Dull. I'm really getting bored. There's not a lot to do in [city], especially if one doesn't drink or smoke.

Health

Valerie's health habits, although she neither smoked nor drank, were inconsistent. For example, she ate no breakfast, ate either a school lunch or something from a fast-food restaurant, and overate in the evenings. She had a very small body frame and was about 15 pounds overweight. She worried about her weight but exercised only occasionally when she had the time or motivation.

She reported an excellent ability to cope with stress on the health questionnaire but suggested that the one thing schools could do to improve her health was to "remove most (if not all) causes of stress." She stayed home when she felt particularly dissatisfied with school and admitted that the cause was stress. Interestingly, the stress was sometimes linked to physical ailments.

> Diary entry, November 24, 1980: I stayed home from school today. I just didn't feel like going and I was getting hoarse, but no sore throat.

She also talked about going to school when she was sick and expected her students to be more tolerant of her on those days. She assured them she would be considerate of them if they told her they were not feeling well.

Interview, September 1980.

VALERIE: I explained to them that some days you just don't feel like being bothered. I'll respect that. "Tell me and I'll give you an assignment and I'll leave you alone. By the same token, when I come in here and I'm dead, half-dying, sick, or whatever, I'll tell you and then you'll know." I'm very honest with them and I'll tell them, "I'm not feeling well today so let's just try to take it slow and quiet."

Valerie began having serious periodontal problems due to lack of regular appointments with a dentist. She was in great pain while at school and was worried about the cost of her dental bills.

CONCLUSIONS: OVERLAP OF HOME AND SCHOOL

The overlap between Valerie's home and school life could be viewed from various levels. On one level she never took work home from school and never spent time in the evenings on school-related work.

Interview, September 1980.

INTERVIEWER: How do you feel at the end of the day?

VALERIE: Great! At 10 minutes before 3 I feel like a new person. It's like reroofing or going into being someone else. You're one person all day but at 10 minutes to 3 when school is out, I'm revitalized because I'm going home and I don't have to be at school any longer.

In addition to never bringing work home, she never shared school problems with her family. For example, she said she never told anyone in her family about the problems surrounding the situation when she did not receive tenure.

However, at another level, her job was constantly on her mind when she left school because she was so desperate to leave teaching. Applying for jobs and to graduate schools took time outside school but was motivated by the stress and anxiety she felt toward teaching—even when she was not in school. Therefore, the work of teaching in the classroom was not a problem to Valerie but the working conditions of teaching were.

Valerie did not mind if her home life carried over into her school life, because she simply took care of problems during the school day if necessary. Her planning and conference periods allowed her free time to make telephone calls, to leave school and go to the bank or post office, or to plan what she would do when she left school at 3 P.M. When students came into her classroom, she concentrated on the work of teaching and was able to switch back and forth between her personal and teaching roles. There were few occasions, however, when her personal life interrupted her work as a teacher. Once, her mother called to tell her that her sister had been arrested for a traffic violation. Valerie was shocked because no one in her family had ever been involved with the police. She went to her bank and withdrew money for her sister's bond, then went to the jail and took her sister home. Valerie did not sleep that night and as a result was sleepy the next day at school.

In summary, Valerie's home life and school life were separate and distinct in some ways but in others, totally overlapping. Her dissatisfaction with teaching and the fact that her salary limited her were pervasive factors both at home and at school.

Epilogue

Valerie quit teaching in 1982 and went back to school yet another time. She enrolled in a nursing school and thus planned to begin a second career in another sex-segregated occupation.

9

Bonnie: A Divorced Secondary School Teacher with Children

Bonnie was a 48-year-old woman who taught English and journalism in a parochial (Catholic) secondary school and word study, composition, and mythology in a college. The secondary school and college were both located in a large city in the Midwest.

Bonnie's case was unusual because she had seven children, whom she had supported for many years after her divorce, which occurred shortly after her last two children (twins) were born. She had exceptional strength, both physically and emotionally, endurance, and resilience. These qualities carried her through many difficult situations, among which was entering the teaching field after all seven children were born. Yet, although unusual, Bonnie's life is representative of many other women with children who deal with simultaneous roles effectively—in the classroom and in their homes—often sacrificing time for themselves.

TYPICAL DAY

Bonnie's alarm clock rang at 5:00 A.M., but she stayed in bed under the warmth of her electric blanket. The temperature outside was below freezing and the temperature inside was only a little warmer, because Bonnie could not afford heating fuel for her two-story farmhouse. She stayed in bed for an hour grading English compositions and then rose to awaken her three teenaged sons—the last of her seven children still living at home. Her sons fixed their breakfast, dressed, and waited for their school bus, and Bonnie got in her old pickup truck and drove the 20 miles to her school. She bounced along the dirt road until she reached the highway, relieved because the truck had not broken down again.

Bonnie arrived at the college a few minutes late for her 8:00 A.M. English composition class. At 9:00 A.M. she checked her mailboxes in the English and language departments and then walked the mile to the parochial high school where she began a four-hour teaching day. Before class, she had time to relax in the teachers' lounge, smoke a cigarette, eat crackers and peanut butter provided by Sister Teresa, her principal, talk with other teachers, and read a bulletin that said, "Don't forget to supervise the corridors between classes. Are you beginning your classes with a prayer? They are needed."

Bonnie taught two sophomore English classes, using the same lesson plan for both. They reviewed a grammar lesson orally and Bonnie frequently asked questions to ensure that the students knew the principles behind their answers. She was upset because a few students were not prepared and asked them to stay after school to complete their homework assignments. Although this would lengthen Bonnie's day, she felt strongly about students coming to class prepared and knew her decision would be supported by the principal.

At noon, Bonnie decided to skip lunch and grade papers in the teachers' lounge. While she was there, the principal asked her to substitute for a teacher who had gone home sick. This meant that Bonnie would be particularly rushed to get back for her class at the college, but she agreed because it was expected and because she did not want to anger Sister Teresa, who was not happy about her split commitment to the school and the college.

Bonnie's high school journalism class was held in the art room. Students were writing articles for an upcoming issue of the school newspaper and Bonnie reminded them several times that they would have to work more quickly if deadlines were to be met. After substituting in the other teacher's class, Bonnie walked back to the college and taught a mythology class, which lasted until 5:00 P.M. Checking her mailboxes again, she found a message from her oldest son. She called his school and found that he had missed the school bus and had walked 5 miles toward home before getting a ride. Because Bonnie's office was 20 miles from home, she knew she would not have been able to pick him up even if she had received the message sooner. Bonnie felt frustrated about the situation and went to her office, which was located in a small frame house across the street from the classroom building. She had office hours until 6:00 P.M., when her night class began.

At 8:00 P.M. Bonnie drove home and ate her first meal of the day. Her sons had eaten earlier, cleaned the kitchen, and kept a fire in the fireplace while they watched TV. She rested briefly but left the room after settling an argument between the boys. She lay in bed under her electric blanket, with a neck brace for her back problems, and graded papers until midnight. She was exhausted but felt relieved when she thought back to the days when she had milked 40 cows before and after school. She felt even more relieved as she thought about the impending sale of the farm and looked forward to living in the same town where she worked, transferring her sons out of their rural school and having money to pay her bills.

At 2:00 A.M., Bonnie's oldest daughter called to talk about her marital problems. Her husband, a violent man, had taken their two children away. She did not know where they were and was afraid of her husband. Bonnie promised to help her. After a restless night, Bonnie arose at 5:00 A.M. to begin another day's work.

PERSONAL HISTORY

Growing Up

The first years of Bonnie's life were spent in a situation much like that described in Steinbeck's *The Grapes of Wrath* (1939).[1] Victims of the midwestern dust bowl and suffering dire poverty, Bonnie's farming parents packed their seven children into a battered old car and went west. When they reached the coast, they camped outside with hundreds of other displaced workers. One of Bonnie's earliest memories was of her mother crying in the night because she had nothing to feed her children. They eventually settled in a southwestern state, first picking cotton and then growing their own crops on land gradually purchased by Bonnie's father. Every family member was expected to pick a quota of cotton so that the total amount was a bale (1200 pounds). Bonnie's mother picked 100 pounds of cotton a day even when pregnant. She once miscarried and Bonnie's father wrapped the baby in a towel and buried it in the desert. Her mother returned to the fields the next day. Bonnie's working life began at age 4 and she picked 50 pounds of cotton daily.

The strain of supporting seven children resulted in alcoholism and rages in her father. He beat every one in the family. At age 13, one of Bonnie's brothers ran away from home. Bonnie was with her father when he found him hiding in the desert. Her father beat her brother until he fell to the ground and then he kicked him repeatedly. When Bonnie was 16, her father left and neither Bonnie nor her brothers and sisters saw him again—nor did they have any desire to do so even though they knew he was still alive.

Bonnie resented her mother's inability to extricate herself from the situation. She had begged her mother to leave but her mother told her she could not support seven children.

Conversations with brothers and sisters, June 1981.

BONNIE: She [mother] let all of us be hurt the way we were constantly and didn't do something about it. She remembers that she did it. She says that she took the blows sometimes. That's not good enough for me. I used to beg her to leave and she wouldn't do it. I guess I was angry at her for a long time for allowing me, a little, bitty skinny thing, anemic, B-1 shots every other day, to be slammed around like that. It took me a long time to get gentle feelings toward my mother. I don't know if I'd kill for my kids but I wouldn't let them be treated like that.

Bonnie's father's violent, aggressive behavior and her mother's passive behavior led to constant marital discord. Her father frequently had affairs with other women and this sometimes motivated her mother to become more assertive.

Diary entry, September 22, 1980: Today I saw a woman enter a barber shop (or was it a beauty parlor?). She carried (or did she wear?) a purse on her left arm in the way of 1930s, 1940s women, left arm close to the body and left hand spread open against the stomach, rather heavy, sharp body held straight, shoulders squared. She wore a country-woman plain cotton dress.... I remembered my mother carrying a purse like that the day she dragged me, an 11-year-old, through the park as she fiercely strode along on her way to hit a blonde whore over the head with her purse. My sailor father mixed up his love letters and mailed the wrong one to my mother.

When Bonnie caught her father with another woman, her father paid her not to tell her mother.

Bonnie thought about her childhood with anger and sorrow but even some joy. She remembered being beaten and belittled by her brothers but also remembered the enjoyable, sometimes dangerous games and pranks they played on one another. Therefore, it was with considerable anxiety that she visited her mother but thought her sons should meet their grandmother. Bonnie described her mother as an "old" 70 years because she needed help dressing and washing and was very forgetful. Bonnie thought she would die soon and was saddened.

Diary entry, June 29, 1981: When I walked away, I kissed her goodbye knowing it was probably the last time and I clung to her like a child, unable to do any other thing ... "All the Empty Gestures." What a great song title. As long as the world knows the forms—mothers act like this, daughters act like that—we can somehow keep the whole thing going. I went home to make my peace with her, or with my idea of her, and I ran again. There is so much pain there. Maybe I'll never get that in hand.

Personal Relationships and Education

At age 16, Bonnie married a construction worker. During the following 20 years, she watched her husband become a verbally abusive alcoholic, while she raised their seven children and worked to supplement their meager income. Bonnie said she thought she was unconsciously trying to gain her mother's favor by producing the same number of children, including a set of twins, though she also said she had seven children because they could not afford birth control. The twins, her last children, were born 16 years after her first child. Her pediatrician, a woman with whom she became personal friends, encouraged her to stop having children and begin college. Bonnie graduated from college while pregnant with the twins, began teaching, and finally got herself out of her marriage.

Bonnie supported all seven children on her salary, until her daughters began to leave home. She had several jobs simultaneously until she married a farmer, quit teaching, and helped care for their dairy herd. She returned to teaching when her husband told her she had to in order for all the bills to be paid. Bonnie taught, continued to work on the farm, and finished her master's degree in English. After several years, her husband left the farm, their marriage, and their three sons who still lived at home. Bonnie and her sons then had to run the farm. They milked the cows before and after school, took care of sick animals, fed animals during snowstorms, and planted crops.

Bonnie felt guilty at times for having her sons assume adult responsibilities when they were barely 10 years old but knew it was necessary to their survival. Survival was difficult but Bonnie was successful. She first sold the cows and later the farm for a good profit. She thought she had proven herself in a man's world.

Because Bonnie's four daughters left home when they were teenagers, her relationship with them was different from that with her sons. She had raised two separate families. She had been distant from her daughters for several years, although they called her when they had problems—to asking for money, shelter, or solace. Since the birth of grandchildren she had become closer to her daughters, but at age 48, Bonnie felt the need to stop mothering and have some time for herself.

> Diary entry, November 21, 1980 (A daughter and her husband had come to visit Bonnie): I think he [her daughter's husband] reminds me of the children's father and it seems all the daughters so far have chosen killer types, uneducated and violent. I spent 20 years in a marriage with an ignorant, narrow, drunken man, and now each daughter had brought home to me someone very like their father. Why do they bring them to me? My feeling is lately that I will have to move the nest—sell my house to get away from them. I congratulate myself daily on being alone and responsible only to me but every evening the TV shows, the walking through the house, the whispered conversations that are supposedly out of concern for me all are driving me nuts; and feeding and housing two more people is something I can't do.

Yet at other times, she felt differently.

> Diary entry, May 1981: Seems I have somehow to thread my way through emotional chaos my daughters seem to find themselves in. I guess it's flattering they call and ask for help but I don't know why it is. I always say to them,

"You have to solve your own problems." They always want to talk and my experiences are somewhat parallel to theirs and it's good for them to hear what's happening to them. I hope it's good for them to hear how I've lived through some of those experiences. But, gee, I really don't want to live their lives. And I hope in there somewhere there's a friendship that brings them here for conversation, not dependence.

Bonnie felt the same mixed feelings about her sons. At times she was frustrated and angry because they did not do their chores, fought, or did not do as well in school as she thought they should. At other times, she was very protective and strict, and the boys were not allowed to do the things their sisters had done or what other kids their age did—date, drive, go to parties, make independent decisions. And at other times, she was proud of them for their achievements in school, sports, and music—all activities she had worked and sacrificed for.

> Diary entry, March 1981: It always pleases me when my children are that sensitive and that aware of different levels of feeling and commenting. It's a great pleasure to me to see [her oldest son] growing and in the right direction ... very sensitive to people and what they say and why they say it.
> They're really nice people, my sons. It's a matter of irony to me that I spent so many years giving to my daughters, giving in terms of support and money, trying to help them go on to college and learn to grow. Probably he will be most like me in the sense that he will appreciate music and books and will go on to college and maybe some day write. I guess that's one of life's little ironies. I find he's an instant replay of his mother.

And a few days later.

> At one point in the day there was a lot of conflict with the boys. When I ask for their help and I don't get it, I get very frustrated. I left my bedroom and heard a noise and went into the kitchen. The twins were physically battling it out. I was just very upset and took them by the hair and smacked them across the mouth—outraged. So I thrashed them and very much resented that in the midst of all the chaos we live in that they would do that. I suppose it's fairly normal. I don't know how much that helped me. I always feel guilty after that kind of corporal punishment.

Work

During Bonnie's 15 years as a teacher, she had taught in seven different school districts and therefore had never received tenure. Except for her current position, all her other jobs had been in small districts in the Midwest. She had taken some of these jobs because no other openings were available, and others because of the location of her husbands' jobs.

At the beginning of the study, Bonnie taught in a small district close to the farm she and her sons maintained. The district had problems similar to numerous other small rural districts observed in the study. These problems

—low pay, poor facilities, and adverse working conditions—were primarily linked to economics. Other problems stemmed from the authoritarian administrators (one principal and one superintendent). There was high turnover (up to 50 percent) among the teachers because administrators fired them in an effort to keep salaries at the lowest possible level. Experienced teachers were too expensive and were threats to an administrator's authority because they sometimes tried to change things. Teachers who joined unions were harassed and fired and teachers who stood up for their rights were also eliminated. School board meetings were closed regardless of the laws prohibiting it.

Student discipline was strict in Bonnie's rural district. In the elementary school, a small room (two feet by four feet) with a window high on the wall was used as a detention room. Children who misbehaved were put in the room by themselves for a day. If parents refused to allow their children to be punished by being put in the room, the children could choose an alternative—either three paddles or an F. If the parents were powerful enough, their children were not punished. Powerful parents influenced school board decisions. Bonnie was fired because she gave a B+ instead of an A− to a board member's child. Probably, however, other factors entered into her case. For example, Bonnie thought her role as a teacher extended beyond her classroom. When she did not agree with school policies or thought a policy or punishment unfair to students, she confronted administrators and fought for change. She also attempted to organize a union. Such behavior is not accepted in rural districts in the Midwest and is threatening to administrators.

After Bonnie left the rural school district, she attempted to prosecute the superintendent for sexual harassment. He had kissed her during an interview and told her if she kissed him every morning she would never have anything to worry about. However, the union lawyer did not think there was sufficient evidence so the case was dropped. She did win a suit against the district, however, because a coach and the principal had forced her son to play basketball after he had broken his arm. The suit was settled a year after she left the district.

Bonnie spent the summer searching for a job. She suspected she was not considered for several jobs because the administrators in her old district made negative comments about her to administrators in other districts. Finally, late in August, Bonnie signed teaching contracts with a parochial high school and a college. She taught five college classes plus three high school classes for a total yearly salary of about $10,000. During that year, she sold her farm, moved to the city, and transferred her sons to her school.

A statement of Bonnie's teaching philosophy was found in writing she included with her diary entitled "Letter from an Unemployed Teacher." Bonnie never actually sent the letter but thought it was approporiate for administrators at several small schools where she had taught.

... All [her teaching] was designed to produce thinkers, not "yes" students. Kindness and consideration for each other in the classroom were responses discussed openly and expected in the classroom. As a group, we knew there were "clods" and there were real human beings....

I tried at all times to be honest with my students, admitting any lacks and mistakes. I tried to appreciate them for being real human beings and thought I set high standards of conduct for them as students and people. If I did not participate in faculty matters such as committee work, I felt I owed my strength to my students.

I still feel thereby lies my responsibility as a teacher. I feel the kind of student-teacher relationships I have described kept a lid on trouble for the school, gave an outlet for troubled students for self-examination....

I felt I touched the lives of some of my students. I thought that was what teaching should be.

SCHOOL LIFE

Cultural Setting

Bonnie's school was located in a large city in the Midwest. The population of the city was growing and in the past 20 years, the school district had grown from one public high school to five. There was one large state college (where Bonnie taught) and several small private colleges. The city was near a large resort area to which residents traveled on weekends and in the summer. There were many small industries in the city and a proliferation of churches, which ensured the city of a central position in the nation's Bible Belt. The city's rapid growth was a surprise to residents such as Bonnie, who regarded the city as medium sized, easy to get around in, and safe from crime. Shopping areas, restaurants, highways, residential areas, and even crime were recent developments.

Students in Bonnie's school were primarily from the city, but some were from surrounding areas. Parents paid tuition, were usually Catholic, and expected the high standards and strict discipline they did not think existed in public schools.

School Administration

When Bonnie left her job at the rural school, she considered leaving teaching because her experiences had been difficult, depressing, and degrading. She attributed these experiences to the lack of respect, integrity, honesty, and intelligence among rural administrators for whom she had worked. After a year at the parochial school, however, she changed her mind because she respected and admired her principal, Sister Teresa. Sister Teresa was quite supportive of teachers, treated them with kindness and consideration, allowed them to express their opinions, planned social events, and frequently patted teachers on the back throughout the year. Bonnie had some difficulty adjusting to positive comments and pats on the back.

> Diary entry, September 12, 1980: I keep on looking, hearing, waiting for someone (something) at the high school to say, "Fooled you. We really don't mean it." They seem to be telling me it's all right for me to practice the art of teaching. I'm not naive enough to believe that I've found "Oz," but it's as close as I've been in some years. I know there must be flaws, festering places. It would not be a human situation otherwise. But I have been shown kindness and caring, and best of all, beyond the honesty is humor. My God, coaches with a sense of humor—intelligent, witty coaches! A principal with concern, real concern, for the immortal *souls* of her students. A lady who is warm and lonely but who takes her responsibility very heavily toward her charges, both students and teachers. She chooses the hard path, that of conscience. It makes me smile a little the several views of her I have had from students and teachers. Hope I'm not making another mistake.

Although Bonnie thought that Sister Teresa was sometimes unreasonably strict and inflexible, she respected her ability to maintain strong control of the school and students, support teachers, and allow teachers a central role in the school's organization.

Interivew, December 29, 1981.

BONNIE: She really is Mother Superior, and everybody knows, including all those men up there, that when she decides something they may as well throw the towel in because that's it. There will be no conversation about it. And the kids too really walk the line ... the rule is the rule and it *will be*! It's arbitrary, but on the other hand she's really kind.

The overlap between church and school was total because it was a parochial school. Characteristics important to religious philosophy, such as love, kindness, and charity toward others, underlay the school's policies and Sister Teresa's administrative decisions, as seen in this bulletin she sent the teachers.

> To the Faculty, Bulletin, September 24, 1980: *Warning*: Money is being taken from lockers in the school section and in the locker room. Do not bring large sums to school or if you have to, check the money in at the office. Locks are available in the office but if you take one, it must be used properly. Let us combine our prayers for the one or ones who are responsible for the thievery. I hope these individuals realize that they are putting all of us in a very uneasy environment.

At the end of Bonnie's first year at the school, Sister Teresa told her she was a very good teacher and hoped to keep her around. It was a verbal evaluation. At the end of the second year, a formal instrument was used for the evaluation and Bonnie felt she was not evaluated as highly as the previous year. She was rated average in some areas. One of these was her participation in extracurricular activities. However, she did not know how she could improve in this area because she had two jobs and could not attend some after-school functions.

Teachers were expected to attend ball games at night to show their support of students. Because Bonnie often taught at night or was exhausted, she did not attend many games. The principal knew of her second job and family responsibilities, but she still expected her to come to the games.

At the college, Bonnie was hired by the department heads of the two areas in which she taught. They hired her on an adjunct basis from semester to semester and she had no contact with other college administrators. The determination of class schedules and her relationship with department heads were informal.

School Facility

Bonnie's high school was an old but exceptionally clean, well-kept brick building located near the central part of the city. Adjacent to the school were an elementary school, a convent, and a church. Bonnie's classroom contained 35 student desks, a teacher's desk, a lectern, and a bookcase. There was little on the walls except a crucifix and a clock. Because she shared the room with other teachers, Bonnie carried her books and papers around with her or stored them in the small wooden locker that was provided for each teacher in the lounge.

The teachers' lounge was the hub of teacher activity. It contained tables and chairs, two new couches, and a coffeepot and refrigerator. There was a loose, friendly rapport and much joking among the teachers and between the teachers and the principal, when they met in the lounge.

Bonnie's college classes were held in a modern building with poor acoustics. Noise from the hallways and adjoining classes could be heard throughout Bonnie's small, crowded classes. She shared office space with graduate students in a small frame house across the street from the classroom building. (As adjunct faculty she shared a similar status with graduate students.)

Teacher Morale

The positive morale at Bonnie's school was due in no small part to Sister Teresa's creation of a supportive atmosphere. Although pay was low (starting salary was $8500 in 1981), working conditions were good—facilities were adequate, students were well disciplined, academic standards were high, teachers were encouraged to improve themselves, and a spirit of camaraderie and congeniality prevailed. Bonnie felt these conditions were positive, reinforcing, and motivating factors in her own teaching.

> Diary entry, June 1981: The faculty at the high school is fairly young, bright, very active, and very energetic and move in all kinds of areas of life; I find that refreshing. They accept me as I am. They know who I am. I have not had to hide behind any pattern or caricature. The lunch hours are usually filled with talk and laughter. They know I'm a strong female, a strong human being, and they seem to like that. None of them seems to have any great need to cut me down and make me fit into some preconceived pattern, and I appreciate that very much.
>
> They are sometimes childish, with Sister. She acts like the mother and they act like the children, but they're basically nice people—have good standards and all of them want to grow personally and communicate with people who think differently from them. Sounds like an ideal situation. There must be something in there that's going to be bad.

Bonnie was proud of being a part of a college faculty, regardless of the marginality of her role. She held professors in high esteem and felt stimulated by being able to talk go them on a daily basis. Bonnie knew she had to obtain a doctorate to be able to become a permanent member of the college faculty; she looked forward to the day when her sons would graduate from high school and she would be free to pursue her own education and eventually become a professor.

Students

Bonnie's high school students were middle class or above, fashionably dressed, and well behaved. Their good behavior was not only due to Bonnie's strong classroom control but also to the religious norms and rules of the school, which required students to behave properly and be civil to peers and teachers.

> Diary entry, September 30, 1981: The door of the room I'm sitting in was left open, as the school secretary just entered and then left. I got up to close the door to shut out the noise of the gym. Two fellows in the class had gotten up, and as I closed the door, they quietly turned and sat down. Each had indicated earlier that I needed quiet in order to work ... how gallant of them. Funny how when I'm in the pits and wish I were anywhere but in school teaching kids, they do something special and I change my mind.

Most of the school's 150 students participated in extracurricular activities and talked to Bonnie about their parties held outside school. Drinking was the norm, although if Sister Teresa found out about it, students were punished. For example, several football players were suspended from the team for drinking at a party during the football season.

Although students trusted Bonnie and confided in her, when they were allowed to evaulate her, they were quite critical. Bonnie said she was "devastated" by their response. Students commented that she was too strict, taught as though they were in college, had no school spirit, and sometimes sat on her desk with her legs apart. Bonnie decided not to discuss the evaluations with her students; she perceived that they appreciated that decision and were therefore warmer toward her.

Classes

Starting two new teaching situations required innumerable hours of preparation and grading piles of compositions. Bonnie was overwhelmed during the first weeks of school trying to adjust to five college courses and three high school classes.

> Diary entry, August 21, 1980: School started today. Sophomores at the high school attentive. Fairly well behaved. I wore a new, tailored, pale-pink summer suit. My hair was up and I was told I looked very pretty. I felt I looked like a bum. My hair hangs limply in back and curls in front where it should be smooth. I was well prepared. I have no doubt I can handle *that* aspect. . . . I feel I'm jumping out into the abyss Kierkegaard spoke of. I don't expect there will be anything [anyone] there to catch me. I'll have to supply my own net at some point along the line. Perhaps the farm sale will be finalized. Still wish I could stay. Still want to go. Hell-of-a-note. Why can't some things in life be total? Scares the hell out of me that the college is so casual about my having only a weekend to prepare three college classes. My friend said just pretend the first day. Christ! Pretend? I have no decent clothes. My hair is in strings. Something must be done.

By the second semester her routine was simplified—not because she taught fewer classes but because she could use her first-semester preparations and lesson plans. The college courses, mythology and word study, were somewhat routinized, because workbooks were used in word study, and in mythology, laboratory sessions were often held in which students took notes on films. Bonnie could use a fairly standard procedure from class to class and semester to semester. The remaining difficulty was that she assigned compositions in several classes and had to spend hours grading them at home. However, she knew there was no other way for students to learn how to write well.

> Diary entry, September 18, 1980: Getting good written papers from my students at high school and college. I can't believe the honesty I'm getting. I had lectured on searching for their own voices, their own idiom. Many use cliche's and trivia, but they are achieving or reaching for real feelings, real people, and real events about which to comment.

Bonnie's hours of preparation were reflected in her class presentations and organization. Students were expected to come prepared and to concentrate completely on the hour's work. Students had to be able to support their answers and comments with well-thought-out rationales, because Bonnie believed the purpose of teaching was to enable students to think for themselves. She interspersed her lessons with humor, references to students' personal interests, stories about her sons, philosophy, mythology, literature, and explanations of the meanings of words gleaned from her experience as a language teacher. The facts that she expected good performances from all students, had high standards, accepted only thoughtful explanations for answers, and expected every student to be doing the work at all times may have influenced students' evaluations of her as strict and as teaching at a college level.

Bonnie was as organized in her college classes as in her high school classes but was less formal in style. There were no discipline problems, students were older, and Bonnie did not have to worry about the same sanctions of her behavior as she did under Sister Teresa. Her humor, comments, and examples were more relaxed and appropriate to older students.

Bonnie's teaching schedule left her physically and emotionally exhausted. She often looked tired and Sister Teresa expressed concern that her exhaustion would affect her teaching effectiveness. While Sister Teresa had no evidence that this was happening, her feeling influenced her evaluation of Bonnie's teaching. Bonnie knew she was less tolerant and patient with students (and her own children) when she was tired—but also knew she had no choice but to hold both jobs until her financial status was more stable.

Leaving School

Bonnie planned to teach a third year at the parochial high school and would receive the highest salary of any faculty member—$12,500 (in 1982). Cutbacks at the college had eliminated some classes but she hoped to continue teaching as many as possible. Bonnie was fearful she would not be able to support her family on her salary.

HOME LIFE

Bonnie's home life changed in important ways when she moved from the farm into the city. Farm work added a third job to her two teaching jobs and demanded her full attention in the summer. The period on the farm, despite Bonnie's love of the outdoors and the quiet she sometimes enjoyed, was filled with worry about finances, constant concern over the weather, and physical exhaustion. A drought ruined all her crops one year and she was forced to go on unemployment to supplement her disaster relief checks. Therefore, she was looking forward to selling the farm and ridding herself of the problems and uncertainties that went with it.

> Diary entry, August 22, 1980: The weather is still wiping me out. Fields all brown. Often I drive over the hill and I look at my fields carefully, hoping for some sign of growth, of green, and I say, "You son-of-a-bitch. Why? Why?" It is gross and obscene if someone is manipulating us all. Lately I refuse to hope, refuse to look at the sky, will not run to fling open the door when it thunders to

check hopefully for rain. The hell with it. I will not be manipulated anymore. I refuse to hope for rain. I refuse to be disappointed. I refuse to be afraid. Farming is only a part of my life and it's not the heart part. It's more like the vaginal part. . . . Still, on moonlit nights I watch and try to absorb, store up for when I will no longer be here. Coming home at twilight I watch the movement, try to touch the colors with some part of my self that I will remember. I have felt a part of this place. A part as the cows were a part. I have often walked along but not felt alone. I have seen dangers but have not been afraid. I have been sick with exhaustion yet continued to work. I have valued cleanlines but have not hated my manure-covered hands and feet. I have been locked in by snow and felt I was completely free. I think (guess) (feel) I choose now, know now, it's time to go.

With the $50,000 profit from the farm, Bonnie moved to a two-story brick house with a large yard and an extra lot with trees, in a middle- to lower-middle-class neighborhood. She made a substantial down payment, bought new furniture, clothes for her sons, and a new car, sent her sons to a sports camp, and put the rest in a savings account. Life was easier in the new, comfortable house, with a car that ran and a short commute. But by the end of a year, Bonnie had to use some of her savings to meet her monthly bills and had invested most of the rest in a new publishing company which was publishing a biography she had written. Her investment would cover the costs of printing, but unless she sold several thousand copies, the investment would be lost and so would her house, because she had mortgaged it to the maximum amount.

Interview, June 4, 1982.

BONNIE: Last year when I left the farm, I thought, "I'm free at last. I'll be solvent forever." Now I'm considering how I got into this. How do I get into these things? I've got to find a way to stop this!

But Bonnie was not sorry she invested all her money in the book company and might lose her home, because her life-long dream was to be a successful, publishing writer, and she thought she was near that goal.

Household Duties

Bonnie's sons were expected to do most of the household jobs—cooking, cleaning, laundry, and yard work. Although Bonnie cleaned some things on the weekends, she had little time to do housework during the week. Because the boys were there more hours than she, she thought it reasonable to have them do all the work and became angry if she came home and they had not done it.

All three sons fixed their own breakfasts. One son was expected to cook dinner while the other two had cleaning chores. Bonnie bought a microwave oven and kept a freezer stocked with food so there would always be food if she was not at home for dinner.

Financial Conditions

Bonnie's entire life was overshadowed by financial problems. From the time when she divorced her first husband and supported all seven children by working at two jobs, through her years of struggle in farming, up to her current dual teaching jobs for $10,000, Bonnie had only one brief respite from near-poverty—when she sold her farm. But even with the profit from the farm, she could not make payments on necessities without drawing heavily from her savings. Money, therefore, was a constant concern.

> Diary entry, September 19, 1980 [while still on the farm]: Life is austere. Desperate even.

> Diary entry, January 28, 1981 [while still on the farm]: We've been living in this house for the last month and there've been two snow storms and we've had no propane.

> Diary entry, September 26, 1981: [while in the city]: I am not earning enough to support my family. I'm running about $200 behind expenses.

> Diary entry, September 30, 1981: I've had a certain resentment toward my life lately. I'm not sure why. Perhaps because no matter how hard I work, I can't make enough money to cover our living expenses.

Bonnie's change from teaching in rural schools to teaching in a parochial school and as an adjunct college faculty member had changed her financial status very little. Unless her investment in the publishing company was successful, she would be in an even more devasting financial position in the future.

Leisure Activities

Because of Bonnie's poor financial status and heavy work schedule, she rarely had leisure time. Most days consisted of 18 hours of work. After selling the farm, she took a one-week trip to Europe with some college co-workers and later took her sons to meet her family in the West, but normally she did not travel or take vacations. On rare occasions, she went out to dinner with friends or for a drink or went to a theater performance. Typically, however, Bonnie's only leisure activity was to lie in bed and rest, preferably when her sons were out.

> Diary entry, December 28, 1980: The long Christmas holiday is over I spent it alone. All the TV commercials told me that it is spent with family—not true. It was quiet and and peaceful. I did not put on clothes for two days. Spent most of that time in bed. It was very cold. I still have not bought propane for heating and am using only the fireplace. With my electric blanket, I was quite comfortable. Four days alone I spent reading, thinking, dreaming.

> Diary entry, September 30, 1981: I love Sundays. I love to sleep late. Not dress at all. Do my class preparation at a leisurely pace. Watch good movies.

Generally be a slob responsible to no one. I do not answer the door or the telephone. I feel cut off from all responsibilities. Well, most responsibilities.

As Bonnie's publication date for her book drew closer, she spent more time working alone at night, treasuring solitude. Her leisure was her work, but she saw her writing as enjoyable and even therapeutic.

Health

Although Bonnie had few illnesses (colds, flu, and so on) and never missed a day of school, she often felt tired, was in pain, ate irregularly, and smoked too much. It is not surprising that she felt tired, given her 18-hour workday, lack of sleep, and the fact that the stresses of her life caused emotional exhaustion as well. One outcome of this exhaustion was chronic back pain and/or muscle tension in her shoulders. She found some relief by seeing a chiropractor, doing exercises, and wearing a neck brace, but she could not afford to continue seeing the chiropractor and had no time to do the exercises. Therefore, she wore the neck brace whenever possible, usually while sitting in bed grading papers or writing. Bonnie also suffered because of her years of hard work on the farm and took large quantities of aspirin to alleviate the pain.

Bonnie's hectic pace also affected her eating habits. She skipped breakfast and often skipped lunch and therefore overate at dinner. She worried about being overweight and periodically tried to lose the 15 pounds she thought was excessive. In times of stress, she overate and smoked more cigarettes. She disliked that kind of behavior but kept repeating it during stressful times.

Once, after a day of teaching at high school and college, Bonnie taught an extra hour for a teacher who was absent from high school, went home to eat with her children, went to a high school Latin Club meeting, took the students out for pizza and to a theatrical performance, and drove two students home who lived over 25 miles from the school. Arriving home at 1:00 A.M., she overate while trying to relax.

> Diary entry, September 16, 1981: I sat in front of the TV eating and trying to relax. I no longer see very well. My eyes are "fogging up." My body hurts like hell. I took three aspirin the moment I came through the door. My bones ached. I lay down knowing that the next day teaching would be painful.

CONCLUSIONS: OVERLAP OF HOME AND SCHOOL

Bonnie's home and work worlds often overlapped. At home while supervising her sons' housework, homework, and arguments, listening to and helping solve the problems of her four daughters, and carrying the financial burden of supporting the family, Bonnie graded dozens of papers and wrote lesson plans for eight classes. Increasing pressure from her principal led Bonnie to participate in extracurricular activities, but that meant she spent even less time at home with her family or that she got less sleep so she could grade papers.

At school, the events or problems of home life impinged on her thoughts and time. As mentioned previously, the fact that she was often tired and looked tired concerned her principal and affected the principal's evaluation of her. But Bonnie could not lessen her work schedule, eliminate the problems of her children, or sleep more. The endless cycle between home and work problems resulted in a negative reinforcing pattern. Ironically, the very things that would have allowed her to be most effective as a teacher—sleep, relaxation, and focus on one job—were unattainable because the conditions under which she worked and her salary forced her to work harder, lose sleep, and experience stress.

In addition to Bonnie's exhaustion affecting her teaching, other instances of Bonnie's home life affected her school life. She was called out of her classes to accept phone calls from her sons' school when there were problems; for example, when one broke his arm, one vomited all day, and one missed the school bus. She had to resolve the problems in some way—very quickly—so that she could return to teaching, however preoccupied her thoughts. In addition, calls and visits from her daughters took time away from paper grading and class preparation.

> Diary entry, May 1981: This is just an uproarious time—trying to prepare finals. I would set my alarm for 4:00 A.M., planning to work a few hours, and the phone would ring [calls from her daughters]. I'd work for a while and on the phone would be somebody with a brand new tragedy. So I'd go to work, to school, unprepared and somehow get through the day.

> Diary entry, September 21, 1981 [a phone call from a daughter had come at 1:30 A.M.]: I could not go to sleep so I stayed up until 4:00 A.M. preparing classes for the week. I hate to go into any class unprepared although that has happened. I stopped by the English department to say hello to the secretary. She told me I had a class at 4:00 P.M. I had not been notified, had no books, was frazzled, and had no lipstick on. I walked into the class, held them for the whole hour with a lecture, and assigned their first essay. I did not appreciate the surprise. I got up at 7:00 A.M. Felt like death warmed over. The whole day was tough.

Another area of overlap was Bonnie's roles as a parent and as a teacher. After Bonnie left the rural school, her sons remained enrolled. She suspected that the administrators vented their anger at her (for forming a union, threatening a law suit, and so on) on her sons. The most serious example was when a coach and the principal forced her son to continue playing basketball after his arm had been broken. The success of her law suit over the incident gave her satisfaction, but she gained even greater satisfaction by removing her sons from the school. Bonnie also became angry and got involved when her sons' teachers' discipline or teaching methods disagreed with her own. It was at those times that her roles as teacher and parent most closely intermingled. One example was when a basketball coach grabbed her son, shook him, and took him off the team when he missed a crucial basket in a game.

> Diary entry, February 1981: I had started the pickup and started to move, and I was suddenly absolutely totally livid with rage. I stopped the pickup and threw open the door and my foot hit the ground and I was on my way into the gym. I had it instantly clear in my mind that I was gonna walk in and, in front of the whole town, was gonna take the coach by the collar and say, "You son of a bitch, you ever touch my kid again and you will be sorry." The picture even flashed through my mind of picking up a bucket of water and dumping it over his head. Another of just smacking him across the mouth.

Her son begged her not to talk to the coach and she stopped herself. By the following Monday, the coach was in a good mood, put her son back on the team, and simply benched him for a few games.

All Bonnie's reactions to teachers' treatment of her sons were not so explosive. When her boys were enrolled in her parochial school, however, she had difficulty understanding or accepting the teaching styles and methods of other teachers (even those whom she respected). For example, she was upset that some teachers rarely gave homework and therefore had few papers to grade. She viewed this as laziness and thought that if she had time to grade papers, so did other teachers. She complained that she had to teach her sons the things that other teachers ought to be teaching them.

In summary, the overlap between Bonnie's school life and home life was complex; her life could not be separated into neat categories. One area merged into the other with a particular role or area emerging as most important depending on the setting. For example, while at school, home concerns were not forgotten or invisible, but teaching was predominant.

Bonnie's history showed a pattern of struggle—often for survival. Since childhood, her escape had been through books—first, fairy tales and later, the classics, poetry, mythology, and philosophy. She viewed life with humor and intellectual curiosity, as a kind of mysterious joke with a grand scheme she did not fully understand. She often spent time trying to understand how she fit into the philosphical, psychological, and mythological essence of that joke. Despite the pace and responsibilities of her life, she thought it was fairly typical, that it was not that different from anyone else's. She only knew she sometimes felt overwhelmed by circumstances. On one occasion, she was sitting in an unemployment office after she lost all her crops in the midwestern summer heat and drought and before she found her current teaching position.

> Diary entry, August 1980: She opened her purse and fished uneasily for a compact. Was her eye makeup smeared? She hated to look like a raccoon, black circles around her green eyes. She flipped open the mirror, one-half

plain, one-half magnified. She found herself staring into the magnified half. "Oh, my God! I didn't realize I looked so old." She was holding the mirror in her purse at an angle close to her chest and looked down her nose into it. Huge wrinkles seemed to be running up her throat, and the bags under her eyes could not be ignored or rationalized away. They, too, were lined. The freckles she had hated all her life were still there, no amount of being told she was beautiful would remove them, and the red hair pulled back in a wad on her neck for coolness and neatness in the 100° weather looked faded and old to her.

When asked how she coped with the complexities of her life, Bonnie replied, "I just go from crisis to crisis."

Epliogue

Bonnie continued to teach in the parochial school and taught courses whenever possible at the college. Two events occurred that affected her deeply. Her oldest daughter died in an automobile accident and Bonnie mourned her death while assuming care for her grandchild. Thus, while mothering her child ended, mothering a new generation began. The sale of her book, although moderately successful, left her financially devastated because of misdealings of the publishing company in which she invested all her savings. Bonnie continued her lifelong battle with financial problems. Despite these serious problems, Bonnie maintained her commitment to teaching and to high standards for students. Incredible strength carried her through another difficult period of life.

NOTE

1. In the summer of 1981, Bonnie went to a family reunion, where her mother and most of her brothers and sisters met after many years of estrangement. Bonnie taped their conversations and allowed me to read them. Her childhood memories were substantiated by her brothers' and sisters' accounts.

10

The School and Home Lives
of Fifty Women Teachers

In this chapter I have integrated descriptions of the lives of the women presented in the previous eight chapters with those of the 42 women who were interviewed only one time.

A DESCRIPTION OF THE TOTAL SAMPLE

In Chapter 1, the typical teacher was described as a white woman in her thirties who taught for 12 years and often has a master's degree. The average age of the sample of 50 teachers was 32 years and the range was 23–57 years. Most of the teachers were white (82 percent); the rest were black (16 percent) or Hispanic (2 percent). The highest level of education of more than half the teachers (56 percent) was a bachelor's degree, while 42 percent had master's degrees and one person (2 percent) had a doctorate. The average teaching experience was 7.5 years, although the range was quite wide (1–19 years).

The secondary school teachers specialized in traditional academic areas—English, social studies, math, science, languages, speech, business, home economics, and physical education. The elementary school teachers represented all grades, and they either taught most subjects in a self-contained classroom or were specialists in reading or math. Most of the teachers (86 percent) taught in "regular" classrooms, where they instructed groups of children for given periods of the day; three of these teachers taught classrooms of severely mentally retarded students. The other 14 percent of the teachers were "specialists"—counselor, social worker, librarian, speech therapist, two resource teachers, and a special education teacher for the learning disabled—and they saw students individually.

BACKGROUND CHARACTERISTICS

Family Socioeconomic Status

Teachers were asked to give their fathers' and mothers' occupations at the time they entered college. In the sample, 12 percent had fathers who were deceased or retired. Occupations of the working fathers were divided into two categories: farm or blue-collar (for example, mechanics, janitors, factory workers) and white-collar (for example, school principals, bankers, professors, physicians). Of the working fathers, more than two-thirds (69.8 percent) were farm or blue-collar workers, while the remainder (30.2 percent) were white-collar.

Teachers' mothers' occupations were divided into three categories: farm or blue-collar (for example, school cooks, factory workers, clerks), white-collar (for example, teachers, nurses, or social workers), and homemakers. Over one-third of the mothers (34.7 percent) were home-makers of those who worked, about 60 percent were farm or blue-collar workers and the remainder (38.7 percent) were white-collar workers.

The predominance of farm or blue-collar workers among teachers' parents is similar to national statistics, which reveal an increasing heterogeneity in teachers' social-class backgrounds, with larger numbers of teachers coming from lower-middle and upper-working-class families (Havinghurst & Levine, 1979). Although studies show a drop in the number of teachers from farm families and an increase in those from urban, working-class families, the average education student tends to come from a small city or a rural area (Yarger, Howey, & Joyce, 1977).

Teachers whose parents were farm or blue-collar workers reported a variety of childhood experiences, because their fathers' incomes differed greatly. Some remembered poverty while others recalled a comfortable life-style. Teachers whose parents earned higher salaries or whose families were white-collar recalled having all the necessities of life, although few had luxuries.

Social-Class Background and Perspectives on Life

Vanfossen (1979) reviews characteristics of social classes in American society and the predominant values and attitudes (perspectives on life) that emerge in socialization. Comparing white-collar and blue-collar workers with teachers serves as a basis for understanding differences in teachers' perspectives on life.

Vanfossen writes that white-collar families are child centered and stress the importance of education, getting along with others, obedience, docility, and respectability. White-collar parents want to be regarded as honest, hardworking, and responsible.

Vanfossen's description of blue-collar family life depicts growing up as difficult. Instability and alcoholism are common, so children do not have good role models. Life is viewed as hard and drab, work is boring, tedious, and unpleasant, and early marriages and childbearing lead to further economic problems.

Social-class background clearly had a strong influence on teachers' attitudes, values, and behavior in later life. Socialization, whether in a white-collar, farm, or blue-collar family, had a strong influence on teachers' perspectives on life. To the extent that these perspectives were narrow or broad, teachers viewed their alternatives for changing their lives as limited or extensive. Some teachers did not try to alter destructive personal relations, for example, because of narrow perspectives on life.

Havinghurst and Levine (1979) distinguish three patterns that can occur among teachers from working-class, farm, or blue-collar backgrounds: they can try to live down their origins if they feel a sense of inferiority; they can identify more strongly with students from social-class backgrounds like their own; or they can accept middle-class standards and become more strict toward students who come from backgrounds similar to their own. Three of the case studies illustrate these patterns.

The first pattern, living down one's origins, is exhibited by Lee (Chapter 2), the 26-year-old, single, elementary school physical education teacher. This woman grew up in poverty because her father was retired; by the time she was 2 years old, he was on social security. The encouragement of a coach, combined with a scholarship and a loan, enabled her to complete college. Because she was a teacher, she thought she had succeeded in the world. Regardless of how difficult her teaching situation was, she never viewed it as more difficult than her early life, as was seen in her comment quoted earlier.

LEE: To get a degree and be socially acceptable because I was not socially acceptable in high school. I felt kind of like I wanted to say, "Hey, I got out of this hole, and I made it." I pulled myself up, and I got my stuff together, and here I am. You know, I'm a coach. And even though it's a small town where the school system has less than 200 kids in it, I am still highly respected in the town, because of the social role.

The second pattern, identification with students of one's own social-class origins, was found in the case study of Chris (Chapter 3), the 29-year-old, single, secondary school social studies teacher. She grew up on a farm and lived in a rural area. Her first teaching job was also in a rural area, and she taught six years in a school she thought was ideal. When she moved to a suburb and taught students there, she had a difficult time adjusting. She thought students in rural areas had better values—they worked hard and respected teachers. She viewed her new students as spoiled, inconsiderate, lazy, and rude. Thus, she had difficulty sympathizing with students whose soical-class backgrounds were quite different from hers, and she preferred to teach students whose values and attitudes were similar to her own.

The third pattern, being more strict toward those whose social-class origins were similar to one's own—because of self-denial of those origins—was exhibited by Valerie (Chapter 8), the 35-year-old, black, divorced, elementary school teacher with two children. Although both her parents worked, their family of 11 children was poor and lived in a housing project she described as "rotten" and "a mess." She had earned a master's degree and 30 hours of additional graduate credit and was continuing to get more education. Through a complex set of circumstances, she took a job in a parochial school in the area where she grew up and was not happy about that. Despite her own background, she always blamed parents for children's problems, had little sympathy for the poor, and was critical of the children's poor English and behavior she associated with "poor-boy talk" (that is, black English). She was concerned that people on welfare did not really use their welfare checks for needed items, and she commented that a friend who owned a grocery said the only time he saw Cadillacs was on the day welfare checks arrived. Denial of her social-class background prohibited her from being empathetic toward her students.

Choice of College, Spouse, and Teaching Job

Teachers' social-class backgrounds and historically bound perspectives on life also affected their college, spouse, and job choices. All 50 teachers went to college close to their parents' homes. Only one attended college in a state other than the one in which she grew up, and that college was only a few hours' drive from her parents' home.

Teachers were usually married while in college or shortly thereafter to someone they met in college. They selected spouses who had similar social-class backgrounds and who shared their attitudes and values. Teachers' spouses took jobs near their parents' homes, and because teachers took jobs in the same locations, 96 percent taught near their parents' homes.

Teachers of all socioeconomic backgrounds had many reasons for choosing teaching as a career. Among those most often cited were the following: they enjoyed children or people (21.7 percent); they were pushed into it by another person—a parent or teacher (10.9 percent); they liked school (10.9 percent); they used it as a way of getting into another field or they hoped to save money to be able to choose another career, such as law (8.7 percent).

The 28 women in the sample who went to college between 1960 and 1970 (the mean age of the sample was 32 years) had few career choices, regardless of social-class background. Therefore, distinctions among teachers of different social classes concerning career choices became blurred. While some teachers gave traditional reasons for going into teaching, many others were vague about their occupational choice. They said they simply "fell" into it, had no other choice, or did not know why they chose teaching. Those who said they thought there were no other choices apparently chose teaching by default. They knew women could also be secretaries or nurses but commented that they did not want to sit at a desk all day or could not stand the sight of blood. Eleanor, a 32-year-old, married, elementary school teacher with no children, commented, "My mother always told me, 'Go back to school, get a job in case you ever have to support yourself. A teacher would be good, or a nurse.' I noticed that no one ever recommended that I be a brain surgeon in case I had to support myself."

CHARACTERISTICS OF SCHOOL LIFE

Teachers' comments and concerns about their jobs and working conditions and their teaching and classroom interaction were compared by the grade level they taught (elementary or secondary) and the size of their district and the geographic location of their school.

Elementary and Secondary School Teaching

Elementary and secondary school teachers had similar concerns about their working conditions. Such things as school closings, low pay, and reductions in force affected teachers at both levels. Their working conditions were quite different, however, most obviously in their substantive level and focus.

Elementary school teachers provided total care of students. In addition to teaching lessons, teachers cleaned muddy boots, tied shoes, zipped zippers, cleaned up vomit and other messes created by students who did not make it to the restroom in time, bandaged skinned knees, and monitored bathroom visits. Secondary school teachers were not so intimately involved with students, usually saw them for only one period a day, and expected them to take care of their own personal needs. However, many examples of adolescent behavior were less than endearing. Teachers said a minority of students caused all the problems, but those problems often disrupted their classes. They also expressed concern, anxiety, frustration, and, at times, fear about the behavior of their students. Many teachers—in all sized school districts from rural to urban—thought students had changed in recent years because of increased alcohol and drug use. Teachers noted that it was impossible to teach effectively when some students were stoned or drunk. They remembered students in their beginning years of teaching as motivated, obedient, and courteous. Now they found them apathetic, belligerent, and rude. Incidences of vandalism and violence made the teachers fearful. (One teacher in a rural area carried a gun in her car for protection.) Even teachers who had taught only one or two years were disappointed in students' behavior. They compared them to memories of their own high school classmates and found their students quite different. Some thought changes in students could be attributed to poor parental guidance. Again, comparing their students to their classmates, they remembered strict, hard-working parents who were not indulgent—as seen in the comments of Mary Kay (a 24-year-old, married, secondary school home economics teacher with no children):

> MARY KAY: The poor students, it seems like their parents are not that much concerned with what they are doing. That's also true with the students whose parents have a lot of money. They don't really have a lot of strings attached to what their children are doing. You know, they buy them a car. They're freer, they don't really have a lot of responsibility, and I found that really sad. A lot of parents are divorced and they are self-centered. They are more concerned with themselves and their lives than their children's. I can sympathize with that situation but it really hurts the children and it shows up in their school work and in their personality. They have got the attitude, "If nobody cares about me, why should I care about anything else."
>
> There's a big drug problem. There's even a bigger alcohol problem. There are students who come to school drunk. There are students who come to school every day high from pot and all those other things, pills and stuff. They don't care, and in a lot of cases that's hard for a teacher to work with.

The teacher in this excerpt taught in a small to medium-sized school district in the Southeast. Sylvia (Chapter 5), who taught in a larger district in the Southwest, had similar comments.

> SYLVIA: No wonder they don't like school because when they're "partying"—which is their euphemism for getting drunk or whatever— they're having fun and they're free and nobody is telling them what to do. They're old enough to get drunk and whatever else they do, and then they come to school and here is this diminutive person telling them what to do, making them study boring stuff. They

probably have their preconceived dislikes and apathy and this compounds it.

Secondary school teachers had to deal with a broad range of students' emotions; some, but not all, were negative or related to drugs and alcohol. For example, Jan, a 24-year old single business teacher, said she had only one problem at school—male students fell in love with her.

> JAN: I have a terrible time with boys, senior boys, thinking and misinterpreting my friendship. It's happened four times and I've only been here two years. You know how embarrassing that is? "Well, we heard you were dating so and so on the football team." Maybe he's my student aide or maybe he stayed after school to type three or four times. It's a crush, and I don't mean to sound like I'm anything special but it just happens.

This teacher's principal knew how embarrassed she was about the problem so, although they talked about it, he never noted it on her evaluations. Each time it happened, she had to talk to the boy and hope to end his infatuation without embarrassing him.

Not being able to touch students in affectionate ways was a major difference between secondary and elementary school teaching. Elementary school teachers could discipline students but also hug and kiss them, receive love notes and promises to "be good." Secondary school teachers had to draw clear lines between developing good rapport and being overly friendly. Being too friendly could lead to the problem of the teacher mentioned above. Some teachers also feared they would lose control of their classes if they were too friendly to students. Gaining control of five or six classes of 30 students each was a more complicated task for a secondary school teacher than controlling a single class of 20 or 30 students for an elementary school teacher. However, elementary school teachers also had to monitor children's behavior every moment they were not in the classroom, while secondary school teachers had less contact with students, unless principals assigned them tasks such as monitoring hallways or restrooms. Although elementary school teachers helped children in the restrooms, secondary school teachers were expected to surprise unsuspecting students who were smoking and take them to the principal's office. Teachers found the task embarrassing, particularly because they often had to use the same restrooms as the students.

While size of classes and amount of contact with students influenced the teachers' control of students, another factor was the differences in the physical size of elementary and secondary school students. Clearly, elementary school teachers, at least in the primary grades, had an advantage over their students. Standing over a child with a disapproving facial expression was used as a discipline technique. For example, Phyllis

(Chapter 6), who taught first grade, merely had to touch a child on the shoulder to be able to stop his or her disruptive behavior. Secondary school teachers, however, were at a disadvantage, particularly with male students. Few touched a student who was disruptive; if a situation was uncontrollable, they went to the principal's office and reported the incident. Jan, whose male students occasionally fell in love with her, was an exception. She reported that she never had discipline problems, but on one occasion a male student refused to sit down when he was supposed to be sitting. Instead of working, he began talking to another student and said to the teacher, "Hey, when I'm through, I'll sit down." She walked out of her class and waited for the student.

> JAN: I walked out of the room and slammed the door; I knew he'd come after me, because he knew that that's what I expected. Sure enough, he opened the door and he no more got that door opened than I was just furious. He was a big football player and I grabbed his letter jacket—not very hard, but I just grabbed him and pushed him and he kinda leaned up against the lockers. I said, "Look, you little son-of-a-bitch, don't you ever do that again. I don't like for you to talk to me like that in front of my classes and if you do, you're out of here. I don't want to put up with you." Then I realized what I had said, because I knew I was just frustrated. I said, "Just leave. Don't come back for the rest of the week. Go to study hall."

The 5-foot-2-inch teacher never had further problems with the 19-year-old football player. Although she never used that tactic again, the effect on students from other classrooms who observed her actions with him was significant. She never had discipline problems again.

Other secondary school teachers were more fearful of students because they had been threatened or their property damaged. Sarah, a 27-year-old, single, journalism teacher and librarian, kept a gun in her car because students had once loosened the lug bolts on her tires to cause her to have an accident. Students had been known to shoot teachers' windows in their cars and homes, so the teacher felt she was merely protecting herself by carrying the gun. A similar incident was reported by Lee (Chapter 2), who said students shot a hunting arrow through their principal's living room window, narrowly missing his wife's head. The students were never caught.

Because of the variation in students' behavior and teaching content at elementary and secondary school levels, one of the greatest difficulties for teachers was changing from one level to the other. If teachers had experience with a particular grade level and then changed levels, they usually found the experience negative because their expectations of students' behavior were no longer appropriate. The cases of Chris (Chapter 3) and Sylvia (Chapter 5) illustrate this point.

Chris taught six years in a rural high school. Her classes contained junior and senior students in elective courses. Then she moved to a city and taught a required civics course to ninth-grade students in a junior high school. During the entire school year, Chris complained about the immaturity of the students, their lack of self-control, and their rudeness. She could not understand why anyone would want to teach that age group and was happy when she moved back to high school juniors and seniors —who she thought were easier to motivate.

Sylvia taught seventh grade for over eight years and then moved and taught juniors in high school. She thought the juniors were impossible to motivate, were lacking in self-control, and were rude. She considered quitting teaching and decided if she ever changed jobs she would go back to junior high school, where, in her perception, students were easier to control and more polite.

The cases of Chris and Sylvia suggest that students' ages have little to do with teacher dissatisfaction but that difficulties arise when teachers change from teaching students of a particular age to those of another. Too often, when teachers move to a new district, they are placed in whatever positions are open rather than in positions that best meet their needs and abilities.

A final point of comparison between elementary and secondary school teachers was the amount of school work they took home. Of the 50 teachers in the study, over one-fourth (28.6 percent) took no work home at all.[1] Of those, 85 percent taught special classes on a one-to-one basis or taught special courses to whole classes; for example, reading, the gifted, or the severely mentally retarded. About two-thirds (64.3 percent) of those who took no work home were elementary school teachers. This suggests that when work is taken home, it is at the secondary school level among teachers who teach traditional academic subjects. However, of the five teachers who worked over two hours nightly, three were elementary school teachers. Beginning teachers had more hours of preparation outside school than did experienced teachers, with the exception of English teachers, who took home great quantities of paperwork regardless of their years of experience. For example, two secondary school English teachers, Bonnie (Chapter 9) and Sylvia (Chapter 5), noted in their diaries that they graded papers nearly every night, seven days a week, during the entire school year.

Geographic Location and District Size

In this section, we will examine the effects of geographic location, the size of school districts, and the cultural setting (represented by variations in geographic regions) and make a comparison of rural and urban districts.

Cultural Setting. Although there were insufficient data to make statistical comparisons among teachers in different geographical regions, there was evidence that pointed to the need for considering the effects of regional or cultural variations on the context of teaching. Whether a region had a history of conservatism in regard to education and educational funding had important effects on teaching and teachers. Support for education, as reflected in state expenditures, obviously affected teachers' salaries but also affected ideologies, which in turn influenced what teachers did in classrooms. For example, while students' performances were not assessed in this study, the comments of teachers in supportive regions (14 percent of the sample) included few critical remarks and were overwhelmingly positive concerning students. Whether these positive comments were attributable to differences in students or differences in teachers cannot be determined here, but the fact that regional differences were found suggests further investigation of these issues is advisable.

An observable difference between teachers in various regions of the country was in the quality of their life-styles. To illustrate, we can compare two teachers who had similar characteristics but lived in different areas. They taught in similar-sized school districts, were both married to teachers, had the same number of years of education (nearly completed master's degrees), and had both taught about 10 years. The only difference between their situations was that one had two children.

Julie (Chapter 7), a 37-year-old, secondary school home economics teacher, taught in the Midwest in an area where attitudes toward education were extremely conservative and where state expenditures on education were quite low. Eleanor, a 32-year-old elementary school teacher, taught in the Northeast in a state that had a long tradition of support for education, which was reflected in a higher level of state funding for public schools. Eleanor's salary was slightly over twice as much as Julie's and Eleanor's husband's salary was half again as large as Julie's husband's. Eleanor and her husband's joint salaries were over $40,000 a year while Julie and her husband's were about $24,000 a year (and they had two children). Eleanor lived in a two-story colonial-style home on a triple-sized lot with trees, a stream with a small bridge, and a large garden space. She and her husband shared cooking duties and enjoyed fixing gourmet meals. They went to concerts and the theater in their leisure time, traveled within and outside the country, and belonged to a wine-tasting group. Julie and her husband lived in a modular home in a rural wooded area with other modular homes and some trailers. They ate food grown in their garden and meat given them by Julie's in-laws or that her husband brought home from hunting and fishing expeditions. Julie did all the cooking and housework, and she her husband spent their leisure time watching television, with relatives, or fishing; on rare occasions they saw a movie or ate at McDonald's.

Julie's and Eleanor's life-styles were quite different, primarily because of the difference in their incomes. Comparing the two regions where they lived, housing was only slightly more expensive where Eleanor lived, while food and gas costs were similar. Taxes were higher in Eleanor's state, but utilities were higher in Julie's. In short, while Eleanor made twice as much as did Julie, the cost of living was not twice as much. In fact, it was only slightly more expensive. This example points out the importance of examining the cultural setting or region when making comparisons and points to the need for caution when making generalizations about teachers' life-styles.

Rural and Urban Districts. Teachers were also compared within regions or states by the size district in which their schools were located. Ornstein (1980) compared trends in teachers' salaries by regions and states and found that regional differences remained consistent over a 10-year period (regions that paid well in 1969–1970 paid well in 1979–1980) but that the greatest differences were found within states. For example, he found that within Georgia, teachers in Cobb County made $5000 a year less than teachers in Atlanta. I found a wide range of salaries within states but even larger differences between regions or states because of the economic characteristics of the states in the study (one of the lower-paying states and one of the higher-paying states were among those represented).

The most serious problems were found in rural schools in states where funding for public schools was low. There were low salaries, high turnover rates, teacher shortages, dilapidated, unsafe facilities, and oppressive working conditions. Teachers in rural schools also had frequent complaints about their administrators; typically, a male principal and male superintendent. These men tended to be authoritarian, control their school boards, and sometimes engage in unethical activities including sexual harassment. For example, several teachers reported that when teachers were fired, they were given no advance notice. Because principals never wrote formal evaluations, teachers had no recourse.

The combined factors of poor facilities, lack of administrative support, and administrative mismanagement resulted in pervasive low morale in rural schools. McPherson (1972) also reported low teacher morale in her description of teaching in a rural school in New England. Although facilities were adequate, the major source of dissatisfaction among teachers was the lack of administrative support.

Within larger school districts there was a wide variety of sizes and conditions of school buildings. Some larger districts had buildings that were like small rural schools and also large modern buildings like those in suburbs. In addition, although the poorest facilities were found in rural districts, dilapidated buildings were also found in inner-city urban schools. For example, Valerie (Chapter 8) taught in an urban school that was in terrible repair. It was a private parochial school with insufficient funds to make needed repairs. The paint was peeling, lighting was poor, and there was little evidence of its having been cleaned in recent years. The heavy mesh wire gates that locked the windows and the automatic locks on the doors gave the school a prisonlike atmosphere.

In large districts, central power and control shifted from one or two administrators to several administrators and rules amd regulations were more complicated and extensive. For example, in Sylvia's (Chapter 5) school of 2000 students, extensive records of students' progress were required. Every six weeks Sylvia had to prepare progress reports and grades for her 180 students. She was overwhelmed with paperwork and worked several hours every night trying to catch up. Her school also complied with state regulations by having teachers plan lessons according to a curriculum guide. In these guides, each day's, month's, and semester's activities were listed in detail and teachers were expected to complete the guide within a school year. Those who varied and added activities of their own, such as giving a spelling test while completing a grammar unit, were reprimanded by the principal.

In Sonia's (a 38-year-old, married, secondary school English teacher with one child) school of 2500 students, all records such as grades, absences, and test scores were put on the school's computer. Teachers were often reminded to keep accurate records and to get records in before deadlines. They were sanctioned if key punch cards were not coded correctly. When the computer broke down, there were problems at all levels of the school. Teachers no longer had accurate records of absences, and principals were not able to trace missing students.

Teachers in large schools more often reported a feeling of isolation from other teachers and from their administrators. Although some said they preferred to stay to themselves because it helped them deal with the enormity of the school, others felt lonely and unappreciated. Teacher morale in larger schools depended on numerous factors—geographical location, school facilities, size and content of classes, type of student represented, and administrators' leadership styles. Of all the factors, the administrators' leadership style was most often mentioned as a source of dissatisfaction and low teacher morale. Even when facilities were poor, class preparations extensive, and salaries low, teachers tolerated the conditions if the principal(s) was supportive, flexible, and visible. In larger schools, teachers had an advantage—there were several principals. From the group of principals, teachers tended to select one with whom they felt most comfortable and talked to him or her whenever they had problems.

An important factor that influenced teachers' perceptions and experiences in cultural and geographical contexts was their own personal backgrounds and teaching experiences. Marie (Chapter 4), for example, found that teaching gifted children was ideal because it most closely fitted her own experiences as a student. She was highly motivated and was always at the top of her classes in the cloistered atmosphere of the Catholic girls' school she attended. Teaching the brightest students in a small, closed environment was reminiscent of her own memories of school.

The closest fit between teachers' backgrounds and their teaching situations was found where teachers taught in similar or even the same towns and cities where they had been raised and attended school. Because all the teachers went to college close to their parents' homes and most (96 percent) later took jobs in the same (or same general) area, the fit between teachers' backgrounds and those of the students was close.

Although teachers generally took jobs close to geographical areas where they had always lived, there were examples where moves, even though close, were from smaller to larger districts or the reverse. These moves often produced the most serious problems of adaptation found. A period of culture shock produced even greater disorientation than did changing from elementary to secondary or vice versa. Chris (Chapter 3), for example, experienced culture shock when she began teaching in an affluent suburban school after six years in a rural school. She was raised in a rural area and found that students had values similar to hers in the rural school. However, in the affluent suburban school she thought students were spoiled, indulged, and pampered by their parents. She thought they wanted things "handed to them on a silver platter" rather than working for them. She found them disrespectful and rude when compared to rural students, who she thought worked hard and respected teachers.

MARITAL STATUS AND WORK

Single Teachers

Although single teachers did not have the complications and responsibilities of husbands and children, they often had relationships with other people and ties to families that required time and attention and that were sometimes constraining but at other times were sources of warmth and support. These family ties or intimate dating relationships influenced single teachers' mobility. They stayed in geographic areas near significant others and had frequent contact with them. For example, Chris (Chapter 3) lived a four-hour drive from her mother's home but drove there every weekend when her mother was ill. Lee (Chapter 2) drove once a month to see her senile mother, who had been in and out of mental institutions most of her life. Lee had to gain power of attorney over her mother and clean her house, mow her lawn, and pay her bills whenever she visited.

These examples show the strong ties single teachers maintained with their families. Teachers who dated had difficulty sustaining relationships, teaching, and keeping in contact with their families. School administrators often asked single teachers to accept extracurricular duties, such as being cheerleader sponsors, coaches, or theater directors, on the assumption that they had more free time than did teachers who were married or had children.

Household work was seldom a problem for single teachers because they were not home often enough to create any mess and because cleaning up after one person was relatively easy. Those who shared their houses or apartments with someone else shared house duties. However, single teachers' involvement in extracurricular duties often left them too exhausted to do housework, when it was necessary. Lee commented, "I really need to clean the house, but there's something about leaving at 7:30 A.M. and getting home at 6 P.M. that really turns me off housework."

Financial conditions for single teachers were often strained. Supporting oneself on a single income was difficult, and without the contribution of a second salary, few could hope ever to buy a house. Chris, for example, had to take a job in a school that paid $2000 less than she had earned the year before. Living in a large city on approximately $13,000 a year was difficult, and she had to withdraw money from her savings account each month in order to pay bills.

Because of heavy work schedules and lack of money, single teachers had little time, energy, or resources to enjoy leisure activities. Time out of school was devoted to resting or visiting with friends or relatives. Ruth, a 23-year-old math teacher, described her leisure time, "I really don't allow myself to sit. I cook dinner, that's my sitting. I don't do a whole lot."

Married Teachers

Twenty-six of the teachers in the sample were married. Married teachers' life-styles varied according to their husbands' income levels. Teachers whose husbands' incomes exceeded theirs generally enjoyed a higher standard of living than other teachers. For example, Marie (Chapter 4) was married to a retired military man who had a social service job. The combination of her salary and his salary and pension enabled them to own a large home in an upper-middle-class neighborhood and two cars, travel on weekends and in the summer, dine out, go to the theater, and contribute to a savings account that would allow them to retire early and work on their doctorate degrees.

Teachers whose husbands' salaries equaled theirs (24 percent of married teachers' husbands were also teachers) lived varying life-styles. Their financial status depended on where they lived, because teachers' salaries varied considerably from state to state and region to region. In some states, teachers married to other teachers made sufficient incomes to live as did Marie; in others, the joint incomes of two teachers barely met basic living expenses.

Teachers whose husbands' salaries were lower than theirs had a more difficult time than any other married teachers, even if they lived in an area where teachers' salaries were adeqaute. For example, Phyllis (Chapter 6) was married to a man who taught at a small junior college where salaries were below those of public school teachers. He stayed in the National Guard to earn extra money, but their joint incomes limited their life-style considerably. They rarely bought clothes and never took vacations or did anything that was costly.

Because of the large range of teachers' husbands' salaries, teachers' descriptions of their life-styles varied considerably. Regardless of their incomes, however, no teacher in the study was working to earn extra money for "frills." Most were forced to work. Those few whose husbands made high incomes were committed to teaching and did not plan to quit, unless they took a job in another area.

Where married women taught depended on where their husbands were employed. Although most couples stayed in areas near their parents' homes and where they went to college, teachers' husbands did move from one place to another, within a relatively small radius. Wives were expected to take whatever jobs were available in their grade levels or subjects or, if possible, to gain certification to meet the requirements of whatever jobs were available. Married teachers, therefore, did not choose jobs according to where they wished to live or schools in which they wished to teach.

As pointed out earlier, married teachers and their husbands usually came from the same areas and went to the same colleges; therefore, they shared attitudes and values that influenced their perspectives on life. These perspectives tended to reflect their predominantly blue-collar backgrounds, although they regarded themselves as middle class even when they lived a working-class life-style.

Further evidence of blue-collar backgrounds was seen in married teachers' and their husbands' sex-role attitudes. Weitzman (1979) points out that people of higher social class are less rigid about sex distinctions. Differences between boys and girls are stressed most in lower-class families. Middle-class families encourage some independence and assertiveness in their daughters.

In the study, sex-role socialization was considered a contributing factor to the narrowness or broadness of teachers' and their spouses' perspectives on life. The degree to which they adhered to traditional sex-role behavior influenced the distribution of household work and child care. Traditional patterns reflecting the influence of predominantly blue-collar backgrounds were found among the teachers. While over one-third (38 percent) of the teachers' husbands shared the housework, 35 percent of their husbands occasionally "helped out," "pitched in," or "picked up the slack," and about one-fourth (27 percent) of the teachers did all of the housework. Therefore, almost two-thirds (62 percent) of the married teachers did most or all of the housework. Teachers who did all the housework commented that it was easier to do it themselves than to have to nag family members about helping. By doing it themselves, however, they reinforced their families' comfortable patterns.

There was some evidence that teachers' reports of the extent of their husbands' help were not accurate. Because the case-study teachers were observed at home, their reports could be compared with observations. Julie (Chapter 7) quit her job because she was not making enough money and because her husband preferred that she stay home to take care of the house. Discrepancies were found between her attitudes about men's work in the house and the actual behavior of her husband. She had strong beliefs that household work should be shared and complained about an ex-husband who had never helped. However, her present husband often worked at his school in the evenings and went fishing on weekends, so she was usually left with the housework. He did help her, but the help was sporadic. Because she found it so different to have a husband who helped out at times after a husband who did nothing, she supported his pattern of sporadic help.

Married teachers who did most of the housework also took responsibility for child care. Multiple responsibilities complicated the lives of married teachers who had children because they had more people and events to contend with. Coodinating family members' activities became an increasing problem the more children a teacher had.

Married teachers with children rarely spent any of their time at home away from their families, because they felt guilty about leaving the children with baby-sitters. They said they would never stop working to stay home with their children but still worried that they were not being good mothers. Shelly, a 31-year-old, secondary school English teacher, with two children under age 4, never spent time outside school away from her children but still felt guilty about working.

> SHELLY: I hate to say it. . . . I do feel a little guilty about not being the mother, staying at home, baking chocolate chip cookies for my children. But I think we're all happier for the way it is. I would not be happy staying at home. If I stayed at home all the time, I would be miserable, and I would make them miserable, and we would just all be miserable. This way we are all just real happy. Sounds terrible, doesn't it?

Single and married teachers without children thought their own problems were minuscule compared with those who had children. Some commented that they were undecided about whether to have children because of the complications children would add to their lives. None wanted to quit working to have children, and all said they would take only temporary leaves from their work if they ever did have them.

Because married women, particularly those with children, had responsibilities for housework and often had financial problems, they spent little time in leisure activities. For many, simply sitting and resting was a leisure activity, as was sleeping an hour later than usual on a Saturday morning.

When asked what she did in her leisure time, one teacher with a child simply answered, "Nothing." A teacher without children who was married to another teacher commented, "We don't do anything. We don't have free time."

Teachers who brought little or no work home and those who earned higher incomes participated in a range of leisure activities. Those without children had more freedom and could travel more or participate in activities by themselves when their husbands were not home.

The leisure time of a few teachers; both with and without children, was determined by their husbands' desire that they not take work home from school. Although many husbands worked at nights or on weekends and went with friends on fishing trips or other outings, they wanted their wives to devote their time at home to housework, children, or their husbands. One teacher said her husband not only did not want her to bring work from school but also did not want her to "get hooked" on television shows (such as "Dallas") whose stories continued from week to week, because it would take time away from him and the housework.

Divorced Teachers

Divorced teachers' financial status, household duties, and leisure time varied, depending on whether they had children or not. Divorced teachers who did not have children had life-styles similar to single teachers, as did divorced women whose children had left home. Their financial status, however, was quite different from that of single teachers because they received monetary and other material compensations when they divorced. Some owned houses or had bought properties. Marlena, a 50-year-old secondary school teacher with two children who were no longer living at home, had received a large monetary settlement when divorced from her lawyer husband. She lived in an apartment, had a housekeeper, and never brought work home from school. Consequently, she was able to come home, prop up her feet, and relax, "Just like a man," she said.

In comparison, Sarah, a 27-year-old secondary school teacher had been married to a truck driver who often beat her and threatened to shoot her. She escaped, living at subsistence level for a few months, and then went back to teaching. Although her income was not so high as Marlena's, she enjoyed the same feeling of independence when home. She had time for many leisure activities and had a unique method of housecleaning.

SARAH: Usually what I'll do is get up on Saturday morning early, watch cartoons, and drink some coffee, and then about 10 o'clock, break out the wine and start drinking wine and cleaning house. This one time in particular I finished cleaning about 7 that night and was just bombed.

Divorced teachers with children living at home had the most strained living conditions of all, especially if they received no child support. They worried constantly about paying their bills, had no time to themselves because there was no one with whom to share child-care responsibilities, and had no leisure time. For example, Karen, a 32-year-old elementary school teacher, had two children under age 5 and received no child support. For part of a school year she taught half a day, worked in a doughnut shop for another eight hours, and cleaned houses on the weekends. But even with her three jobs, she had only $12 a week for food.

Trish, a 39-year-old secondary school teacher, had two daughters and did receive child support from her ex-husband but the children rarely saw him. Therefore, she was with her daughters whenever she was not at school. She talked about the difficulties of rearing children with no help from relatives and of her feelings of depression and loneliness.

> TRISH: I don't care how good a friend it is, you hate to really lean on anybody too hard. It's pretty hard, but I feel like everybody's got their own problems. If you don't do those things, if you aren't objective, you're going to drive yourself nuts. And you end up getting depressed, and depression can be a real disabler. I can't afford to get depressed because there's not going to be anybody else who's going to feed the kids. Life was going to be like it is on the "Waltons." That was what it was going to be like for me and, well, it just isn't.

CONCLUSIONS: OVERLAP OF HOME AND SCHOOL

Effects of School on Home

Teachers' home lives were affected by their school lives in several ways. Those who took some paperwork home (71.4 percent) extended their workdays one hour or more. The home lives of those who spent over two hours a night (10.2 percent) on paperwork were significantly affected. The work was never completed, so these teachers could not relax in the evenings or on weekends. Secondary school English teachers usually took inordinate amounts of work home, because they required students to write compositions.

Extensive record keeping and adherence to the formal curriculum guides and lesson plans required by some schools also contributed to teachers' work loads at home. Sylvia (Chapter 5) taught in a school with such requirements and never felt caught up with paperwork, even though she spent several hours every night working.

> SYLVIA: Work has been piling up on me, and I've just been keeping my head above water. The end of the six-week period is

approaching. That means catching up on grading, averaging grades, making up exams, grading exams, and so on. I hate this aspect of teaching; the pressure builds and builds. You lose sleep. As hard as I try, I never have grades figured ahead of time.

Teachers who had extracurricular duties also had limited time at home. Coaches, drama teachers, and cheerleader sponsors were often at school several nights a week for practices, rehearsals, games, or performances. These teachers did not have time to go home for dinner and, on some nights, did not go home until midnight. Their personal lives were almost totally subsumed by their school lives.

Whether or not they took paperwork home or had extracurricular duties, all teachers were influenced at home by school-related factors in ways that made their work ever present. Low salaries, for example, made a significant impact on teachers' life-styles. Constant monetary problems at home made teachers question whether they should stay in teaching. Trish, a 39-year-old, divorced, secondary school teacher with two children to support, worked on a degree in business so she could quit teaching. "I am considering leaving teaching. Not that I really want to, but I've got two kids to support, and living on a teacher's salary is pretty difficult."

Or as Shelly, a 31-year-old, married, secondary school teacher with two children, said, "I like [teaching]. I really enjoy it. I like my students, and I feel like I'm a pretty good teacher, but it's hard. It's a hard life. I just say to myself, 'What am I doing in this?'"

Valerie (Chapter 8) never took paperwork home but thought constantly about leaving teaching. She spent time outside school looking for other jobs, applying for graduate programs, or taking courses so she could qualify for other work. Teaching was an albatross, an unwanted burden to endure until she could escape. Her negative attitude and depression permeated her home life.

In addition to paperwork, extracurricular duties, and poor working conditions, teachers also thought about or worried about specific events and people in their school environments when they were at home. For example, Phyllis (Chapter 6) was excluded from teachers' cliques and even treated rudely during her first year of teaching; as a result, she often went home from school and cried. No matter what tactics she tried throughout the school year to get other teachers to accept her, the situation never changed. She was depressed all year and disenchanted with teaching, which affected her behavior at home.

The most serious effect of school on home was getting fired. Teachers felt helpless and unable to control their own lives when they lost their jobs. Teachers who supported families were particularly devastated and applied for numerous jobs, regardless of where the school was located or the salary.

Effects of Home on School

Teachers' home lives affected their school lives because of personal problems or scheduling complications. Although some teachers reported few problems at home, they vividly remembered days when those problems influenced their teaching. For example, Sharon, a 30-year-old, married, elementary school teacher with no children, described her feelings at school after she had had an argument with her husband.

> SHARON: It's just words. They've been said, and it makes you feel bad whether it was to you or to somebody close to you. It gives you a real yucky feeling. You're not that spontaneous and exciting a person at work, maybe, because that's bothering you.

Sylvia (Chapter 5) remembered an argument with her husband that had a much stronger effect on her teaching than the situation described by Sharon.

> SYLVIA: One of my students kept asking me why my eyes were red and then, "Why are you crying? Why are you crying?" All this attention got me started crying in earnest, and I had to leave the room. On my way into the restroom I ran into a teacher who asked what was wrong, and I just went ahead and told her the truth. Meanwhile, the inquisitive student had followed me to the restroom to find out what was wrong. All this was embarrassing!

Teachers whose personal problems were of such magnitude that they persisted over long periods of time had difficulty functioning effectively in their classrooms. For example, Chris (Chapter 3) went through a period in which an intimate relationship ended and her mother developed cancer. At school, she was depressed; she rarely smiled and was unenthusiastic. She became antagonistic toward students and coped by maintaining strict control.

Teachers who had children also had more complicated home lives, which affected their school lives in several ways. They were physically exhausted if they had babies or small children because they had to carry them, change their diapers, or stay up at night to feed them or care for them when they were sick.

Children's illnesses caused particularly difficult problems for teachers and affected their teaching, because they were tired from staying up at night and worried about the children all day if they were with baby-sitters or had to stay home from school. A good example of this problem was found in the case of Phyllis (Chapter 6), when she left one of her sons with a sore throat at a baby-sitter's. Throughout the school day she received calls from the baby-sitter asking her to pick up her child because he had become more seriously ill. She also received calls from her husband about arrangements to pick up their son and then calls from him from the doctor's office. Later in the afternoon, she found out that her son had bronchitis and could not go back to the baby-sitter. When her students were at recess, she cried for a long time in her classroom. Her principal took over her class so she could leave, but she did not tell her students what the problem was. Her students were upset and worried about her, and little was accomplished the rest of the afternoon.

A final problem for teachers with children was coordinating family members' schedules. Getting children to baby-sitters' homes, schools, doctors' and dentists' appointments, barber shops, club meetings, music lessons, athletic events, or jobs required careful planning before and after each school day. Moreover, children were not always ready on time, often forgot their gym clothes, let their dogs loose, broke the wires on their braces, or left a needed book at home. Therefore, teachers were sometimes late for school, had to take care of emergencies during the school day, could not stay after school for meetings, or were simply distracted during the day thinking about scheduling problems. Teachers' schedules were particularly disrupted when principals called special meetings without advance notice.

Reciprocal Influences

Although, for analytic purposes, throughout this chapter, teachers' home and school lives have been discussed separately, they were typically inseparable. Teachers who said they were able to compartmentalize their home and school lives were rare, and only one among the eight case studies did so. This was Marie (Chapter 4), who had a more affluent life-style than most teachers, shared housework with her husband, and took little schoolwork home. As a child, she had never argued with her parents or her brother and after she married, she did not argue with her husband. Her rational outlook and intellectualizing of affective situations helped her compartmentalize. "I guess I do compartmentalize a lot. When I get to school, I totally forget about everything else till school's over. . . . Gee, I can't imagine being able to worry about problems. There're so many demands on your attention."

Although other teachers would have liked to have been able to compartmentalize, they found it impossible. Instead, relationships in one facet of their lives were interrelated to relationships in other areas. Home and school events were ever-present realities, regardless of differing situational contexts. For example, teachers' salaries and working conditions affected their life-styles and limited or broadened their choices for options or change. At the same time, marital choices, husbands' incomes and job locations, and the number of children in their families also limited or broadened their alternatives for teaching jobs. Dissatisfaction with teaching influenced personal and marital relations, and personal problems influenced teaching effectiveness. The effects of home and school were inextricably interrelated or, as one teacher commented, "There's no difference!"

NOTE

1. Of the 50 teachers, 30.6 percent took work home periodically, 8.2 percent did less than one hour of work at home daily, 22.4 percent worked one to two hours, and 10.2 percent worked over two hours daily.

11

Summary and Conclusions

Teachers have been described in this book as belonging to a quasi profession rather than a profession. In the process of deprofessionalization, teaching has become more similar to working-class jobs in regard to the conditions under which teachers work and live. Work in schools is depersonalized, options for teachers are limited, choices are narrowed, and control is limited. Teachers not only have limited control over their work places but have limited interaction with those in control. Therefore, teachers feel less involved, less committed, and more alienated or burned out. The conditions under which teachers work are characterized by contradictory sets of expectations for their behavior, which place them in double binds that are difficult to resolve. These contradictions combined with the working-class working conditions place serious limitations on teachers' life-styles and home lives. A triple day of work is characteristic of most teachers' lives.

As a result of the quasi-professional status of teaching, few good students want to enter teaching and experienced teachers are extremely dissatisfied. Feistritzer (1983) reports that over one-third of the teachers in the country are dissatisfied with teaching and over one-half would not choose to enter teaching again. As she points out, "This is a shocking increase in the number of dissatisfied teachers. Twenty years ago only 11 percent of teachers polled reported they certainly or probably would not choose teaching if they had it to do over again" (p. 29). Wangberg, Metzger, and Levitov (1982) reviewed several studies related to this problem.

Reed (1979) reported that when New York City laid off 9,000 teachers in a recent year, only 2,400 returned when asked. Apparently, these teachers had found new jobs which were more desirable to them than teaching or than teaching in New York City. Sparks (1979) reported that 46 percent of the teachers in his regional study were dissatisfied with their jobs and would not again choose teaching as a career. A survey conducted by the Federation of Allegheny County, Maryland, Teachers found that more than half of the repondents said they would not again choose teaching. (Cumberland News, 1980) (1982:37)

The effects of widespread dissatisfaction among teachers and of fewer women choosing teaching as a career needs serious study, given predicted teacher shortages in the future. While Feistritzer (1983) points out that there has never been an overall demand for teachers, if the percentages of graduates who enter teaching is similar to 1980, a significant shortage could occur through the 1980s and 1990s, although the shortage would vary by region of the country, content area, and grade level. It is, of course, impossible to predict how the supply of teachers would be affected if the dissatisfied teachers quit.

What can we conclude from this description of teaching? What can be done to professionalize it? What can be done to keep good teachers in schools and attract good students to the field? Can schools keep teachers like Julie, who was willing to teach in dangerous and despicable class-rooms; like Lee, who taught every child in the school by running from one building to the other despite inclement weather, pools of water on the gym floor, and constant illness; like Phyllis, who conducted a full teaching day after vandals had sprayed her room with a fire extinguisher; or like Bonnie, who ran a farm and taught night courses in addition to her school day? To implement any program that does not address the broader issues of the conditions and contradictions under which teachers work may be a "Band-Aid" approach. Indeed, schools must recognize teachers' concerns and examine ways that their lives can be made more flexible, rather than more restricted. Rigid control over teachers or ignoring their personal lives does not result in schools being enjoyable workplaces for women and, one would assume, does not encourage effective teaching. Effective teaching, the concern of both educators and the public, will not necessarily result from increased demands for teacher accountability through testing and the like. Instead, let us refocus the concern—that the public be reeducated to the needs of teachers. If professional performance is expected of teachers, then teachers should be treated as other professionals in our society, with the same respect, esteem, and rewards.

Professional treatment must begin in schools in relationships between administrators and teachers. Because administrators serve as interme-diaries between teachers and the public, if they regard and treat teachers as professionals, a positive image will be projected to the public and a strong case can be made for affording teachers' rewards appropriate to their professional status. However, reexamination of data from the study shows that relationships between teachers and administrators are often strained and that contact is minimal. This inhibits change. For example, 31.7 percent of the teachers said they seldom talked with their principals; among those who did see their principals more frequently, contact was often limited to formal or "businesslike" interaction. Cindy, a 52-year-old elementary school teacher, commented that teachers in her school were reluctant to tell their principal about problems because the principal reacted by giving them negative sanctions. She cited an incident where a teacher received a low evaluation from the principal after going to him for help with a particular child. The lesson learned was that "To ask for help is to admit you're inadequate. You can't admit to being human if you want tenure. The response from the principal is, 'Oh, you can't handle the child!' It becomes a reflection of you—not of the kid's problem." Nevertheless, the teachers in the study tended to accept the power of administrators equitably. If the comments of teachers who were not un-agreed with them. Even when teachers were not fearful of being fired or transferred, they did not want to "make waves." Therefore, they felt little control over their jobs, and continuing not to make waves perpetuated their quasi-professional status.

When contact with administrators is difficult, teachers can seek more formalized means of communication through collective bargaining. However, as Johnson (1981) has reported, simply belonging to unions or engaging in collective bargaining does not necessarily ensure standardiza-tion of work practices. Johnson found that whether or not teachers had grievances, were hostile or cordial, or stuck to their contracts, depended on the role of their principal. If relationships with the principal were positive, fewer labor-related problems were found. However, in states where unions are not universally accepted or where collective bargaining is not sanctioned, teachers have no channels through which to work with administrators equitably. If the comments of teachers who were not un-ionized are compared to those who were, having some means of negotiat-ing with administrators through unions and collective bargaining, regard-less of the lack of receptivity on the principal's part, is better than having no communication at all. In states where unions did not have widespread membership, teachers, except in the largest districts, were pressured and administrators strongly discouraged their joining. In the smallest districts, teachers were prohibited from having union meetings at school and some were fired for joining the union.

Teachers who were members of unions had different perceptions of the limits of their power than did nonmembers, depending on the strength and longevity of union membership. Even teachers who only minimally participated in unions saw possibilities for change and were more willing to express their ideas to peers and administrators, although administrators sometimes questioned their motives, suggested they were troublemakers, and implied they were not dedicated teachers. Teachers with strong union affiliation utilized accepted negotiation processes and had learned the value of selecting an effective negotiator. They felt a greater sense of control over their jobs than did teachers with less union involvement.

Strategies used in formal negotiations extended to informal levels of the school. Cindy, a 52-year-old divorced teacher, taught in a state with a history of strong union involvement. She found that negotiations did not address subtle forms of sexism practiced by her principal. For example, the principal planned a dinner for the school board and asked all the female faculty members to bring the food. As the elementary principal began making a chart of what each woman would bring, Cindy said to the principal, "No, we teach, we don't cook!" When the startled principal protested that dinners had always been done that way and that there was no money available for the dinner, she replied, "That's the way the ball bounces. When we come home from a day we're tired and we don't intend to cook." The principal found the money and they had the dinner, but the women did not prepare it. This teacher's approach to this problem developed from her involvement in union negotiations, where she had learned that teachers' needs are met only if they vocalize those needs and stand firmly behind their convictions.

Union and nonunion teachers should share experiences and develop realistic images of one another. For example, some nonunion teachers expressed a strong fear of unions and imagined members to be mostly angry male picketers whose strike activities threatened the future of schools. These teachers would benefit from meeting women who are not different from themselves, who rear children and care about students but also happen to be members of unions.

Regardless of teachers' union participation, principals' development of an atmosphere of openness and collegiality would help create conditions of closer, more informal rapport with teachers. Frequent, supportive, informal, nonsexist interaction with principals outside the formal constraints of evaluation would help teachers feel a part of school organization and would enhance their sense of personal recognition and self-esteem—they should be treated as professionals.

> If teachers work in a school with a principal who cares, who works with the kids, cooperates with the faculty, and creates a supportive environment, then those teachers will most likely be positively reinforced, and emotionally will feel rewarded.... But if teachers have a principal who creeps around corners rather than being open, then morale will drop and teacher absenteeism will increase. Teachers become emotionally exhausted and starved for positive reinforcement. Not long after comes the physical manifestation of frustration and stress. (Bernhagen, as quoted in Harlin & Jerrick, 1976 p. 57)

While principals must treat teachers as professionals, they and other school administrators must also concern themselves with the public's perception of teachers as professionals; and they must develop realistic expectations for teachers' behavior in accordance with those perceptions.

However, merely acknowledging teachers as professionals or giving them control over their work places ignores the problems that result from poor wages—low status in society, a working-class life-style, and widespread dissatisfaction.

Poor wages also means that the better people are not attracted to teaching. As long as there are teachers who live at subsistence levels, whose children qualify for free lunches, who never buy new clothes, who cannot leave home because they cannot afford a baby-sitter, who have never had a vacation, and who must work at extra jobs to support their families, teaching will never achieve professional status and the quality of education will be seriously affected.

Appendix

METHOD AND PROCEDURES

Sample Selection

Case Studies.   Only eight teachers were selected for case studies so that their lives could be examined in intimate detail. Several considerations were taken into account in the selection process: teachers' geographic location; their willingness to share personal information about their lives on a long-term, intensive basis; and their ability to articulate feelings and recount events. Other selection criteria were related to conditions thought to affect teachers' home-school relationships: their marital status, the grade level they taught (elementary or secondary), and the size of the district in which they taught.

The eight case-study teachers were selected from those I had known as a teacher or observed as a researcher or who were recommended by others. The sample included four elementary school teachers and four secondary school teachers, who were classified in one of four marital categories: single, married without children, married with children, and divorced.

Comparative Data.   A larger pool of teachers' names was collected from school districts in several states, and from this group, 42 teachers were selected to be interviewed once. These teachers were chosen on the same bases as the case studies—marital status, level taught, and district size.

Teachers in the comparative sample were contacted by telephone and asked if they would be willing to discuss their work and what they did outside school. All those contacted agreed to be interviewed. The results include teachers in more than 60 schools, 30 school districts, and 6 states. The six states represent four regions of the country: the Midwest, Northeast, Southeast, and Southwest.

Data Collection

Interviews.   Formal interviews were conducted with all 50 women. (Because of missing data, some of the percentages reported represent a sample of less than 50.) The open-ended, in-depth interviews covered four major areas: (a) personal histories—thier families, experiences growing up, experiences in school, and reasons for choosing teaching as an occupation; (b) teaching experiences—work histories, descriptions of current classrooms, schools, and school systems, relationship with students, peers, and administrators, and perspectives about all aspects of teaching; (c) home lives—events and relationships that influenced current statuses, relationships with family and friends, life-style (where and how they lived), housework, leisure activities, and the overlap between home and school; and (d) staff development—past experiences and suggestions for change.

All interviews were tape recorded and conducted by me or one of three trained research assistants. All three assistants were women who had master's degrees in sociology, knowledge of interviewing techniques, and good interpersonal skills. The interviews lasted 1½ to 5 hours and were held in teachers' homes to free them from any constraints they may have felt about discussing school problems while at school. Being in teachers' homes also allowed us an opportunity to observe and gain some sense of the teachers' life-styles, as reflected in the kinds of homes in which they lived; in some cases, we were also able to observe family interaction.

Informal interviews were conducted with the eight case-study teachers throughout the study. Interviewers tape recorded conversations when possible or took notes either during the interviews or as soon as possible afterward. Teachers were interviewed either face to face during observations or by telephone in order to maintain contact over time. The initial formal interview questions provided a general framework around which to organize questions concerning teachers' life histories.

Observations. The case-study teachers were observed periodically at home and at school for about 19 months, including the last 3 months of the 1980 school year, the summer of 1980, the 1980–1981 school year, and the beginning of the 1981–1982 school year. There were approximately 1200 hours of observation, or 150 hours per teacher.

Diaries. Throughout the observation period, the case-study teachers kept diaries. Teachers were instructed to write or tape record their diaries as often as possible during the observation period for a stipend of $25 per month (a total of $300). Teachers were asked to write in as much detail as possible about their school days and home activities. They were told that no events were too mundane for inclusion—what they had for dinner, a child's illness, or a broken appliance were all considered important to understanding their daily lives. Teachers were provided examples of the kinds of information that could be included, and further instruction was given after initial entries were written. Occasionally teachers were asked to write about particular entries, but most missing or vague entries were discussed in interviews.

Organization of the Data. Each of the 50 teachers filled out a form that provided basic demographic and background information and a health data form. Responses to the forms were coded and recorded on master sheets according to teachers' marital status, grade level taught, and school district size. All tape-recorded interviews, field notes, and diaries were also transcribed and coded. Data for the cases and comparative interviews exceeded 4400 pages.

One set of interviews, field notes, and diaries was initially coded and sorted (also with a trained assistant) by categories used in the interview schedule. After the second set of transcriptions was read many times, two sets of codes were developed inductively—process codes for the case-study data and strategy codes for the entire sample. A master sheet based on process-coding categories was made for each of the eight women and used as the basis for writing their life histories. Notation of codes included reference to specific quotes from interviews and diaries, for illustrative purposes and to support points made in teachers' life histories.

Strategy codes were developed to address the major purposes of the study: understanding the ways teachers coped with their home and school lives and the extent of overlap of the two. As coding categories were developed, transcriptions were reread to see how closely they fit the data. Category development and rereading continued until all data were taken into account.

The results of the study should be regarded as exploratory. They suggest directions for further study, perhaps using the same methods and different cases or using different methods in order to test finding.

References

Adkison, J. A. Women in school administration: A review of the research. *Review of Educational Research*, 1981, *51*(3), 311–343.

Carew, J., & Lightfoot, S. *Beyond bias*. Cambridge, Mass.: Harvard University Press, 1978.

Drabick, L. Perceivers of the teacher role: The teacher educator. In L. Drabick (Ed.), *Interpreting education: A sociological appraoch*. New York: Appleton-Century-Crofts, 1971.

Edgar, D. E. & Warren, R. L. Power and autonomy in teacher socialization. *Sociology of Education*, 1969, *42*, 386–399.

Eisenstein, Z. R. *The radical future of liberal feminism*. New York: Longman, 1981.

Feiman-Nemser, S., & Floden, R. E. *The cultures of teaching*. Manuscript. Michigan State University, 1984.

Feistritzer, C. E. *The condition of teaching: A state-by-state analysis*. Princeton, N.J.: The Carnegie Foundation for the Advancement of Teaching, 1983.

Feistritzer Associates. *The American teacher*. Feistritzer Publications, 1983.

Geer, B. Occupational commitment and the teaching profession. In H. S. Becker, B. Geer, D. Riesman, & R. S. Weiss (Eds.), *Institutions and the person*. Chicago: Aldine, 1968.

Glenn, E. N., & Feldberg, R. L. Degraded and deskilled: The proletarianization of clerical work. *Social Problems,* 1977, *25*(1), 52–64.

Grant, W. V., & Eiden, L. J. *Digest of education statistics,* Washington, D.C.: Government Printing Office, 1982.

Grimm, J. W. Women in female-dominated professions. In A. H. Stromberg & S. Harkess (Eds.), *Women working*. Palo Alto, Calif.: Mayfield, 1978.

Grimm, J. W., & Stern, R. N. Sex roles and internal labor market structures: The "female" semi-professions. *Social Problems*, 1974, *21*(5), 690–705.

Harlin, V. K., & Jerrick, S. J. Is teaching hazardous to your health? *Instructor*, 1976, *86*, 55–58, 212–214.

Havinghurst, R. J., & Levine, D. U. *Society and education*. Boston: Allyn & Bacon, 1979.

Hoffman, N., ed. *Woman's "true" profession*. Old Westbury, N.Y.: The Feminist Press, 1981.

Johnson, S. M. Collective bargaining at the school site: A varied picture. Paper prepared for the conference Creating Conditions for Effective Teaching, sponsored by The Center for Educational Policy and Management, The University of Oregon, Eugene, Ore., July 1981.

Katz, D., & Kahn, R. Consequences of role conflict. In D. Johnson (Ed.), *The social psychology of education.* New York: Holt, Rinehart and Winston, 1966.

Kounin, J. S. *Discipline and group management in classrooms.* New York: Holt, Rinehart and Winston, 1970.

Lightfoot, S. L. *Worlds apart.* New York: Basic Books, 1978.

Lortie, D. C. *Schoolteacher: A sociological study.* Chicago: The University of Chicago Press, 1975.

McPherson, G. H. *Small-town teacher.* Cambridge, Mass.: Harvard University Press, 1972.

Metzger, D. J., & Wangberg, E. G. Many female teachers would choose other jobs. *Kappan,* 1981, *63*(3), 213.

National Education Association. *Prices, budgets, salaries and income.* Washington, D.C.: National Education Association, February 1983.

Nelson, M. K. The intersection of home and work: Rural Vermont schoolteachers, 1915–1950. Paper presented at the annual meeting of the American Educational Research Association, New York, March 22, 1982.

Ornstein, A. C. Teacher salaries: Past, present, future, *Kappan,* 1980, 677–679.

Pleck, J. H. The work-family role system. *Social Problems,* 1977, *24*(4), 417–427.

Ravitch, D. *The troubled crusade: American education, 1945–1980.* New York: Basis Books, 1983.

Rubin, L. B. *Worlds of pain.* New York: Basic Books, 1976.

Ryan, K., Newman, K., Mager, G., Applegate, J., Lasley, T., Flora, R., & Johnston, J. *Biting the apple.* New York: Longman, 1980.

Shakeshaft, C. *Teaching guide to accompany "woman's 'true' profession."* Old Westbury, N.Y.: The Feminist Press, 1981.

Simpson, R. L., & Simpson, I. H. Women and bureaurcracy in the semi-professions. In A. Etzioni (Ed.), *The semi-professions and their organization.* New York: Free Press, 1969.

Steinbeck. J. *The grapes of wrath.* New York: Viking Press, 1939.

Sutton, R. I. Job stress among primary and secondary schoolteachers: Its relationship to ill-being. *Work and Occupations,* 1984, *11*, 7–15.

Vanfossen, B. E. *The structure of social inequality.* Boston: Little, Brown, 1979.

Waller, W. *The sociology of teaching.* New York: Wiley, 1932.

Wangberg, E. G., Metzger D. J., & Levitov, J. E. Working conditions and career options lead to female elementary teacher job dissatisfaction. *Journal of Teacher Education,* 1982, *33*(5), 37–40.

Weitzman, L. J. *Sex role socialization.* Palo Alto, Calif.: Mayfield, 1979.

Wright, B., & Tuska, S. From dream to life in the psychology of becoming a teacher. *The School Review,* 1968, *76*, 253–293.

Yarger, S. J., Howey, K., & Joyce, B. Reflections on preservice preparation: Impressions from the national survey. *Journal of Teacher Education,* 1977, *28*(6), 34–37.

Zurcher, L. A. *Social roles: Conformity, conflict, and creativity.* Beverly Hills Calif.: Sage, 1983.

Index